ENTERPRISING WOMEN

ENTERPRISING
WOMEN

LESSONS FROM

100

OF THE GREATEST ENTREPRENEURS OF OUR DAY

A. DAVID SILVER

amacom
AMERICAN MANAGEMENT ASSOCIATION

New York • Atlanta • Boston • Chicago • Kansas City • San Francisco • Washington, D.C.
Brussels • Mexico City • Tokyo • Toronto

Library of Congress Cataloging-in-Publication Data

Silver, A. David (Aaron David), 1941–
    Enterprising women : lessons from 100 of the greatest
entrepreneurs of our day / by A. David Silver.
        p.   cm.
    Includes bibliographical references and index.
    ISBN 0-8144-0226-7
    1. Women in business—United States.   2. Women-owned business
enterprises—United States.   3. Entrepreneurship—United States.
I. Title.
HD6054.4.U6S55   1994
338'.04'082—dc20   94-4849
                                                                          CIP

Printing number

10 9 8 7 6 5 4 3 2 1

Contents

Acknowledgments

This book owes its origins to the entrepreneurial spirit of my mother, Sylvia Werner Silver, who has devoted her life to improving the lives of others in her community, never seeking recognition, always opening up paths for others to follow. While living in and raising a family in a segregated town she helped start an integrated summer camp and sent her children to it. She helped families escape the terrors of Nazism. She was an active Zionist leader in her community long before there was an Israel. She created schools, camps, community service organizations; published newsletters and directories; raised money for her charities and pulled money out of people for her most beloved charity, the Hadassah Hospital in Israel. Sylvia Silver has been an inspiration to hundreds of women, and the mover and shaker behind the hand that wrote this book.

Shasheen Shah did an outstanding job of collecting and assimilating data for this book and in conducting some of the more illuminating interviews. He worked unstintingly to complete the final product. Other significant participants were Serene Sandoval and Charlene Maes.

Introduction

The purpose of this book is to describe the entrepreneurial process by example. Women entrepreneurs walk a different path than men entrepreneurs. They start businesses for the same reasons that men do—to solve a problem for a large number of people, to do something important with their lives, or to put food on the table. But they go about the launch process somewhat differently.

For instance, women entrepreneurs do not have the same access to capital as do men entrepreneurs. To overcome this deficit, they frequently start companies in which the customer pays up front for the product. These are trust-based businesses in which the customer pays for the product or service before the entrepreneur ships or delivers it. Parenthetically, there are very few women who have been convicted of commercial fraud. Accordingly, one can draw the conclusion that women entrepreneurs are people we can trust.

The number of women who are starting new businesses is enormous. It is greater than the number of men entrepreneurs. This is a paradigm shift. Business journalists, management consultants, securities analysts, business school professors, and economists who do not catch this wave will be swept under by it. The woman entrepreneur of today is the woman CEO of tomorrow and many businesses will be headed by women managers. To understand their journeys is to understand their outlooks, their missions, how they plan, how they operate. Do they vertically integrate? Do they seek to go public? Are they acquisitive? Are they going to dominate the huge caring and curing industries in which they have set down such magnificent roots?

My selection process was one of identifying the 100 greatest women entrepreneurs of our day from a list of more than 250. I asked every business writer working for a major newspaper or magazine to supply the names of their candidates, people they had written about, and many of them graciously obliged, particularly Sharon Nelton of *Nation's Business*,

Joseph Mancuso of the Center for Entrepreneurial Management, and Rieva Lesonsky, the former editor of *Entrepreneurial Women.* My research associate, Shasheen Shah, then contacted all of the candidates and requested biographical data and company histories. A handful of women declined to be in the book, some because they were writing books of their own.

The standards for inclusion were as follows:

The women entrepreneurs had to have created valuable, sustainable companies that solve problems for large numbers of people. A high degree of social utility was frequently a deciding point in the inclusion process. Real estate developers and extractive-industry entrepreneurs were excluded because the problems they address—shelter and energy—have been around a very long time and there have been no unique delivery systems or elegant solutions to these problems since prehistoric times.

We used the base line of $10 million in sales or $15 million in estimated or actual market value, but varied these figures if the entrepreneurial company was still quite young and intensely socially useful. The woman entrepreneur had to have either started the company or co-founded it with a spouse but held onto the CEO position, or, if her father started the company, she had to have increased sales by more than tenfold. This was sufficient to persuade us that the wife or daughter was responsible for designing the company's mission statement and creating its marketing channels.

The wealth created by the 100 entrepreneurs profiled here exceeds $6 billion. The amount of capital raised to launch these enterprises was a mere $30 million. Subtract the five high-technology companies, and the total start-up capital raised by the ninety-seven other women was $2 million or $20,000 per company. The 100 women have created more than 500,000 jobs, most of them held by women. But the most significant statistic is the problem-solving machines that these companies have put into motion.

The women entrepreneurs profiled are legitimate heroes. All of them have brought about positive change that would very likely not have occurred without their intervention. They have all made the improbable happen. They delight in being alive at the right time and in control of events at critical moments in the histories of their markets. They thrive on change. The infinite possibilities of the unpredictable future offer endless opportunities for spontaneous improvisation and for the imaginative, bold strokes that bring about changes in the lives of millions of people. Strength comes to these highly successful entrepreneurs from their clear, brightly colored vision and passionate faith in their views of the future and in their power to mold it; they know where they are going, by what means and why. This strength enhances their energy and drives it to new heights.

Listen to the voices of the woman entrepreneur. The tone is controlled, calm, and self-assured. It does not know bitterness, even when failure seems imminent. The woman entrepreneur is personally aware of the randomness of events, the shortcomings of everyone with whom she deals, and the nucleating power of the law of reciprocity that places *trust* at the heart of her business.

One

The Uniqueness of the Woman Entrepreneur

The woman entrepreneur is someone dissatisfied with her career path (though not with her chosen field) who decides to solve a problem that is causing her, and many other people, she believes, intense dissatisfaction. Many people experience dissatisfaction with one irksome thing or another. They have insight into a solution to the problem, but they lack the energy to build a company that will convey that solution. Indeed, they may set about solving the problem in a caring environment, one client, one classroom, or one patient at a time, with the result that they are paid a salary or a fee for service. Teachers, nurses, doctors, researchers, and therapists are not entrepreneurs, although they solve problems for people. Shopkeepers, consultants, brokers, and agents are not entrepreneurs because these businesses are not sustainable unless the proprietor comes in every morning and flips on the lights. Entrepreneurs create lasting value.

Entrepreneurs experience dissatisfaction, develop the insight into a solution, and have the energy to build and launch a company to convey, on a continuing basis, the solution to the problem. As we approach the twenty-first century, the catalytic power of entrepreneurship is female.

What Drives Her

The woman entrepreneur is not only energetic but single-minded in pursuit of her goal; she has a mission and clear vision; she intends to create out of this vision a product or service in a field many have determined is important that will improve the lives of tens of thousands of people. Yes, the entrepreneur will probably make a lot of money and she knows it; exactly when, who knows and who cares?

What drives this kind of person? Why will she forgo the conventional path, ignore all warnings about the likelihood of failure, take on enormous financial burdens, assume responsibilities such as management decisions or marketing plans for which she is poorly trained, toss aside the tranquility of home and marriage as if possessed by this single goal?

At what point does the entrepreneur jump into action? What is the personal history behind such determination? And what does she say are the driving forces?

At the time she takes the leap, the woman entrepreneur is typically between thirty and thirty-six years old, married, the mother of one child, and employed by a faceless corporation; she lives in the city, votes liberal, and has no material assets.

This archetypal individual represents—to some—a contradiction. Until the time she conceived her entrepreneurial venture, she worked fully within the bounds of traditional societal values, for a corporation, perhaps, or for a laboratory, a school, or a government agency. She had been hired, she believed, for her creative potential and was rewarded, she also believed, for her creative contributions. She was well satisfied.

Lurking in the wings, however, was a foil. Although initially she trusted that the organization valued her and rewarded her principally for her creative potential and output, as she became more energetic and required increasing latitude and funding for her ideas and projects, the organization's commitment to creative output and its willingness to invest in her personal research and development efforts emerged as less than she wanted, less than she expected. At first surprised, she became increasingly dissatisfied, though for a time she did nothing, said nothing.

At the same time, as her trust in the workplace faded, a strong commitment to her own capabilities was unfolding. More and more, she experienced a sense of directedness; an inner voice was asking her questions about personal values, about the expression of self-worth and self-sufficiency. She was not necessarily asking the abstract philosophical stock-taking questions that observers and analysts of mid-life change report are raised so frequently by people in their mid-thirties and forties, questions like, "What have I accomplished in my life?" "What have I sacrificed?" "What will I do with the rest of my life?" Those questions are as likely to come to the entrepreneur as to anyone else. At this point in her life, the Big Question for the woman entrepreneur was: "What will I do with my creativity?"

She was intense, deadly serious about homesteading somewhere, and so being able to exercise her confidence in herself. Before she even knew it had started, the entrepreneurial race was on. For a time, as she continued to do her job for her employer, dissatisfaction increased and the idea for the one product or service she would develop—one that would take the marketplace by storm—was putting down roots in her mind. The first growth might be a primary shoot that withered, but the root system was secure. And, as I will discuss in more detail, she will be protected by an enormous capacity to replenish psychic energy, by intense pleasure in her activity, and, if she is to be successful, by excellent communications skills and exquisite judgment.

At this stage, potential entrepreneurs frequently seek out other entrepreneurs, mentors, and venture capitalists. Women entrepreneurs frequently speak of male mentors, fathers who encouraged them or bankers who gave them small loans and financial advice. Some speak of the influence of their mothers, but you will note that the mothers were dissatisfied, energetic, insightful and not shy people.

Who Is the Woman Entrepreneur?

Entrepreneurs are complex, intense, determined, imaginative people who have faith in themselves and whose energy isn't sapped by anger, bitterness, or disappointment. The workplace has not been satisfying, true, and hasn't rewarded what she most respects in herself; the not-yet-active entrepreneur has put in a lot of time and has tried to contribute her best. She has become dissatisfied and to some extent disillusioned. And she is not politically adept, so pure commitment to human potential irritates rather than inspires management, making it impossible for her to maneuver budgets and other forms of influence the way others can to make the organizational dynamics work for, not against, her.

Nevertheless, though she resents the system and continues to be disillusioned, she goes on to create her own reality; thus, *the true entrepreneur does not feel victimized.* She doesn't plot and plan retaliation. Rather, she accepts that the organization will not provide a place for her to do what she wants to do and believes should be done, and she decides to create such an organization on her own.

Acceptance of reality brings determination, not depression, distraction, or diffuse, flailing attempts to get even, to show them.

It brings dedication to building on her own strengths rather than to demonstrating the weakness of the organization (and thereby deluding herself that this would change anything with respect to her position). She knows she cannot reduce its power, so she decides to establish her own.

And since personal goals and needs have been emerging as the strongest forces, they take over to govern her behavior, and she directs her psychic and creative energy into building on the emotional self-sufficiency that has been slowly, steadily taking hold. She does this with an ease that astounds people who know or hear about her.

The creative intelligence she brought to her employer's business is now directed toward designing a product or service and positioning it for the marketplace. She examines opportunities, perhaps for licensing, sees none she likes, may work for a short time as an independent consultant or for a consulting firm, continues to see the needs she herself identified, and finally decides to create her own opportunity.

She is getting ready to break ground, carve out her niche, and build her place in the sun. Not an empire, for empire building is not what she is about. Rather, she is planning for, and is after, self-reliance, a quality-controlled provision for creative output. She talks about building an organization where people will not get lost; where creativity will be rewarded; where salaries and benefits will be just; where participative management (though she doesn't call it by that name) will be the rule, not the exception. And to the amazement of people who are not able to turn anger, energy, disappointment, and dissatisfaction into focused personal directedness, she begins to experience intense pleasure. An undercurrent of basic optimism and trust in her professional power, the certainty that has always existed that her expertise in her field is unequaled, govern a clear decision to be on her own and to succeed. She has no fear of failure, though she makes careful, detailed plans to avoid it. Statistics on new business and small-business failures offered to her by well-meaning friends and family are dismissed as irrelevant. "Sure, lots of people fail, but since I'm going to succeed, why are you telling me these numbers?" she demands. Then she goes on with her phone calls to bankers, target customers, possible franchisees, friends of friends, presentations end to end. Failure is simply not a possibility. She has spotted an opportunity and is leaping forward to take advantage of it as rapidly as possible.

With confidence, optimism, courage, focus, and determination, the would-be entrepreneur sets out to look for money. What happens then depends on whether she hires a business partner and whether the product or service is, in fact, one for which a market exists.

Choosing a Business Partner

To succeed not only in finding start-up capital but also in building a successful business, the would-be entrepreneur must be able to lead her team by exercising good judgment, by knowing the right thing to do at the right time. But since she may not have a clue about *how* to do the right things, she will eventually get tangled up in the snare of trying to plan a business. Without knowing word one about functional areas like strategic planning, sales projections, market research, or even simple accounting practices, she will at this point select a manager who does, one who can at the same time allow the entrepreneur chieftain to maintain leadership.

The higher the entrepreneur reaches for a manager, the more likely is her business to succeed. Entrepreneurs exhibit the keen judgment they are known for when they ask a certified achiever, someone who has demonstrated first-class management ability in a growth situation, to join them.

What might make others topple into confusion and frantic despair nourishes her spirit and her spirited intellect. Out of the complexity she pulls the necessary interim funding—usually the day the bank loan interest is due, and from the most unlikely sources: a first-rate franchisee group representative, a corps of dedicated dealers or distributors—and determination and confidence enough to refuse equity-hungry venture tempters. Those would-be entrepreneurs who have the product or service and the character prerequisites will become wealthy; those who don't will be wiped out in the marketplace.

You know who some of these successful entrepreneurial women are, those who have told of transformations overnight, abrupt decisions to do something on their own: There's Mary Kay Ash, who used to fly around the country from city to city to train men for her employer so that they could advance in the corporate hierarchy while she could not because she "was in the wrong body." And Lane Nemeth, founder of Discovery Toys, who while teaching in a day care center became dissatisfied with the absence of quality educational toys. She thought at first she would quit the day care center and open a toy store. Her husband suggested instead, "If you have this idea of teaching parents about toys, why don't you market educational toys like Tupperware does?"

The Parents of the Woman Entrepreneur

The successful entrepreneur carries a certain kind of emotional luggage that gives her her characteristic courage, drive, and heart. Her parents admired, and worked toward a place in, the status hierarchy. They valued a traditional, socially acceptable, orderly life in which they would have a position vis-à-vis others. They trained their daughter to succeed for them, to "make us proud," to do something positive with her life. The father, a busy but frequently absent figure, taught her to be competitive, to demand the best from herself. Family life was held together by a devoted, attentive mother who was very ambitious for her children.

Doing double duty, the mother pushed for achievement, competence, and public recognition of her daughter's accomplishments. It is no surprise that the successful entrepreneur starts her professional life seeking to work in a well-regarded "establishment" organization, and that when she leaves she has the motivation to succeed at all costs.

Here are four brief entrepreneur vignettes:

SANDRA DIXON JILES's father, a fruit cart proprietor, encouraged independence of thought and independence of career choice. All four of his daughters earned Master's degrees and Sandra has built UBM, Inc., one of Chicago's premier construction management firms.

SYBIL FERGUSON founded the Diet Center in 1968 by giving advice to friends and neighbors who, like herself, were unable to keep their weight down. She weighed 186 pounds, but although she needed surgery, her doctor said he would have to postpone the operation because Sybil was suffering from malnutrition. After three blood transfusions, Sybil had her surgery, recovered successfully, and went to the local library in Rexburg, Idaho, to read all the material there was about nutrition. "I taught myself how to feed my body correctly and to lose weight with a different method than counting calories," she told us. Sybil lost fifty-six pounds on a diet consisting of foods that have the highest nutritional value, such as proteins to rebuild cells and roughage to remove waste. Sybil's doctor began sending her his patients, and the news spread throughout Idaho. Sybil's husband said, "Sybil, I think I'll quit my job and help you. If you can teach people to do what you are doing, I can sell franchises." That was in 1971. Twenty-two years later, there are 900 Diet Center franchises strung out from Maine to Alaska.

Sybil told me about her parents: "My mother always worked, but she raised five children. She was always interested in me as a person, but when I wanted to talk about my dreams and the things I wanted to become, I went to my father." Sybil felt the pain of exclusion as a child. During her elementary school years, Sybil didn't speak or smile or play with others because she was so afraid of being teased about her ugly teeth. When the mouth had grown and Sybil could be fitted for false teeth, her pent-up determination to become somebody blossomed.

GAIL KOFF, co-founder of Jacoby & Meyers, Inc., owner-operator of more than 350 storefront law offices across the country, was raised to "do something with my life." She was the only daughter and youngest child in a family of four. Gail's mother was the pragmatist ("If you want to go to law school, you'll have to pay for it yourself") while her father listened to her dreams. Gail told me, "It became an obsession with me to become a lawyer, and at that time, the 1960s, there were very few women lawyers. I put myself through law school, which meant going at night, and when I finished there was disillusionment. I felt that myths had been created about the law to give society a feeling that there is a structure and there is authority, and these myths, supported by lawyers, ended up placing the law very far above the people instead of people having access to lawyers and being able to use the law." Gail joined a large firm in New York because she needed to have an income, but her heart was in using the law for social change. She practiced corporate law for four years, but chaired committees of the state and city bar associations dealing with the issue of bringing legal services within reach of the common person.

Then two things happened at once. Gail became dismayed at how the lawyers in her firm prepared wills for clients: "The lawyer would just chat with the client for a few minutes and even forget to ask certain questions because there was no checklist . . . then charge them more than they needed to." And Gail discovered Steve Meyers, who had begun opening legal clinics in California and advertising for clients to have their wills prepared for a few hundred dollars. She told us, "I thought it was fabulous and I knew there was a business here."

Gail became a partner with Messrs. Jacoby and Meyers, changing the name of the holding company to JEMKO. She opened more than 150 offices on the East coast, raised over $35 million of venture capital from the largest venture capital fund in the country, wrote a book about her experiences, got married, had three babies, and furnished three houses all in the space of six years. Although she admits to having very little social life or time for herself, Gail loves the fact that she is making an impact. She says, "The entrepreneurial process has to touch you emotionally, and if it does that, it will get you through all the problems you are going to have."

LUCY MACKALL, founder of Have A Heart, Inc., who has brought us brightly colored canvas shopping bags, fanciful shoelaces, and myriad heart-adorned consumer products, speaks eloquently and with considerable experience about the energy required to be an entrepreneur. "When I realized I had to work Saturdays," she told me, "I didn't notice that it was Saturday. It was just another day." Lucy says she learns from her mistakes. "You're going to make them, so you might as well be aggressive. When you get too cautious, you don't take the risks you might otherwise have succeeded in."

Lucy has always been a high-energy person. Born into an upper-class family, she received encouragement from her family to "have complete confidence in myself, to be totally independent, and to take care of my own life." Rather than go to camp or loll around the family compound on the shore in Amagansett, New York, Lucy told us, "Most summers I felt like I had to do something interesting or money-making or different or challenging. One summer, when I was sixteen, I had a business where parents would pay me to pick up their kids and do something interesting with them. The kids and I had fun and I made a lot of money, and I was still very young."

These four women entrepreneurs typify the three concurrent sparks that must be lit by the spirit of enterprise to turn a reasonably content, hard-working young woman into a driven, focused, fanatical entrepreneur: dissatisfaction, insight, energy—such as Gail Koff's dissatisfaction that the law was not being made available to the common person; Sybil Ferguson's insight into the role of proper nutrition in dieting; and the high energy level Lucy Mackall brought to being an entrepreneur, constantly trying new products in the marketplace and winging it on optimism and grit. Sandra Dixon Jiles's drive to do something important with her life to *honor her father* is a covenantal statement that explains the singular importance of the chase that goes to the very heart and sinews of entrepreneurship. Each of the four experienced dissatisfaction, had the insight into a solution, and had the energy to work the long, lonely hours needed to solve the problem they had identified in order to make an impact.

The Caring and Curing Characteristics of Their Businesses

One or two other surface characteristics bear pointing out. Although entrepreneurs were frequently sick or suffered some form of deprivation at some time during their childhood—one source of their monstrous drive—adult entrepreneurs are almost never sick. There are two explanations for this: (1) They are having too much fun to miss a day of work; or (2) entrepreneurs do not know how to delegate responsibility and therefore cannot afford to be absent.

Women entrepreneurs are positively evangelical about their businesses. They tend to form businesses with many marketing people who must continually be encouraged to believe in the cause, to care deeply for the customer, to look deep within themselves for the courage to leave their homes every day and sell the company's particular brand of goodness. Why marketing and distribution businesses? One reason is that these companies are largely customer- (or franchisee-) financed, which minimizes the woman entrepreneur's need to raise venture capital. The flip side of that coin is that venture capitalists, most of whom are male, are extremely reluctant to invest in women-owned businesses. Is it intimidation? I don't know. Is it fear of having to make demands on women? I don't know.

Another reason is that women entrepreneurs are frequently adept at embroidering their products in packages marked "caring" and "curing" and convincing a large number of people that they mean it. Debbi Fields, the founder of Mrs. Fields Cookies, Inc., says that her stores may appear to be selling cookies, but they are actually selling "warmth." In a high-technology world, the need for nostalgic items such as old-fashioned chocolate chip cookies and shoelaces with hearts on them increases proportionately. Joan Barnes, founder of Gymboree Corp., franchisor of wellness-oriented day care centers, said that she is in the business of "small kids and parenting," but what gives her an equally large thrill is "to grow other businesswomen, because all the franchisees are women."[1]

The words that women entrepreneurs use in their companies are unique and often connected with the notions of caring and relationships. At Discovery Toys, for instance, when a new recruit is to be trained by the geographically nearest marketing representative, the training assignment is referred to as an "adoption policy." Lois Vana Marshall, founder of The Marshall Group Personnel Franchise Corp., says about her franchisees, "I am living with people who are going through the growth pains every day and it really is a leveling experience. It doesn't allow me the opportunity to be comfortable in success because I have to help guide them and direct them and lead them to success. Which is wonderful. To see these people flourish before your eyes is almost like a relationship situation."

Don't Mess With Their Integrity

Rose Blumkin, age 99, came to the Midwest from Russia in 1917 without a penny to her name. Left with only $500 and two children when her husband died suddenly when she was 43, Blumkin began selling furniture out of her living room and basement. She had helped her husband

---

1. Barnes sold her interest in 1991 when the direction changed and the venture capitalists came in.

run their pawnshop, so selling was not new to her. Nor were obstacles. In 1917, Blumkin bribed her way past a Russian border guard, then came to America via China and Japan on a peanut boat. Her drive to be free got her out of Russia and her drive to do something with that freedom created the 250,000-square-foot Nebraska Furniture Mart. Every day of her life was another day of getting farther away from the border guard. She sold her company to Warren Buffett in 1983 for $60 million, and three years later, at age 93, started a new company because she was dissatisfied with the new management's practices.

Entrepreneurship is gift giving. Entrepreneurs are society's altruists. When we compete in the marketplace, we are attempting to give gifts of great value to our customers. "Competitions in giving," George Gilder writes, "are contests of altruism . . . the contest of gifts leads to an expansion of human sympathies. The circle of giving (the profits of the economy) will grow as long as the gifts are consistently valued more by the receivers than the givers."[2]

Entrepreneurs compete with one another to see whose gifts will be perceived as having the greatest value. Entrepreneurs are altruists who achieve great wealth in a land of egotists. The functional role of the entrepreneur in the community is to develop new markets that will create productivity and employment, to solve problems that affect large numbers of people, and to create wealth that will lead to reinvestment and further giving.

Our society has gift givers other than entrepreneurs, but they usually generate large incomes, psychic or spendable, rather than great wealth. Service professionals—doctors, lawyers, teachers, consultants, artists, and accountants—are problem solvers, who desire to be paid for their gifts rather quickly. Entrepreneurs, on the other hand, understand that if they build a gift-giving system to reach the maximum number of receivers, their gifts are likely to be considered valuable by more people, will touch the lives of more people, and will produce wealth both for themselves and for their investors.

But to wait for payment means to incur debt, to ask for favors, to persuade people to join the caring system, to leverage suppliers to wait for payment, to buy time, and to carve time away from one's family and friends. These activities are entered into only by fanatics—people whose hearts are bursting with the need to do some one thing, and to do it well, for a large number of people.

My gift in writing this book is to show that women have unique entrepreneurial opportunities in the areas of caring and curing—our

---

2. George Gilder, *Wealth and Poverty* (New York: Basic Books, 1981), p. 22.

largest markets. Dozens of women entrepreneurs have become exceptionally good gift givers, and my goal is to describe the process of entrepreneurship clearly and concisely so that women with high aspirations can become successful entrepreneurs without having to tackle as many problems in business as their predecessors did. We are speaking here about entrepreneurs, problem solvers, and gift givers. The difference between an entrepreneur and a small-businessperson is that an entrepreneur goes into business for *others*. A small-businessperson goes into business for *herself*. The distinction is important.

Many women on our list of the 100 Greatest Entrepreneurs of Our Day are into wellness, including aerobics, weight loss programs, wellness magazines, and running apparel and shoes. *Wellness* is *personal entrepreneurship*: solving the body's problems and receiving "physical rewards." The problems in our society are endless—violence toward women, child abuse, sexual discrimination, cowardly politicians, drugs, crime, disease, the homeless, the poor—and women entrepreneurs, with guidance and capital, will solve or mitigate many of them. They have already begun the task.

The Heart of the Entrepreneur

The first step in the evolution of an entrepreneur involves taking an inventory of one's physical and mental state. Entrepreneurship will occur only to a woman who becomes *dissatisfied* with the state she is in, who has the *energy* to effect a dramatic change in that state, and who has *insight* into how to change it. The potential entrepreneur becomes aware of the uselessness of much of her work or life, seeing that this uselessness conflicts with her moral imperative to live a more meaningful life. Women who have evolved to a high level of motivation and health desperately seek self-fulfillment. If at this moment they have insight into the solution for what it is that dissatisfies them and the energy to focus intensively on a single issue for five years, they will become entrepreneurs. This is what is meant by *heart*.

The Patience of the Entrepreneur

"Interpersonal differences in patience can partly explain why one person is wealthier than another," writes behavioral scientist Shlomo Maital.[3]

"The single most important factor in venture capital investing,"

3. Shlomo Maital, *Minds, Markets & Money* (New York: Basic Books, 1972), p. 80.

states venture capitalist Thomas P. Murphy, a *Forbes* columnist for many years, "is patience." If it is true that the only honest methods of achieving wealth are to become a competent entrepreneur or to invest capital and time in the companies they launch, then perhaps there is relevance to the importance of patience.

If patience is a learned as well as a heritable trait, and if it is a causative factor in the creation of wealth, then the wealth-creation process can be learned; moreover, it can be passed on to one's children. "Some people just have a knack for making money." Perhaps this folksy expression has some truth in it. Wealth equals delayed gratification.

The reason that entrepreneurship requires patience is that the solution to one set of problems often generates another set of problems. Entrepreneurial companies are living things, managed by human beings, and random collisions serve to knock them off their carefully laid plans with surprising frequency. Many entrepreneurs set out to solve one set of problems only to have the collision of random forces knock them in another direction.

The ability to be a successful entrepreneur and, by deduction, the ability to generate wealth itself, is heritable. Some people can and some people cannot. Those who can learned patience at some point in their childhood. We know that many successful entrepreneurs were deprived as children and that this deprivation took the form of an illness or economic hardship or an embarrassing appearance. But, in the families of entrepreneurs, there was an altruist, someone who gave to the other members of the family no matter how miserably they may have behaved. This family member created trust in the children, and people develop patience by trusting in the outcome of an event in the future.

For example, if a child is asked to work and told that she will be rewarded for that work, she will trust the parent or family member who asked her to do so. If there is no payoff, then the child will not develop trust. Or, if there is no parent or family member who is willing to offer an assignment to the child for which she will be rewarded, then patience very likely will not be learned. Note the many entrepreneurs who grew up on farms. In a farm family, everyone works and the rewards are shared by all, as well as such hardships as fallow land, poor harvests, and falling prices for agricultural products.

Lou Brum Burdick, founder of Brum & Anderson, Inc., a public relations firm, told me:

> I think I learned a lot of things growing up on the farm that
> have proved invaluable for my business. My business is

founded on teamwork. I am the eldest of nine children, so I have always been real comfortable assigning duties and putting people in charge of things. It's very instinctive. Everybody works hard on a farm, and everybody does, at whatever age, what they are capable of, and they contribute to the whole. So early on, it is ingrained in you that every member of the family depends on everyone else in the family. Plus, farming is a business. We grew up very conscious of the price of corn and wheat.

The father or the mother is responsible for engendering trust and cooperation. Women entrepreneurs frequently say that this role was played by their father. Where the father was absent because of death, divorce, or other reasons, the mother was the family altruist. Sybil Ferguson recalls her father giving her the inspiration to follow her dreams, to see problems as opportunities, and to trust in her special vision of the future. Nancy Heller went to work in her father's coat factory. Harriet Gerber Lewis's father took her on sales trips when she was fourteen years old. Jean O'Ffill told me, "My dad and I were very close. I adored him. I was twenty-five years old before I recognized that my dad wasn't perfect."

Most economists ignore the role of the family and the teaching of *patience*. Economists tend to see the marketplace as having products and services in supply and a demand curve interested in them at a certain price. Entrepreneurs create markets by identifying potential demands and creating products and services that will fill those needs. However, at least one economist believes that the methods and models of psychology can be enlisted to give meaning to economic phenomena. Nobel Prize winner Gary Becker of the University of Chicago has enunciated a theory of family behavior that has implications for entrepreneurs. His theory states: "Within the family, the presence of an altruist who can deal out material rewards or penalties has the effect of making all other family members *behave* altruistically toward one another, no matter how selfish or 'rotten' they are."[4]

Note how Becker's "rotten kid" theory contrasts sharply with the legendary "survival of the fittest" theory put forth by economists. In this theory, "the cupidity and egoism of self-interested individuals, minimally constrained by bonds of law and custom, work to create the

4. Ibid., p. 61.

wealthiest of societies."[5] Whereas a "survival of the fittest" approach, or operating exclusively in one's own self-interest, is a successful strategy for competing companies, it is not a successful strategy for an entrepreneur. Moreover, entrepreneurs admit to the importance of patience, cooperation, heart, and other values and rarely proclaim that they were more competitive than anyone else in a particular arena.

Women entrepreneurs frequently attribute their success, at least in part, to the values that they learned at home during childhood. Of these, patience and trust are foremost because there are so many random events that knock entrepreneurial companies off their business plans. New problems are created for the entrepreneur when this happens, and frequently the entrepreneur is incapable of dealing with them unless she has learned patience and to trust in herself and her co-workers.

It is not simply bad luck or bad planning that causes the solution of one set of problems to generate another set of problems. Living systems operate that way. They interface with other systems and all components of other systems. One system's output is another system's input, and vice versa. The interactions of systems are usually asynchronous, and sometimes very much so. There's always a time lag in the adaptation of one system to another. Competent entrepreneurs understand that they must be patient and suffer through these time lags. Frequently, the random event that pops out of the interface of two living systems creates an entrepreneurial opportunity along with the problem.

For example, the imposition of seat belt laws has reduced the number of vehicular fatalities. On the other hand, it has increased the number of paraplegics. And fewer vehicular fatalities has reduced the number of organ donors. This has created a problem for the people who need compatible organs to survive. Many of them die while awaiting a transplantable organ. The entrepreneurial opportunity in body parts has not gone unnoticed. The Jarvik heart used by Humana Hospital in Louisville, Kentucky, is one of several transplantable hearts recently developed by entrepreneurs.

Competent entrepreneurs and their investors are not perfectionists. They strive for satisfaction only. Perfection is either not attainable or too costly to achieve. Rather than spend the time and capital on an attempt to achieve perfection, entrepreneurs spend less time and capital to achieve *satisfaction*. Carol Mann, president of Triage, Inc., a workout and turnaround consulting firm, says, "In the turnaround business, there are no

5. Ibid.

touchdowns, only the occasional first down to make us cheer. If you hope to get touchdowns, you will be dumped behind the line and turn over the ball." In the entrepreneurial process, random collisions are the norm rather than the exception. Perfection is not possible in that environment. Perfectionists do not make good entrepreneurs.

Patience has been studied by behavioral scientists with some interesting results. As psychologists W. Mischel and R. Metzner write: "A person's willingness to defer immediate gratification depends to a considerable degree on the outcomes that he expects from his choice. Of particular importance are the individual's expectations that future delayed rewards for which he would have to work and/or wait would actually materialize."[6]

The time value of money, expressed by the word *interest*, explains quantitatively the value of delayed gratification. To an entrepreneur, plowing back today's profits into more research and development in order to enhance the value of the gift means building a gift-giving system that the community may at some future time applaud in the form of wealth for the entrepreneur.

Giving Up Social Contacts

Sociability is one of the least important characteristics of successful entrepreneurs. Randall Keith Filer writes: "Sociability—a person's liking for social activities, conversation and having many friends—is negatively related to earnings."[7] Filer evaluated 4,300 persons between 1967 and 1977 in terms of their sex, education, salary, cognitive skills, training, profession, occupation, and industry. The personality characteristic that correlated most positively with high earnings in the Filer study was drive. Earnings and wealth are different, but achieving either requires drive. Patience can lead to wealth, but not to high earnings.

Women entrepreneurs speak of their sacrifices, chief among them being delaying the start of a family and giving up friends and social events for a number of years.

6. W. Mischel and R. Metzner, "Preference for Delayed Rewards as a Function of Age, Intelligence and Length of Delay Interval," *Journal of Abnormal and Social Psychology* 64 (1962), pp. 425–431.
7. Randall Keith Filer, "The Influence of Affective Human Capital on the Wage Equation," in Ronald G. Ehrenberg, ed., *Research in Labor Economy*, Vol. 3 (Greenwich, Conn.: L. A. I. Press, 1981).

Middle-Class Values at Home

Relatively few women entrepreneurs emerge from the hopelessly poor or the extremely wealthy. The latter have lost their drive and are merely part of the process of dissipating the remaining wealth of a previous entrepreneur, perhaps a railroad baron of the mid-nineteenth century. The hopelessly poor are much too involved in putting food on the table, keeping a roof over their heads, and paying for heat in the winter to think about the issues of patience and trust. The very poor are typically unable to cite examples in the community of patience having been rewarded. In fact, the opposite is the case. Erik Erikson writes that a child learns trust in its first two years when its cries are consistently answered by loving, caring hands that reach out to pick up the child and change its diaper or give it a bottle.[8] With many hopelessly poor families lacking a father, the child's mother must necessarily find work, which means that the baby is left with neighbors or a relative. Perhaps all of her cries are not answered. When this is the case, she will not evolve into the next stage of development, but rather lack the necessary trust to evolve into a self-sufficient individual.

Further, it is difficult to speak to a child about studying hard and planning for a future that includes a big home, a spacious lawn, and a swimming pool when there is no heat in that child's rat-infested South Bronx apartment in the middle of February. Lacking aspirations, the hopelessly poor live from day to day. Neither planning nor patience is part of their vocabulary.

Parents teach patience. In the case of women entrepreneurs, if the father is frequently or permanently absent, it is the mother who teaches this virtue. She is strong, self-reliant, with energetic and hopeful attitudes toward life. The mother has a respect for education, for a fully formed personality, for solid achievement in every sphere, together with a clear-eyed, concrete—possibly irreverent—approach to all issues. Above all, she respects effort, honesty, faith, and critical ability. "Don't be a sinner," she says, "but worse than a sinner, don't be a sucker."

Mary Kay Ash founded Mary Kay Cosmetics, Inc., in 1963 with $5,000 in savings and the advice to refrain from heeding every male friend, adviser, and counselor who knew her. It was Ash's mother who urged her to go forward. Ash's husband died suddenly during the first

---

8. Erik Erikson, *Childhood and Society,* 2d ed. (New York: W. W. Norton and Co., Inc., 1963).

few months of operations and she had to pull her eldest son, Richard, out of college to help her. Ash's goal was to create a company in which women could become as wealthy and successful as they allowed themselves to become. Cosmetics was the means to Ash's end: a system for caring for highly motivated women. Ash has been the altruist and gift giver to over 300,000 women. More women earn over $100,000 per annum working for Mary Kay Cosmetics than for all other companies in the United States combined.

Wherever they learned patience and trust—on the farm, from a parent or mentor, or as a result of an early employment experience—entrepreneurs would be lost without it. Their market research would be done too hastily, their product would leave the laboratory too soon, the marketing effort would be inadequate. Then, when nothing worked right, when the product was shipped back due to bugs, when critical suppliers demanded payment in advance, when the bank called the note, and when the salespeople quit, all in the same week, the entrepreneur without patience would throw in the towel. But competent entrepreneurs have the capacity to see the weaknesses in themselves as well as others and the potential for mistakes that these weaknesses can produce. They review in their minds all the potential disaster areas and develop strategies and new directions should any of these events occur.

The Ability to Cooperate

Entrepreneurs are the most resolutely self-reliant people. During the problem formulation stage of the entrepreneurial process they frequently withdraw into themselves. A curtain is pulled down around them and many of their former friends and acquaintances are not permitted to come near. The nascent entrepreneur is going through a period of intense dissatisfaction with her job and at the same time formulating a problem that she thinks might be soluble. All these thoughts involving leaving the security blanket of the job and planning a new company are new to her. Who can she turn to?

Frequently the spouse loses communication with the budding entrepreneur as well. In our survey of over 200 women entrepreneurs, approximately 33 percent became divorced either in the pre-entrepreneurial period or in the early stages of entrepreneurship. Many entrepreneurs are unable to speak about what they are thinking at this juncture. They fear their husband will not be sympathetic. After all, there will be a loss of income, a drain on the savings account, and possibly some borrowing. Debt is not very well understood in the best of circumstances, but going into debt to start a new company in a brand-new field is perceived as tantamount to suicide. Knowing this, the entrepreneur keeps very quiet. The husband foolishly says something like, "Do you love me or do you love that damned company you're starting?" There goes the marriage.

The budding entrepreneur is evolving at this point. She is getting her heart back. The evolution, although noble, is not painless. She is developing an affirmative attitude toward one very large problem that affects a large number of people. She is beginning to see that she can aid in making the life of every person who has that problem easier and more beautiful. That vision can sanctify a life. The entrepreneur begins to see herself as part of a community and to understand that she will owe her life to the people in that community who have the problem, and that they will owe their gratitude to her. Becoming a gift giver forces the entrepreneur to evolve from an egotist to an altruist.

Why do people cooperate? What makes it possible for people to cooperate is the knowledge that they might meet again. If people were absolutely certain that they would never ever meet again, they would treat one another egotistically. However, there is no certainty that in the future when the people meet once again the previous behavior will be reciprocated. To optimize reciprocity in future interactions, therefore, people cooperate in the present. Robert Axelrod, perhaps the leading student of cooperative behavior, writes:

> What makes it possible for cooperation to emerge is the fact that the players might meet again. . . . It would be best to cooperate with someone who will reciprocate that cooperation in the future, but not with someone whose future behavior will not be very much affected by this interaction.[9]

One of the best marketplaces in which to examine cooperative behavior is the U.S. Senate. In this forum, the 100 members know with absolute certainty that they will interface on many future occasions over a six-year period, and perhaps beyond that. Therefore, they treat each other with courtesy, respect, and, in some cases, obsequious behavior.

9. Robert Axelrod, *The Evolution of Cooperation* (New York: Basic Books, 1984), pp. 12 and 16.

They refer to one another as "distinguished colleague" even though their real feelings may be quite different. Their cooperation takes the form of trading votes. Senator A agrees to give the gift of his vote to Senator B's bill if Senator B will reciprocate with the gift of his vote on some future bill proposed by Senator A. The system works well for the senators but tends to isolate them from the people in other marketplaces with whom they do not interface as frequently or with as much certainty. For example, U.S. senators are not as cooperative with their local constituencies as politicians who are required to stand for election more frequently. Accountability has an ability to enforce cooperation.

Axelrod attempted to measure the winning strategy for behavior between two people. He invited professional game theorists, sociologists, and mathematicians to submit their favorite strategies for playing The Prisoner's Dilemma, a simple game in which the solution that a player chooses tells a great deal about the player's willingness to cooperate.

In The Prisoner's Dilemma, two young people who do not know each other and who may never meet again in the future (or, on the other hand, may meet again in the future) get off a plane together in an unnamed foreign country to which neither has ever been, and they commit a very minor crime together and share the proceeds. The two young people are immediately apprehended by the local police and taken to a jail. Each is placed in a separate room and interrogated separately. Each is told that the other person is being asked the same questions about the crime and that each has the opportunity to say that the other person is guilty (in which event he will go free) or to admit to the crime in the hope that the other person will also "cooperate" (in which case they *both* will serve a short sentence). The tendency is to "defect," to claim one's innocence and implicate the other person. However, the other person could do the same thing. In this instance, both persons serve long sentences.

The Prisoner's Dilemma is simply an abstract formulation of some very common and very interesting situations in which what is best for each person individually leads to mutual defection, whereas everyone would have been better off if they had mutually cooperated.

Axelrod's experts submitted their favorite strategies for solving The Prisoner's Dilemma in competition with one another to see which would be the winning strategy in the long run. The winning strategy was the simplest one, TIT-FOR-TAT. This strategy is the one in which a player cooperates on the first move and then does whatever the other player did on the previous move. Axelrod drew the following conclusions from his contest:

Surprisingly, there is a single property which distinguishes the relatively high-scoring entries from the relatively low-scoring entries. This is the property of being *nice*, which is to say never being the first to defect.[10]

Another reason for the success of TIT-FOR-TAT is "its propensity to cooperate after the other player defected." This property Axelrod calls "forgiveness with the exception of a single punishment."[11]

Therefore, the winning behavioral strategy in an interface between two people (or two groups of people) is:

NICE—PROVOCABLE—FORGIVING

This strategy is stable so long as the people who employ it are very clear with the other players that they are employing the TIT-FOR-TAT strategy. If they are clear, then the players will know what to expect in the future. If one then defects, she can expect a provocation, followed by continual cooperation thereafter. If all the employees of a company practice this strategy and are clear with one another at the beginning, the level of cooperation in that company will be so outstanding that no other form of behavior will be able to invade it. Therefore, one additional factor must be added to NICE-PROVOCABLE-FORGIVING. That factor is CLARITY.

Competent entrepreneurs have evolved morally when they are able to tell each employee upon his or her entry, "I would like you to read this booklet, which sets forth our company's business mission and its ethical standards. If you can abide by the latter, you will be happy here." A substantial number of the women entrepreneurs we interviewed spoke freely about how well their employees cooperated in the formative years and how competently everyone acted in difficult times when the chips were down. Joan Barnes, founder of Gymboree Corp., speaks of the loyalty of her original employees. Lane Nemeth, founder of Discovery Toys, which now employs over 150,000 women as a direct sales force, initially hired teachers whom she knew from her previous background and whom she knew she could trust and count on although their business acumen was underdeveloped. Entrepreneurs frequently rank the ability of their co-workers to cooperate over their competence or brilliance.

10. Ibid., p. 33.
11. Ibid., p. 42.

The great enforcer of cooperation in the entrepreneurial company is the continuing relationship. The players are bonded together through ownership of a significant amount of the company's common stock. They are bonded to their suppliers and customers by that great enforcer, the law of reciprocity. This is the knowledge that one will have to reciprocate gifts again and again with the same players. The first player to defect loses.

The bonds are not as tight in a large corporation. Many employees are envious. Many defect by taking credit that is due a co-worker. Many managers fail to reciprocate the cooperation they receive from their employees. Many others are more clever than clear. It is in the nature of large corporations to disappoint their altruists and to keep their egoists. The altruists dare to become entrepreneurs who form companies that enter a competition of gift giving with the large corporations. The entrepreneurs always win.

An Appreciation for Leverage

The fourth criterion of successful women entrepreneurs is an appreciation for and an understanding of leverage. There are two forms of leverage: financial and communications. Financial leverage means borrowing money, or incurring debt. Communications leverage means persuading people to do things for you that they had no intention of doing until you began communicating with them. Competent entrepreneurs, many people have observed, are perfectly comfortable incurring more debt than they would be able to repay if they were called upon to do so; moreover, they are excellent communicators. In a phrase, they have an appreciation for leverage.

For the entrepreneur, debt is a means of *delaying gratification*, not obtaining instant gratification. Lucy Mackall borrowed on her car to start her company. Barbara Nyden Rodstein took out her last drop of savings to launch a bathroom faucet company. Dozens of women entrepreneurs ran up their credit cards to the limit. Sandra Dixon Jiles personally guaranteed loans. Andrea Grossman, who brought us brightly colored stickers for wrapping gifts, launched her new business because she faced an enormous amount of debt when a client for whom she designed corporate brochures could not pay her and she could not pay her suppliers.

Communications leverage is asking questions, and successful entrepreneurs are relentless askers. They question everything, even if they think they know the answer. The question the entrepreneur fails to ask up front could be the one that nails her. The key questions are: Why are we paying for that? If we must pay for it, can we get a discount or can we barter for that asset? Are other companies paying less than we are? Can we delay the payments? Why don't our customers pay us up front? Can we accelerate their payments without disturbing our core business? Can we sell them something else? Is what we are doing ethical and legal? These are gut questions, but know this: Successful entrepreneurs ask them and get answers.

Beginning without venture capital, women entrepreneurs learn to leverage everything. Without leverage, they might have no capital at all. Leverage provides *float*. Float equals capital. But just what is it? Since Archimedes discovered the principle of leveraging, the word *leverage* has acquired many shades of meaning. Archimedes, we are told, said "Give me a lever long enough and a fulcrum strong enough, and single-handed I can move the world." Two thousand years later, novelist Joseph Conrad, a Pole living in class-dominated Victorian and Edwardian England, said, "Don't talk to me of your Archimedes lever. . . . Give me the right word and the right accent and I will move the world."

So, although leverage still signifies a compelling or inducing physical force, it has also come to mean effectiveness in gaining, or using, influence and power—whether for business, professional, economic, political, or social ends.

Each culture and subculture seems to adapt the concept of leverage to its own needs. Take the financial marketplace:

* In corporate finance, leverage means the amount of debt used to support the operations of an enterprise.
* In the securities market, leverage means using credit to enhance one's speculative investment capacity.
* To the woman entrepreneur, it means convincing customers to pay up front, banks to give instant credit on deposits, and suppliers to wait to be paid.

Entrepreneurial leveraging refers to the use of minimal cash to achieve one's objectives while simultaneously generating more cash. Selective leveraging involves seeking out the company's *leverage points*— its key cash-producing and cash-consuming business activities. The cash-producing activities are then strengthened and the cash-consuming activities are discontinued. The objective is to generate more working capital by extracting as much cash as possible at the least possible cost in money, time, and effort and without damaging the core of the business.

Profound Leveraging

Profound leveraging takes place when you can (1) open new market channels, products, and services to existing customers, and (2) market new and old products and services to new customers through established channels, all with low incremental selling costs and a high return-on-sales payback. The woman entrepreneur's approach to marketing becomes the ultimate leveraging "machine," designed to generate multiple returns on the cash invested in marketing.

To keep her leverage machine going, the woman entrepreneur generates sales leads and then rents lists of these sales leads to other vendors while simultaneously turning the leads into customers.

For example, if she operates a chain of restaurants or retail stores, cashiers with a mushrooming array of equipment add up to a cost center. However, by collecting the names and addresses of customers when they pay their bills, she creates a list of customers that can be leveraged. By simply placing a fishbowl at the checkout counter for collecting business cards and by displaying the prize that will be awarded to the lucky winner whose name is drawn on a certain date, she gathers names for a list she can use to notify these individuals directly about special promotions and new merchandise or that she can rent to other interested parties. It's not terribly sophisticated, yet it's a useful and representative idea.

The important thing for the entrepreneur to remember is that any inquiry coming into her company reflects a generic interest in her product or service area. Although the inquiry may not result in an order, the inquiry itself is a leverageable asset that she paid to generate. She can spread that cost, even recoup it. Again, this is because there are more noncustomers than there are customers. In terms of future dollars, their interest in her products and services is more important than the interest of her customers in her specific area.

This is entrepreneur-think, not tradition-think. It demands a feel for residual leveraging, for capturing sales leads, and for spreading the cost of the lead-capturing process by renting the noncustomer names to others. It requires thinking in terms of fishbowls and envelopes and double postcards as message carriers and lead captures that bring back names, addresses, and telephone numbers for free—because she has spread the costs of the message carriers among other vendors.

Why does the woman entrepreneur understand leverage? Because she has to. It is her capital.

Two

Statistical Information on America's Women Entrepreneurs

Based on research conducted by my staff, the statistical profile of America's woman entrepreneur emerges as follows:

* She was the eldest child in the family 35 percent of the time; she was the youngest 28 percent of the time. Twelve percent were only children.
* She was born and raised in the Eastern United States 38 percent of the time, and in the Midwest, 25 percent. Ten percent were foreign-born.
* Fifty percent reported that they were from middle-class homes.
* Forty-seven percent of their mothers worked.
* Their high school achievements were 27.5 percent academic and 18.5 percent athletic.
* Seventy-eight percent of them graduated from college.
* Twenty-seven percent completed graduate school.
* Slightly more than two-thirds are currently married.
* One-third have two children; 12 percent have one child; and one-fourth have no children.
* Forty percent report that they began their families before they began their companies.

Three

The Fundamentals of Entrepreneurship

The fundamental law of the entrepreneurial process is that the creation of a valuable company is a function of the interrelationship of three variables: identifying the problem, creating a solution that fits the problem, and building a team of people to deliver the solution to the problem. Stated another way, wealth or a high valuation (V) is generated through the process of building a team of people (E) to implement the entrepreneur's mission to solve a problem (P) that is affecting a large number of people by creating an elegant solution (S) and conveying it to the problem through multiple marketing channels. Stated as a formula:

$$V = P \times S \times E,$$

where:

V = valuation
P = the size of the problem
S = the elegance of the solution
E = the quality of the entrepreneurial team

This is Silver's first law of entrepreneurship.

To succeed, an entrepreneur must choose an opportunity that possesses values for P, S, and E. When they are multiplied times each other, the result is a large value for V, and wealth is created thereby. Time and capital are lost or wasted when positive values are believed to exist for P, S, and E, but one or more of them is discovered to have zero value. Zero when multiplied by any other number results in zero.

Identifying the Problem

Problems are markets in search of solutions. All successful entrepreneurs have a unique ability to formulate problems. In economic terms, this means identifying a market or a problem in search of a solution. One of the compliments managers pay to entrepreneurs whom they join goes something like this: "She has the ability to see the whole market, from those customers who are ready to buy to those who need years of education."

One measure of how urgently people need a problem solved for them is to see if they will pay up front for a solution. Well over one-half of the most successful women-owned entrepreneurial companies were launched with customer (or dealer, franchisee, and distributor) financing.

Women entrepreneurs also find problems in services undertaken by the government but usually done poorly. Several outstanding entrepreneurs whom we profile in this book, such as Raydean Acevedo and Laura Henderson, solve problems for government agencies.

How do you problem-formulate? As successful artists do, it is necessary to adopt a problem, index its many features and parts, and then begin arranging and rearranging the parts until you identify areas that appear to be receptive to solutions.

When I first learned that I could solve problems for entrepreneurs, only one aspect of the problem appeared to me: raising venture capital for them. I subsequently learned that the universe of entrepreneurs was quite broad, and some segments of it needed entirely different kinds of solutions than other segments. For example, I estimated that approximately one million people in the United States annually consider the possibility of becoming entrepreneurs. I based this on readership of entrepreneur-oriented magazines and attendance figures for franchise, small-business, and new-technology conferences. These people were probably at the dissatisfaction and energy peaks of their personal development curves, but lacked insight into what to do about it. A possible solution was to steal a page from Gloria Steinem: Index the problems of becoming an entrepreneur and the many resources available to entrepreneurs, how to access them, and when. The perfect product was a book.

A smaller group of would-be entrepreneurs, perhaps 100,000 per annum, has a different set of problems. They want to share their problem with others, and discuss specific areas such as attracting a manager, packaging a product, and dealing with suppliers. This group of entrepreneurs would prefer to come together in a conference room environment. The multiple solutions for this group are seminars such as Venture Capital Clubs, conferences, and discussion groups.

A yet smaller group of entrepreneurs has completed its journey through the tunnel, put it all together, and is ready to write a business plan to raise venture capital. I estimated that approximately 10,000 entrepreneurs go through this rite of passage each year.

Finally, approximately 1,000 entrepreneurs will seek the assistance of an investment banker each year to help them find a merger partner or to raise venture capital or other forms of capital.

Thus, when I problem-formulated the market for my services, I saw four tiers, each interested in a separate and distinct product having its own price, payment terms, and means of conveyance. Exhibit 3-1 tells the story better.

Exhibit 3-1. The market of new entrepreneurs.

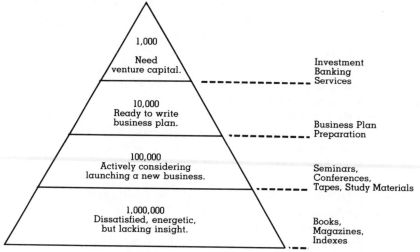

By addressing only one segment of the market, for example, investment banking, I would have been ignoring much larger aspects of the market, which not only feed into one another but can also be serviced easily and profitably by the overall entity. The pyramid method of problem-formulating seems to be applicable in a wide range of new business opportunities.

Creating the Solution

Entrepreneurship is not creating a solution to a problem that is already defined. Rather, it is the formulation and reformulation of the problem until a solution emerges through the process of raising all the questions, examining the problem from all angles, and restating and reframing the problem until it has been examined as thoroughly as possible. The entrepreneur who formulates the problem in a thorough, exhaustive manner will develop a larger P and more elegant S than will the entrepreneur who invests in a superior S without examining all the nooks and crannies of P. The latter is usually done by inventors; they are a far different breed from entrepreneurs.

If the process of entrepreneurial creativity is to be understood fully, the study of what the entrepreneur does cannot be restricted to the visible solution, the finished product. It must include the earlier, crucial step: formulation of the problem to which the solution is a response. In addition, the formulation of the problem is not a constant, but rather a cumulative process of discovery that begins when the potential entrepreneur enters the period of dissatisfaction, extends through the development of insight into the problem, and often does not end even after the entrepreneur appears at the corner of Wall and Broad streets for the listing ceremony on the New York Stock Exchange of her company's common stock.

Thinking, we know, is equated with rational, methodical, unadventurous problem solving—the unfolding of symbolic links from given premises to known conclusions. Creative thinking does not follow the known path. Rather than accepting the premises of a structured problem, creativity fashions a new problematic configuration. Instead of striving to reach a known solution, the cognitive efforts of a creative person are frequently targeted at goals that previously were considered inconceivable or not achievable. If behavioral scientists skilled at structuring measurement systems were to observe entrepreneurs at work, query them continually, and qualify and correlate the results against standards, we would learn more about the creative process that entrepreneurship involves than we would from my or any other observations.

One method of measurement would be to put twenty significant problems on pieces of paper, have the entrepreneurs select the one that they would like to build a business to solve, and then formulate the business plan. The launch itself would require capital aplenty, not a long commodity at universities these days; thus, measuring the competence of an entrepreneur by the success of the business against her creative process will probably have to be postponed until there is funding for the full study. Still, behavioral science is sufficiently developed to measure the creativity in the entrepreneurial process.

The creative process in entrepreneurship has not been investigated thoroughly, and is only now being studied in artists and scientists.

However, the studies by D. N. Perkins and Anna Roe provide a large body of ideas from which we can draw to learn more about the creative process as it applies to entrepreneurs.[1] D. N. Perkins provides us with good principles of creativity:

> *Try to be original.* If you want to be creative, you should try to build into any outcomes the property of originality. This sounds almost too silly to mention, but I don't think so and have given some reasons for that. Many supposedly intrinsically creative pursuits like painting can be pursued in very humdrum ways. Major figures in the arts and the sciences often were certainly trying to be original. Creativity is less an ability than a way of organizing your abilities toward ends that demand invention.
>
> *Find the problem.* This recalls the Getzels-Csikszentmihalyi concept of problem finding. Early in an endeavor, explore the alternatives freely, only gradually converging on a defined course of action and keeping even that flexibility revisable. The evidence is that creative people do this. The principle makes all the more sense in that later on in the process is often too late—too late to build in originality or intensity or other qualities you might want.
>
> *Strive for objectivity.* Problems connected with accurately and objectively monitoring progress pervade creative activity. The judgment of the moment could prove quite different tomorrow, the revisions of today wrong in a week. Makers have adopted many strategies to cope with the caprices of their own impressions, such as setting a product aside for a while. Learning to fashion products that have a potent meaning for others as well as for yourself is a complex process. Beginning with the child's first experiences of language and picturing, the problem of reaching others reappears throughout human development in more subtle guises, and it plagues even the

---

1. Anna Roe concluded that creative physician-scientists were (1) very open to experience, (2) highly observant and prone to see things in unusual ways, (3) extremely curious, (4) accepting of unconventional thoughts, (5) ready to recognize and reconcile apparent opposites, (6) tolerant of ambiguities but liking to resolve disorder into order, (7) appreciative of complexity, (8) highly independent in judgment, thought, and action, (9) self-reliant, and (10) not responsive to group standards and control.

expert maker. Sometimes, it may be best to ignore such hazards and freewheel for a while. But if you always freewheel, you never really take advantage of your own best judgment.

Search as seems necessary and prudent. That is, explore alternatives when you have to because the present option has failed, or when you had better because taking the obvious course commits substantial resources that might be better spent otherwise. Of course, the conventional advice of many works on creativity is to explore many alternatives routinely.

Try, but don't expect, to be right the first time. The research found that people tend to trade quality for quantity. Aiming at fluency, they lower the standards governing their production of ideas, select imperfectly, and achieve no net gain. This is advice against doing just that. Instead, ask your mind to deliver up the best possible results in the first place. Note that this does not mean fussing over initial drafts, trying to make them perfect by editing as you go. Neither does this say that the results will be right the first time. They very likely will need revision, maybe extensive revision, and maybe the wastebasket and a new start. That is why you have to adopt a paradoxical attitude: trying, while being perfectly comfortable about falling short. The point is to bias the quick unconscious mechanisms that assemble the words we use, the gestures we make, toward doing as much of the work as possible and leaving as little as possible for deliberate revision. To put it another way, ask yourself for what you really want, and you may get it, or at least some of it.

Make use of noticing. The ability to notice patterns relevant to a problem is one of the most powerful gifts we have. This can be put to work deliberately by contemplating things connected to the quest. Suppose, for example, you are designing an innovative house and need ideas. Walk around a conventional house and see what transformations suggest themselves. Or examine a conventional house in the mind's eye with the same objective. The latter can be particularly powerful for the body or billfold. Often books on creativity recommend exposure to seemingly unrelated things to stimulate ideas. This certainly works at times, as Darwin, Archimedes, and others have taught us. But, in my experience and judgment, sensitive scrutiny of things related to the task at hand usually yields a richer harvest of ideas.

When stuck, change the problem. Early on in the space race,

NASA spent much time and effort seeking a metal robot strong enough to withstand the heat of reentry and protect the astronauts. The endeavor failed. At some point, a clever person changed the problem. The real problem was to protect the astronauts, and perhaps this could be done without a material that could withstand reentry. The solution, the ablative heat shield, had characteristics exactly opposite to those originally sought. Rather than withstanding the heat, it slowly burned away and carried the heat away from the vehicle. Let me generalize this and similar examples into a heartening principle. Any problem can be solved provided you change the problem into a related one that solves the same real problem. So, ask yourself what the real problem is, what constraints have to be met, and which ones can be changed or sacrificed. (There may be more than one way of formulating the real problem.)

When confused, employ concrete representations. Darwin's notebooks, Beethoven's sketchbooks, a poet's drafts, an architect's plans—all are ways of externalizing thought in process. They pin down ideas to the reality of paper and prevent them from shifting or fading from the memory. All of us do this at one time or another. However, despite such habits, we may not realize that making thought concrete can help to cure confusion on nearly any occasion. When paths lead this way and that, circle back, and refuse to show the right way, make notes, make drawings, make models. Think aloud or form vivid mental images because such internal concreteness helps to clarify the problems.

Practice in a context. Most advice on how to be creative urges the learner to apply it everywhere. However, sometimes "everywhere" is so indefinite and daunting a notion that it turns into nowhere. When people want to improve their creativity, my suggestion is for them to choose some activity they often engage in and try hard to be more creative in that. Focus breeds progress. No need to hold back in other activities, but be sure of one.

Invent your behavior. That is, people should think about, criticize, revise, and devise the ways they do things that are important to them. Too often, inventive thinking is limited to the customary objects of invention—poems, theories, essays, advertising campaigns, and whatnot. But part of the art of invention is to select unusual objects of invention—objects like your own behavior. This isn't just nice; it's needed. Performances do not necessarily improve, even when you do them frequently. Indeed, it's common lore that people often end up practicing and entrenching their mistakes.

These, then, are some possible plans up front, another contribution to that young and hopeful technology of thought. These principles and others like them try to define and impart the limited but very real "edge" that is about the best you can hope for from very general principles. Perhaps the plans mentioned are hard to take, at least as advice. Their prescription is too broad, too much in the direction of telling the daydreamer to pay attention or the grind to daydream more. Just what they mean in particular cases and how one persuades oneself to behave accordingly are serious questions. But take them as general principles and take seriously the problem of translating them into practice, and then they make more sense. There's no reason why the right principles have to be as easy as a recipe for boiling water.[2]

The elegant solutions come to the deeply committed entrepreneur, not as the result of invention but frequently after she has worked with all the elements of the problem, much as Monet painted the church façade at different times during the day in order to capture sunlight on canvas. Clearly he did not, but he produced some beautiful impressions of sunlight.

Selecting the Entrepreneurial Team

Successful women entrepreneurs typically select an experienced corporate "achiever" to oversee the business aspects of the new company. This person is occasionally, but not always, the entrepreneur's husband. The achiever is strong in finance, administration, dealing with suppliers, and handling red tape. Together, they draw up the new company's organizational plan.

The organizational plan defines the functional areas that must be staffed and the characteristics of the people who should staff those functions. Frequently, an entrepreneurial team is unbalanced because friends get together at a large corporation and leave to implement the product idea that the corporation rejected. The friends might be perfectly capable

2. D. N. Perkins, *The Mind's Best Work* (Cambridge, Mass.: Harvard University Press, 1981), pp. 215–219.

engineers but unable to manage others or persuade customers to purchase the product they have designed. Entrepreneurs are frequently reluctant to delegate responsibility to others, either because no one else can do the job or because they think that is the case. The company crawls when it should trot for lack of a barn-burner marketing person or a thorough production person or a financial officer.

It is exceptionally difficult to form effective entrepreneurial teams. My research indicates that, in the most successful entrepreneurial teams, corporate achievers are somewhat older than their entrepreneur partners. The development stages of the entrepreneur and the achiever are markedly different. Their personality characteristics and social values overlap in relatively few areas. The social values of the entrepreneur are usually more liberal. This could be a function of age and life experiences, but a thirty-seven-year-old entrepreneur and the forty-two-year-old former corporate manager that she selects are bound to have different views of life. An entrepreneur is more likely to have few assets, live in the city, and drive a European car. The manager has a house in the suburbs and other assets, and drives an American car. They vote differently and have different opinions on marijuana, politics, premarital sex, music, and use of their leisure time.

The unifying factor is that both members of the team want to build a successful company. The manager's goals are perhaps more capital-gains oriented, while the entrepreneur's goal is to do some one thing extremely well. But the partners need each other for several important reasons, the chief of which are: (1) Entrepreneurs need managers around to direct their talents, focus their energies, and orchestrate the increasing number of employees and departments; (2) managers need energetic, innovative, imaginative entrepreneurs to provide them with growing companies to which they can apply their managerial talents.

The entrepreneurial team works somewhat as follows: Two people decide to go on a photographic safari to Africa. The first person boards the plane in casual attire, unburdened by carry-on luggage. The second carries six cameras, filters, guidebooks, camping equipment, a tent, and other paraphernalia. The plane lands in Kenya and the two set off on foot into the jungle. The first traveler goes out in front and the second decides to stop and put up the tent. The first is about a mile away from where the tent is being set up when a tiger jumps out from behind a tree, growls, and charges. The first traveler spins around and runs back to the tent as fast as can be, with the tiger in hot pursuit. The tent is part-way up, and the tiger's would-be prey runs into the tent, swings around the pole, and heads out in the same direction, shouting back at the busy partner: "This tiger is for you. I'm going to go back for mine."

An entrepreneur can generate weeks of work in the first three hours of the day, drop it off on the manager's desk to be organized and implemented, and then change her mind by the afternoon. Managers are delighted by the opportunity to clean up after the entrepreneurs. They are used to making management decisions; now, for the first time, they own a meaningful portion of the company that they manage. Ownership is the glue that holds the entrepreneurial team together through some dark, scary times.

Demonstrable Economic Justification

Prior to launching a new company, the woman entrepreneur is well-advised to perform the DEJ (demonstrable economic justification) Factor Test. The entrepreneur asks: Does this opportunity meet all the requirements of the DEJ Factor Test? If it possesses all eight of the following factors, it is my experience that the entrepreneur can be almost assured of success. And, the cost of entering the market will be less than $20,000.

As you review the eight DEJ factors listed in Exhibit 3-2, think of the

Exhibit 3-2. The DEJ Factor Test.

DEJ Factor	Ask	What Will It Cost?
1. Existence of Qualified Buyers	Are the consumers to whom this product or service is marked aware that they have a need for it?	Advertising to find buyers
2. Large Number of Buyers	Are there lots of consumers who need this product or service?	Competitive pressure on price if there are too few customers
3. Homogeneity of Buyers	Will the market accept a standardized product or service, or must it be customized?	Manufacturing, tooling, die costs to customize each product

(continues)

Exhibit 3-2. (continued)

DEJ Factor	Ask	What Will It Cost?
4. Existence of Competent Sellers	Is the product or service so complex to explain that customers will need 90 days or more to test it?	Salespersons' salaries and expenses if "brilliance" needed to make sales
5. Lack of Institutional Barriers to Entry	Is there a requirement for governmental or industry association approval before the product or service can be marketed?	Working capital that burns while approval is awaited
6. Easy Promotability by Word of Mouth	Can the product's or service's merits be described by consumers by word of mouth?	Advertising if lacking word of mouth promotability
7. Invisibility of the Inside of the Company	Is there a need to reveal profit margins to the public?	Competitive pressure on price once profit margins are publicly known
8. Optimum Price/Cost Relationship	Is the selling price at least five times the cost of the goods sold?	Restrictions on the number of marketing channels if profit margins are too low

new company you are hoping to start and be brutally objective when answering the questions.

Entrepreneurs who fail to ask these eight questions and to act accordingly risk introducing a new product or service into a market and meeting with failure. The DEJ Factor Test is a predictor of success and a measure of the cost of seizing the opportunity. Here's the rule:

* *Super DEJ:* If the new market possesses all eight DEJ factors, entering it will cost less than $20,000 and the probability of success will be about 99 percent.
* *Majority DEJ:* If the new market possesses seven out of eight DEJ factors, entering it will cost around $1 million, and the probability of success will be about 90 percent.
* *Marginal DEJ:* If the new market possesses six out of eight DEJ factors, entering it will cost up to $20 million and the probability of success will be about 80 percent.
* *Low DEJ:* Below six DEJ factors, the new market will reject the product or service at a cost of more than $20 million. The new company will fail.

So, if the company you are thinking of starting possesses all eight DEJ factors, and if there is a large *P*, an elegant *S*, and some experienced *E*'s to help you, then run, don't walk, to get that company going.

Profiles
of
100 of the
Greatest
Entrepreneurs
of Our Day

Raydean Acevedo

Name of Company:	Research Management Consultants, Inc.(RMCI)
Location:	Camarillo, California
Date Founded:	1987
Description of Business:	Provides high-technology consulting services to corporations and government agencies with 200 or more employees.
Description of *P*:	Acevedo identified the opportunity under the Small Business Administration (SBA) 8(a)—minority contracting—program to solve technology-based problems for government agencies such as the Federal Administration Agency (FAA) and its corporate contractors.
Description of *S*:	Acevedo hired the best people she could find and sent them on-site to the locus of the problems RMCI was solving with the attendant result that SBA District Director Michael E. Lee calls RMCI "one of the SBA's most successful and sophisticated 8(a) firms."
Members of *E*:	Walter Jenkins, executive vice president Cyndi Burns, director Finance and Accounting Mary Draper, director Human Services Deborah Hanley, director Contracts Division Ron Kaiser, director Contracts Division John Buddy, director Maintenance and Repair Task Force Ralph Chapuis, director Environmental Service
Size of V:	The company is privately held and not required to publish its financial statements. Revenues are believed to be $16 million per annum.

Social Utility: Acevedo is business director of the Hispanic
                                         Association of Colleges and Universities,
                                         planner for the Global Woman's Summit, on
                                         the advisory board of Leadership America,
                                         and a member of the W. K. Kellogg
                                         Foundation, National Coalition of Women
                                         Appointees, and Selection Committee for the
                                         Partners of Americas.

Principal Source of
Venture Capital: Personal savings and cash flow from business

RAYDEAN ACEVEDO has always been an entrepreneur. When she was in the eleventh grade the principal of her school died of cancer. Saddened by this loss of one of her role models, she decided to raise money for the American Cancer Society in his honor. She organized a carnival, doing everything from selling tickets to setting up games and prizes and making the food. Her entrepreneurial zeal and warm-hearted concern for the people around her would continue and is responsible for her being one of the 100 greatest entrepreneurs of our day. Research Management Consultants tackles large, tough assignments for the FAA, the U.S. Department of the Navy, and government contractors including the Raytheon Corp., EG&G, and the Reed Group, a specialist in gathering data in the medical and insurance industries. Acevedo worked around the clock for the first year and a half before she took a salary. With conservative economic projections and careful investment, Raydean Acevedo has watched her company blossom into one of the fastest-growing companies in the United States. She says that she has yet to take a two-week vacation. However, she loves what she does and is dedicated to her staff. She makes it a point to make herself visible to all her employees and is committed to ensuring that they are working in an environment in which they are comfortable.

A big part of the company's success, Acevedo believes, is a highly trained and educated staff of professionals, most with advanced degrees, and an organization structured for maximum response to client needs. Unlike the multilayered government and corporate organizations that RMCI typically serves, she explains, her company functions under a compact, two-level structure: the technical consulting team, and a division director. She herself focuses on overall operating direction. "I believe in people. I believe that they do the right thing as long as they are in the right working conditions. I have learned that I have had to be a good listener and that sometimes my expectations are different from others'."

With a staff that is diverse both in their technical capabilities and their backgrounds, Acevedo says, "It can be very challenging." However, she claims, this gives her a good perspective in the final decision-making process and is the source of strength for her company. The key, she says, is "hiring the best people you can, and I do not only mean on paper but making sure that they hold the same values of integrity, quality, and service that are important to me."

The company is also decentralized geographically for maximum proximity to client sites. Although RMCI is based in Camarillo, California, and does its accounting there, four of its six divisions are located in Mclean and Norfolk, Virginia, handy to Washington, D.C. These four divisions are: Information Systems; Maintenance, Repair, and Testing; Contracts; and Human Resources. The Environmental Services Division is headquartered in Denver, along with the company's training center. She has other branches in San Diego and Bakersfield, California; Atlanta, Georgia; and offices in Maryland. Reed Group President Dr. Presley Reed applauds Acevedo's strategy of customer service, describing RMCI as "the most customer oriented firm" he has dealt with, a quality he believes contributed to the success of a tailored software program the company developed that allows his employees to reference complex national disability data for use in their medical and insurance work.[1]

Such kudos have led to formal recognitions as well. RMCI was named the Federal Aviation Administration's Woman Owned Business Enterprise of the Year in 1990, three years after its start-up, and again in 1991, marking the first time a company had won the award in two consecutive years.

RMCI's decentralization applies to new business development as well as to customer service. For government and corporate contracts alike, new work is secured through personal contacts rather than from advertising.

Acevedo's staff of 225 is 60 percent female, with a liberal sprinkling of African-Americans, Asian-Americans, and Hispanics as well.

Acevedo is not only an all-star player in her field but she is also an outstanding member of her community. She is actively involved in various women's and Hispanic organizations and invests both her money and her precious time and energy in these organizations. When asked how she found the time to manage her company and be so involved in the

---

1. David G. Rouguilo, *Hispanic Business* No. 130, June 1993, p. 124.

organizations she supports, she responded, "How do you not find the time? Giving back is as much a part of business as looking at the cash flow projections. . . . My parents always told me that I could do anything and that we were here to make this world a better place." She does, and continues to be a role model not only for Hispanic women and other women in business but for all business leaders—men and women alike.

Mary Kay Ash

Name of Company: Mary Kay Cosmetics, Inc.
Location: Dallas
Date Founded: 1963
Description of Business: The company produces and sells cosmetics through an international network of marketing consultants, using the Party Plan Method.

Description of *P*:   Many women prefer to purchase facial cosmetics in the privacy of their homes, where they can experiment more freely than they can in a store. Avon has proved this with annual sales of more than $3.1 billion. Mary Kay Ash added another feature: creating high incomes for her women marketing consultants, liberating them from the chores of the housewife, and gaining their loyalty for life.

Description of *S*:   There is nothing proprietary about the Mary Kay line of cosmetics. However, the delivery system is not easily duplicated: over 250,000 independent beauty consultants operating in five countries with an evangelical leader who continually inspires them with the courage to believe in themselves. At a recent convention she told these women: "If you are here today you are too smart to go home and scrub the floors." They have rewarded her with overwhelming sales.

Members of *E*:   Richard Rodgers, president

45

Size of V:	Ash and her son led a management buyout in 1986 that bought the company from the public for $250 million.
Social Utility:	The company has generated employment and a high sense of self-worth for over 250,000 women. In addition, 1,500 people are employed at the Dallas headquarters. More women earn over $100,000 per year working for Mary Kay Cosmetics than they do for any other company in the country.
Principal Source of Venture Capital:	The founder's life savings of $5,000

MARY KAY ASH founded her own company in 1963, about three months after retiring from another direct sales company in which she had worked for twenty-five years. She entered the direct sales business as a divorced mother of three children. She wanted to create a company in which being a woman would not hinder upward mobility and financial rewards and in which motivation was based on the goals and objectives that are important to women, not to men. Her entrepreneurial genius was to create a unique motivational system that would attract, hold, motivate, and reward an all-woman marketing organization. The unique product or elegant solution to a large problem was not part of Ash's initial formulation, although clearly the product would have to possess economic viability for her company to be successful.

She chose a cosmetic that she had been using for years, a skin care line based on formulas developed by a hide tanner, which until Ash's endorsement of them had been sold only by the man's granddaughter. She rented a storefront in a Dallas office building and began selling the products to generate revenue. She pulled her son, Richard, then age 20, out of college to assist her. Ash immediately began recruiting and training beauty consultants to begin home demonstrations. Although practically every male friend, adviser, and counselor tried to dissuade her, Ash was given the courage to succeed by her previous successes in direct sales and by her mother's advice and encouragement.

Revenues grew slowly in the 1960s but reached $31 million in 1974 and have since grown tenfold. The company has consistently earned more than 20 percent before taxes and its stockholders' equity exceeded $140 million (at the time Ash repurchased it), of which cash ($25 million) was approximately 20 percent. The company had virtually no long-term debt. Moreover, Ash has built a cash-generating machine that has turned more than a quarter of a million women into self-employed businesswomen with lots of ability and "handsome bank accounts." As in many party plan companies, the wives began outearning their husbands.

How did Ash accomplish this? She created a feeling of family in her company and a hierarchical organization that had a system of rewards and penalties, as with any family. Through frequent seminars attended by the independent beauty consultants, Ash "preaches to her women like a tent-meeting" evangelist. Typical of her gospel are the following precepts: "If you are here today you are too smart to go home and scrub the floors. You are spending one-dollar time on a one-penny chore." This admonition not only gives the women pride but encourages them to hire housekeepers so that they can spend more time recruiting additional beauty consultants and selling more cosmetics. "I created this company for you," she tells them. This and similar preachments enhance the spirit of family and create the excitement of a crusade.

Mary Kay Cosmetics depends for its success on the continual recruitment of new independent beauty consultants. After training, they purchase their initial inventory and begin calling on friends to have parties. The company does not advertise for women but, rather, relies on word of mouth. Thirty percent of its 250,000 direct sales personnel are college graduates. When the economy is weak and inflation is strong, women flock to Mary Kay in greater numbers than when the economy is buoyant.

Out interviewer, Charlene Maes, told me that "Mary Kay can look through a person's eyes right into their heart and persuade that person to do more with her life; and the fix takes hold immediately and lasts a long time."

Joan Barnes

Name of Company:	The Gymboree Corporation
Location:	Burlingame, California
Date Founded:	1976
Description of Business:	Gymboree offers developmental classes for toddlers and their parents in a fun, safe, creative, and interactive environment. It has six company co-owned play centers in northern California and 350 franchise-operated play centers in the United States and in seven foreign countries. The company also operates more than 150 retail stores that sell its infant and children's apparel.
Description of P:	When Joan Barnes gave birth to her first child in 1973, she had recently moved to northern California and did not know anyone there. She found it difficult to find programs for children under five and like-minded mothers and children for herself and her new-born child to socialize with.
Description of S:	Barnes created Gymboree, a specially designed play program for children three months to five years old and their parents. The company focused on socialization, play, and sensory development.
Members of E:	Bud Jacobs, franchise sales development Linda Rasmussen, franchise services Nancy Bott, finance Karen Andersen, public relations and marketing

Size of V:	The company has approximately 11.7 million shares of common stock outstanding and a market value in early 1994 of $493.5 million.
Social Utility:	Barnes supports her local Jewish Community Center and the Jewish Federation.
Principal Source of Venture Capital:	Personal savings of $6,000. In 1982, she received $300,000 from U.S. Venture Partners and several million dollars of additional funding from U.S. Venture Partners and five other venture funds over the next four to five years.

JOAN BARNES, born in Winnetka, Illinois, and raised by a working father and a stay-at-home mother, was unable to find a suitable play program for her two children in the mid-1970s. She had recently moved to California and felt isolated from like-minded mothers. "It was the middle of the 'me' generation; no one was having kids," says Barnes. "I felt isolated and lonely; I really did not know anyone." Barnes had found a new job in California and was the children's program director for a community center in San Rafael. "There were no programs for kids under five," says Barnes. She consequently persuaded one of her supervisors to allow her to organize a development program for toddlers. When it became instantly successful, a colleague suggested that she open her own center and she invested $3,000 toward her equipment and rent. Those classes became a hit, and Barnes bought out her partner for $6,000—her total investment in Gymboree.

She kept her job, which paid $5,000 a year, until four centers were up and running. By 1979, there were eight, and the requests for franchises were tumbling over the transom. Barnes sold them for $5,000 initially, and the franchisees needed an additional $5,000 each for equipment. In return, the franchisees received exclusive territorial rights to markets of at least 75,000 people and subsequently, the right to sell additional products developed by Barnes' management team, including toys, videos, and clothing along with on-going training support and marketing programs.

"I never dreamed of a big empire," says Barnes. "I just put one foot in front of the other. I was driven to make it work." Barnes attributes her intensity to growing up with a stay-at-home mother. "I saw my mom as a frustrated housewife whose strength was languishing by staying at home. I did not want to be like that. During the mid 1970s, women finally got their chance. I wanted to prove it [my idea] was possible."

Her family was skeptical. Barnes continues: "They gave me the guilt trip about leaving my kids." However, Barnes found the emotional support she needed from her husband, who was the political editor for a local newspaper at the time. "My husband was a Mr. Mom character—a homebody. I was lucky. He was a real contributor."

Barnes credits her success to having a good handle on the big picture and being able to visualize the concept and seeing how to make it happen. Barnes comments, "Many entrepreneurs do not know how to delegate. They may be brilliant but are unable to let go, and, therefore, inhibit their ability to grow."

Learning from her involvement in consciousness-raising groups of the 1960s, Barnes organized the centers to involve the parents *and* the kids. Although one of the purposes of the centers was to lend support to like-minded mothers and to give them a place to socialize, she did not want to create rap centers. "I wanted everyone to feel upbeat and engaged," says Barnes.

While Barnes had been exposed to business at a very early age, she had no formal training in business and finance. "I majored in English and dance," says Barnes. "I have always been very entrepreneurial. I ran my own dance classes, I sold real estate, and I ran a small antique business. Business has always interested me. I remember when I was a kid, I wanted to hang out with the men. I never was interested about what was going on in the kitchen. The men were always talking about the real estate deals they were working on. This excited me."

When someone suggested she should start franchising, Barnes knew nothing about franchising. Barnes says, "I think I knew McDonalds was a franchise at that time." Nevertheless, she wrote her first franchise agreement herself with no help from a lawyer. The Federal Trade Commission had recently imposed regulations on franchising, and there was new literature available to the public. "I just went down to the Department of Corporations and learned how to do it. There was nothing legal about it; it was just tedious," says Barnes. However, when she tried to trademark her company name, which at that time was KinderGym, the name was rejected as too generic. "I freaked," says Barnes. "Everything I was doing was under the name KinderGym. I hired a trademark attorney, and we chose the name Gymboree and trademarked it."

Franchising proved to be very successful, and three years later Barnes decided to seek venture capital. "I feld I needed to begin to start to grow purposefully or not grow at all," she says. She wrote her first business plan and was able to attract a venture capital firm to invest $300,000 initially and then several million over the next four to five years.

As the company began to grow bigger and bigger, Barnes says she began to lose interest. Barnes says, "It became too sophisticated; the creativity was gone. It was starting to be a formula business by then." In addition, the business began to take a toll on her personal life. "Personally, it was very hard on me. I had been giving all my energy to the company. My marriage was falling apart, and I began to have medical problems."

Consequently, Barnes handed over the reigns of the company and decided to leave the business. She continued to help out for a couple of more years. But Barnes says, "It was the beginning of a new life. I began a period of personal transformation. I went from spending 7 AM to 7:30 PM working at the office to having a lot of time to myself." Barnes began focusing on her own personal life, and today—as Barnes puts it—"smelling the roses."

Today, in any given week, 100,000 children, grouped according to age, attend various Gymboree classes across the United States, Canada, Australia, France, Israel, Korea, Mexico, Columbia, and Taiwan at an average of $90 for twelve classes. There are 370 Gymboree centers in operation throughout the world.

And today, as a happy stockholder of the company she founded herself, Joan Barnes enjoys spending time with her kids and has become an avid athlete, enjoying mountain biking and hiking the hills of northern California. She says that she even has time to read and enjoys the time to herself. That's quite a shift for this energetic, enthusiastic, and enlightened entrepreneur. Barnes admits, "I'm an entrepreneur by spirit," and she is currently looking into a couple of new ventures. What's next for Joan Barnes? No one is quite sure, but don't close the book on Joan Barnes just yet—there may be another chapter already in the making.

Joyce Beber

Name of Company:	Beber, Silverstein & Co.
Location:	Miami, Florida
Date Founded:	1971
Description of Business:	This advertising agency has developed some stunningly imaginative campaigns for its clients.
Description of P:	John Dewey once wrote that the most important sign in communication is the pointed finger, which conveys a message about the location of something. This translates into the purpose of advertising: pointing to a product or service. The complexity of the advertising business is that a large number of fingers are pointing at once.
Description of S:	Joyce Beber brought a unique asset to the advertising industry: her life experiences.
Members of E:	Elaine Silverstein, co-founder and partner
Size of V:	The company's revenues in 1993 were in excess of $52 million and growing.
Social Utility:	The company does a great deal of pro bono and advocacy work, for Junior Achievers, the Dade County Public Schools, and others. Beber has been honored for her community service work by Big Brothers, Big Sisters, and Women in Communications.
Principal Source of Venture Capital:	$700 in personal savings

"I became an entrepreneur," says JOYCE BEBER with a smile, "because I was naive and had guts. My partner Elaine and I had a healthy mixture of ignorance and confidence. I wanted to make my mark."

When Beber began her advertising agency, practically all her clients were men. "They didn't respect our toughness, which we thought was a unique feature. They wanted ads that would generate sales," she said.

So how did the two young women distinguish themselves?

"From the very beginning, Elaine and I had an obsessive concern for consumer response. If the ads didn't work, we would change them at our own expense," Beber said.

In time, Beber, Silverstein's ads began to take on a different look. The company developed the "Queen" campaign for The Helmsley Hotel chain, and it was the first advertising agency to run three ads on the same subject in individual media.

Beber, Silverstein was one of the first ad agencies to implement the association-based marketing strategy that is today a buzzword with "Frequent Flyer," "Frequent Buyer," and similar programs. In the early 1970s, a florist asked Beber to help him increase sales at nonholiday times. She thought about the problem and came up with the idea of a subscription club for the florist's customers. This encouraged them to buy flowers year-round in order to accumulate membership points.

Beber, Silverstein's different approach attracted national clients such as Cordis, the pacemaker developer, Humana, Knight-Ridder, and Florida Power & Light, among others. One of their clients of which the partners are most proud is the National Organization for Women. They were in charge of NOW's campaign to push the Equal Rights Amendment through Congress.

"Economic need was not the reason I became an entrepreneur," Beber says. "I just wanted to feel I was doing something important.

"I think it is critical to love what you're doing. And we love our business."

Beber learned business from her mother, an antiques collector who used her home as a shop. "She bought and sold antique furniture all the time. You might go to sleep in an antique bed and wake up on a couch in the living room because Mom had sold the bed."

Watching her mother enjoy her avocation while doing it profitably laid a foundation for Joyce Beber to achieve success in her own business.

Lynn Tendler Bignell and Janet Tweed

Name of Company:	Gilbert Tweed Associates
Location:	New York City/Boston
Date Founded:	1972
Description of Business:	One of the fastest-growing executive recruiting firms in the country, Gilbert Tweed Associates (GTA) not only fills position specifications for its clients but also offers them a series of unique services that ensures an effective and thorough search.
Description of *P*:	The anxiety and stress involved when an executive relocates, especially with a family, is one of the leading causes of search failures. Consequently, the effectiveness and quality of the search become compromised. GTA deals with these issues before they become problems, with the result that their searches are complete and successful.
Description of *S*:	Innovative programs developed by GTA, such as InSearch, ReloSearch, and SpouseSearch, which provide a thorough evaluation of the clients' business and staff, an internal/external executive search, and the availability of counsel and support for relocating executives and families, have made GTA one of the top executive search firms in the country.

Members of *E*:	Lynn Tendler Bignell and Janet Tweed, co-founders and principals Achilles Perry, chief operating officer
Size of *V*:	1992 billings of approximately $6 million
Social Utility:	To celebrate its twentieth anniversary, GTA donated over $100,000 in executive search, consulting, and training services to twenty nonprofit health care and educational organizations and has extended invitations to other nonprofit organizations to attend these seminars free of charge.
Principal Source of Venture Capital:	$320 chipped in by the co-founders along with two phones and two desks

Lynn Bignell and Janet Tweed, co-founders of Gilbert Tweed Associates, have been leaders in the executive search business ever since they first began their careers in the 1960s. Originally hired by Dunhill Personnel, they were the first women ever to be hired by this recruiting firm, which placed only sales*men*. After becoming the top producers at Dunhill, both Bignell and Tweed, seeking new challenges, started their own separate firms: J. G. Tweed Associates and Gilbert Associates. While Tweed specialized in recruiting engineering managers, Bignell recruited sales and marketing executives. Neither Tweed nor Bignell had been in business for long before they decided to combine their talents in the partnership of Gilbert Tweed Associates. They had no prior experience in running their own companies and really had no grand business plan. As Bignell put it: "We just put one foot in front of the other. . . . The one thing we did know was that we would never compromise how we selected candidates, and our clients would always get 500 percent of our focus. . . . It paid off because the business kept coming in." Before their merger both Bignell and Tweed had developed loyal client bases while working for Dunhill. Bignell attributes their success to the fact that they are "good relationship builders." "The clients we had twenty years ago are still our clients today."

In a virtually male-dominated field, Bignell and Tweed did not see themselves as "women." "We were just two people who wore skirts some of the time who were doing their thing." Because they realized that there were men who would have difficulty accepting a woman headhunter they learned helpful techniques early on that enabled them to recognize how the relationship between prospective clients and themselves would work out. "We would chat and look for pictures. We would see if they had daughters and find out what their wives did. We would listen to how they spoke about their wives and their daughters . . . you could hear the chauvinism in some people . . . and then we knew that this wasn't going to be a fruitful relationship. There were others who were so proud of their wives who had their own businesses and proud of their daughters who were in med school or law school or had their own careers. When they talked about women like that we knew that we were in a circle that was acceptable to them."

This was only the beginning. They both knew that if they were to succeed in this business they would have to "cast a larger shadow" and take the "perceived risk out of their firm." Consequently, Bignell and Tweed aggressively sought out interviews with major business publications and made their name and story available. They successfully developed good relations with the press, and their name began to appear among the top executive search firms in the country. In addition, they opened up four new offices, three of which failed within the next three years. But this did not stop them. In 1986 they realized that they were spreading themselves too thin and decided to conduct their own search for a chief operating officer for GTA. Since then the company has tripled in size and now has five domestic offices as well as partners in nine countries and fifteen cities abroad. The growth and success of Gilbert Tweed is attributed to the tenacity, balance, and partnership of the founders, their extraordinary intuitive instincts, their openness and receptivity to the advice and counsel of their board, recognizing the need for a chief operating officer, their ability in developing a team of unbeatable professionals, and their strategy to build niche practice areas.

Rose Blumkin

Name of Company:	Nebraska Furniture Mart, Inc.
Location:	Omaha
Date Founded:	1937
Description of Business:	The company owns and operates a large retail furniture store.
Description of *P*:	The problem that furniture solves is the same from one merchant's goods to the next. Thus, Nebraska Furniture Mart must have been doing some unique things to generate sales of $90 million per annum out of one location.
Description of *S*:	Blumkin's secret of success, she told *The Wall Street Journal*, is to "sell cheap, tell the truth, don't cheat nobody, and don't take kickbacks."[1]
Members of *E*:	Louis Blumkin, president
Size of *V*:	Berkshire Hathaway, Inc., whose CEO is the legendary Warren E. Buffett, acquired the company in 1983 for $60 million.
Social Utility:	The company has created 500 jobs, and Blumkin is a living testimonial to the finest qualities that entrepreneurship stands for.
Principal Source of Venture Capital:	$500 personal loan

1. Frank E. Jones, "Furniture Czarina Still a Live Wire at 90, A Retail Phenomenon Oversees Her Empire," *The Wall Street Journal*, May 23, 1984, p. 1.

ROSE BLUMKIN came to the Midwest from Russia in 1917 without a penny to her name. She has built an empire by hard work and by selling quality furniture at prices lower than the competition's. The ninety-nine-year-old, 4-foot-10-inch czarina of Nebraska Furniture Mart moves through her 250,000 square feet of selling space on a motorized three-wheeled cart. She speaks with vendors, salespersons, and customers, making buy-sell-hold decisions as she buzzes around her store. In 1983, New York University awarded Blumkin an honorary doctorate in commercial science, the first woman to be so honored.

When asked by *The Wall Street Journal* reporter Frank E. James why the illiterate daughter of a poor rabbi should be thus awarded, Blumkin replied in broken English: "I'm born, thank God, with brains. In Russia, you don't have no adding machine or nothing, so you have to use your head. So I always used it." Laurence Tisch, a member of NYU's board of trustees, said: "She's more of a business leader than anyone we've ever honored before."[2] Other recipients of NYU's award include the chief executives of Citicorp, Exxon, and General Motors.

Blumkin began in the basement of a pawnshop at age 43 with a borrowed $500. She had helped her husband run the pawnshop until 1950, renting shotguns and selling the miscellany that comes into pawnshops. When her husband died, Blumkin had to make her own way in the world. Where that might have crushed other single mothers, this single mother had already faced far greater obstacles in her life. In 1917, she had bribed her way past a Russian border guard, then come to America via China and Japan on a peanut boat. Her drive to succeed was an offshoot of her drive to be free. It seems that in the case of immigrants-turned-American-entrepreneurs, there is no such thing as being "too far" from the border guard.

Running hard and being smart is not sufficient to assure entrepreneurial success. Blumkin understands leverage. During the Korean War, she borrowed $50,000 for ninety days from a banker when she could not pay her suppliers. Blumkin was fearful that she would not be able to repay the banker. So she rented a hall and had a three-day sale that generated $250,000 in cash, enabling her to pay off the loan. Since then, Blumkin has dealt in cash and achieved its leverage by shrewd and careful buying, giving attention to detail, and selling quality products at 20–30 percent below the prices charged by other retailers. Having all the furniture under one roof helped keep overhead down as well.

2. Ibid.

Her reason for selling to Warren Buffett's Berkshire Hathaway, Inc., in 1983 for $60 million was to resolve her estate. Buffett trusted Blumkin so much that he bought the store without an audit. Buffett, generally known as the "Smartest Investor Alive," told *The Wall Street Journal*: "Put her up against the top graduates of the top business schools or chief executives of the *Fortune* 500 and, assuming an even start with the same resources, she'd run rings around them."[3]

Following the sale of Nebraska Furniture Mart in 1983, Blumkin continued to work a seven-day week as head of the carpet department. In 1989, she left because of a managerial disagreement and opened up her own operation next door in a large building that she had owned for several years. In her new business, Blumkin ran the carpet section but leased out other home furnishings departments.

In late 1992, Blumkin decided to sell her building and land to Berkshire Hathaway, but she continues to run her carpet business at its current location. She doesn't want to slow down while the new business is still in its infancy. Nebraska Furniture Mart will expand its business into her former building.

Afraid of having a partner become a competitor a second time, Buffett asked Blumkin at the age of 99 to sign a noncompete agreement. She graciously agreed to do so.

There are dozens of women who came to America under difficult conditions, fought poverty and the problems of dealing with a new language, then started businesses to make ends meet. Some of these women have done remarkably well with skills such as sewing, inventing, acting, or designing. But Rose Blumkin has done it with brains, hard work, and "no adding machine, thank God."

3. Ibid.

Gertrude Boyle

Name of Company:	Columbia Sportswear Co.
Location:	Portland, Oregon
Date Founded:	1938
Description of Business:	Manufacturer and distributor of general outerwear, skiwear, rainwear, windwear, sportswear, a denim collection, footwear, accessories, and hunting and fishing apparel
Description of P:	People who love outdoor sports need specialized clothing. The consumer who skis in the winter is going to be hiking and fishing in the summer. Outdoor sportsmen need quality clothes to keep them dry and warm.
Description of S:	Columbia Sportswear offers a complete line of clothing for the outdoor sportsman's seasonal needs.
Members of E:	Gertrude Boyle, chairman of the board Tim Boyle (son), president
Size of V:	$135 million sales in 1992
Social Utility:	Is a sponsor and outfitter of the Special Olympics.
Principal Source of Venture Capital:	None; began as a turnaround.

GERTRUDE BOYLE has been with Columbia Sportswear since its founding in 1938, after she and her parents had fled from the wrath of Hitler's Nazi Germany. Originally a small hat and glove company in Portland, Oregon, Columbia Sportswear Co. has grown into an international sportswear giant that can boast of manufacturing and retailing the largest-selling jacket in the history of the ski industry, the Bugaboo Parka.

Gertrude Boyle, better known as Gert, Ma Boyle, or Mother Gert, had helped with the family business ever since she was a child. She graduated from the University of Arizona in 1947 with a degree in sociology and a college sweetheart whom she would end up marrying the following year, Joseph Cornelius Boyle (Neil). Neil and Gert moved to Portland, where Neil joined forces with Gert's father and worked for Columbia. Gert continued to be a part of the business but remained in the background doing what she could while she made a home for her family. In 1960, however, she was responsible for designing the first multipocketed fishing vest, which launched Columbia Sportswear's first piece of outdoor apparel. In 1964, Gert's father, Paul Lamfrom, passed away and her husband Neil took over leadership of the company. At this point, Gert was content to go on being a housewife raising a son and two daughters. Neil began plans to expand; and in 1970, three months before he would die of a sudden heart attack, he took out an SBA loan of $150,000. Their house, Gert's mother's house, and their life insurance policy were all riding on the loan.

After Neil's death, the SBA came knocking at their door. "I had no choice," says Gert. "I tried to sell the company and the only offer I could get was for $1,400. I told him that I could run the company into the ground myself for $1,400." "We just had to take it one day at a time. . . . It took some intestinal fortitude. . . .The biggest problem seemed to be other people. They all told me to get out of it. . . .But I couldn't, my mother's house was on the line." So Gert just did what she had to. She systematically cleaned house, firing people who had a bad attitude or who were not supportive, and started from scratch. "The problem with small companies is that no one writes anything down, and most of the stuff went to the grave in my husband's head." But with the help of her son, Tim, who was finishing up his final year at college, Gertrude Boyle took the bull by the horns and slowly rebuilt her family's debt-ridden company, literally saving the roof over her head and everything her family owned. "What makes Columbia Sportswear so successful today," says Gert, "is that nine-tenths of the employees are working towards the same goal." She also believes that although she has had to run a tight ship, "it is important to thank people and tell them when they are doing a good job."

In 1989, Gert Boyle stepped down as president of Columbia, allowing her son, Tim, to take Columbia into the 1990s. "Tim really has a keen sense about what's good in the industry. He just knows what's going to work and what's not." Gertrude Boyle has continued to take an active role in the company and has been aggressively pursuing the PR for Columbia Sportswear. She and her son have launched a new comical ad campaign portraying old Mother Gert as a cantankerous old mother who still knows what's best for her son. Her dour face is spread over all the ads. This year Columbia introduced its first line of denim jeans and appropriately named them Tough Mothers. Right on the label is a picture of Mother Gert's frowning face. However, Gertrude Boyle maintains that she is really just a "sweet ol' grandmother." "I'm not really like that," she says. While she may be a sweet ole grandmother, the fact remains that Gert Boyle has taken a company from near bankruptcy and turned it into a $135 million outdoor sportswear empire. Now that's one tough mother!

Julie Brice

Name of Company:	I Can't Believe It's Yogurt
Location:	Based in Dallas
Date Founded:	1977
Description of Business:	An international frozen yogurt franchise company
Description of *P*:	"Something that tastes so good can't be good for you."
Description of *S*:	Julie Brice has created an empire disproving that statement by offering the public a healthy and tasty alternative to ice cream.
Members of *E*:	Julie Brice, CEO Bill Brice, CEO Brice Group (ICBIY's parent company)
Size of *V*:	Estimated total revenues for 1992 were $85 million.
Social Utility:	Board of Directors, North Texas Public Broadcasting Inc. Through the Brice Foundation, the company is committed to helping underprivileged children.
Principal Source of Venture Capital:	$10,000 of each sibling's college tuition money

When JULIE BRICE tasted frozen yogurt for the first time, it was love at first bite. She could not believe that it was possible to eat something so delicious while still on a diet. When Brice and her brother Bill were offered positions as managers at two struggling yogurt stores in 1977, Julie was nineteen and Bill was twenty. While other college freshmen at Southern

Methodist University were trying to figure out their lives and enroll in classes to find a major, Julie enrolled in Entrepreneurship 101, taking the job at a small yogurt shop. At this time, frozen yogurt was not very well known. Nevertheless, free spirited and in search of adventure, Julie and her brother viewed the opportunity as a challenge. By the following year, their youthful idealism led them to pool $10,000 of their own college tuition money and buy out the two stores. Still in school, Julie worked around the clock, managing the stores while she also managed to keep up her good grades. She was miraculously able to graduate in four years. By graduation day, she and her brother had opened up yet another store, and she had earned a bachelor of business administration degree with honors. Not too bad for an "idealistic" twenty-three-year-old.

The year 1983 marked the turning point for the brother and sister team, as they made the decision to build their own manufacturing plant and made plans to begin franchising. By manufacturing their own frozen yogurt, they could ensure the quality of their product and keep up the pace with the growing demand for their delicious ice cream alternative. As competition grew, Julie and Bill began to experiment with more and more flavors and toppings to keep one step ahead of the rest.

In 1988, ICBIY introduced the first nonfat frozen yogurt and, the following year, offered the first sugar-free nonfat yogurt to its customers. As their customers became more and more health conscious, two years later the Brices introduced *yoglace*, a frozen dairy dessert, packing only ten calories per ounce. ICBIY's success can be attributed to their high standard of quality and their commitment to continuous innovation. In addition, the franchising system they have set up has been lauded by the critics. Their franchising philosophy is one of partnership and support. In fact, in 1989, ICBIY was awarded the Outstanding Franchisee Relations Award at the twenty-ninth International Franchise Association (IFA) convention. According to Julie Brice, "We spend a tremendous amount of time and energy ensuring that our goals of integrity, professionalism, and motivation are the same as those of our franchise owners." As a result, in 1993, the Brice Group was formed and is now considered one of the foremost authorities on franchising.

To young entrepreneurs, Brice says, "The only limit to what you can do is yourself. You can achieve anything you set your mind to achieve. The following attributes are important to entrepreneurial success: Treat people right, be positive, work hard, be willing to take calculated risks, never give up, and found your business on core values and live by them. Ours are trust, respect, accountability, integrity, commitment, and caring."

This strategy has proved to be very successful. Today, ICBIY claims more than 1,200 stores in the United States and abroad, with annual sales of over $85 million. You can now even find ICBIY served on American Airlines domestic flights. With brother Bill heading the manufacturing plant and Julie heading the retail side, this dynamic duo continues to forge ahead.

Frieda Caplan

Name of Company:	Frieda's, Inc.
Location:	Los Angeles
Date Founded:	1962
Description of Business:	Frieda's markets specialty produce in America.
Description of P:	Specialty food has always had a market in the United States, but large produce importers do not have the time to experiment with new and different foods because they deal in mass volume and high turnover.
Description of S:	Frieda Caplan used her powerful marketing savvy to promote produce never seen in American grocery stores before. She has made success stories out of the kiwifruit, spaghetti squash, jicama, and shallots.
Members of E:	Frieda Caplan, founder and chairman Karen Caplan, president and chief executive officer
Size of V:	1992 gross sales were estimated at $23 million.
Social Utility:	Frieda Caplan is actively involved in various women's organizations and is considered a role model for young women entrepreneurs.
Principal Source of Venture Capital:	$10,000 loan from Caplan's father

If you have had mushrooms on your pizza, sundried tomatoes in your salad, or a kiwifruit for a snack or in a dessert, you can thank FRIEDA CAPLAN, who has single-handedly changed the way America eats. Frieda Caplan began her career in the produce business in 1956 after she took a job with her husband's uncle and aunt, who had a produce stand. Before that she had worked full-time for a nylon thread company. When she had her first child, Karen, now CEO and president of Frieda's, Inc., she could not continue to work her regular schedule and therefore was forced to leave. When she started working for her husband's aunt and uncle, she managed the books, enabling her to work flexible hours while she raised her daughter. One day, when her husband's aunt and uncle decided to go on vacation, they asked if she wanted to work on the floor selling produce. Caplan decided to give it a try and loved it. When her bosses came back she requested to stay on the floor. Within a short time she was phased out of bookkeeping and was selling produce full-time. When one of the local produce vendors decided to go out of business, the owner of the sales facility approached Frieda to see if she wanted to open and run her own produce company. When she said that she had no money, the owner of the building, recognizing Frieda's marketing savvy and entrepreneurial drive, offered her product on a consignment basis. All Frieda had to do was to market and sell her product. It cost her nothing. The only catch was that it was not your average tomato or head of lettuce that she had to sell but rather fresh fungus, better known as mushrooms. Frieda was an instant success. In 1962 she borrowed $10,000 from her father and decided to open her own produce company with mushrooms as her lead item. There were virtually no specialty food stores at that time, and when anyone came to the market with a new or unusual product, people would tell them to go to Frieda, who had gained the reputation for taking anything. She always kept an open mind and looked for new and interesting products to market and sell.

Frieda's marketing ability became clear after she successfully promoted the kiwi fruit. A retailer had asked Frieda if she had ever heard of a Chinese gooseberry. She did not know what it was but quickly sought it out and found it in New Zealand. One of the importers suggested that she come up with a different name for the tasty green and fuzzy fruit. In 1962, Caplan introduced America to the kiwi fruit, named after the small fuzzy kiwi bird native to New Zealand. By the late 1960s, the kiwi fruit had caught on and soon after farmers began to grow this peculiar green fruit. Today there are over 1,000 kiwi fruit farmers in California alone.

Frieda's continues to carry unusual produce, offering the American consumer more than 300 specialty products. What makes Frieda's so successful is her ability to convince the buyers for the supermarket chains to carry her produce. By offering small packages, instructions, and recipes to the consumer, she makes it very easy for retailers to carry and sell her unique items.

Today Frieda Caplan has taken a back seat in the company, handing over the reins to her first daughter, Karen Caplan, who now serves as CEO and president of Frieda's. Her aggressive marketing and sales skills have brought Frieda's from an $11 million business in 1986 to $23 million in 1992. Frieda's offers a full line of customer information, including newsletters, personal responses to consumer letters, and explanatory labels on the products with recipes and suggestions. In addition, Frieda's offers seminars, product selection assistance, and advertising assistance to all retailers in an attempt to educate the public about new products that are available and that satisfy that insatiable need of consumers to find something new. For over thirty fruitful years, Frieda's has been changing the way Americans eat.

Maryles V. Casto

Name of Company:	Casto Travel, Inc.
Location:	Santa Clara, California
Date Founded:	1973
Description of Business:	One of the largest travel agencies and event planners in the country
Description of *P*:	Since the beginnings of mankind, the celebratory occasion has been a constant among all peoples, all races, all groups. Whether it is a sales meeting, an industry expo, or a family gathering, people have always traveled to a festive place to whoop and holler it up among their fellow hunter-collectors or family members. The need keeps on growing and has led to the formation of convention-oriented cities such as Las Vegas and Orlando and to destination resorts.
Description of *S*:	Never merely an order-taking retail travel agent, Casto spotted the desire of people to gather at festive locations and became a significant factor in planning these events, then moving the bodies to them.
Members of *E*:	Maryles Casto, CEO and president Gus Vallejo, chief financial officer Martha Kling, vice president Marketing and Sales
Size of *V*:	The company is privately held and not required to publish its financial information. Sales are believed to be in the range of $50 million per annum.

Social Utility: Maryles Casto has recently been appointed to
                                   the California Council to Promote Women in
                                   Business. She is also very active in her local
                                   community, speaking at high schools and
                                   offering interested students apprenticeships in
                                   her travel company.

Principal Source of
Venture Capital: $1,500 in personal savings

MARYLES CASTO started her business in Silicon Valley, California, at about
the time the area was emerging as a high-technology center. It was not
financial necessity that started Casto down the road toward building a $50
million-a-year company. In the late 1960s she was enjoying a plush life in
her native city of Cebu, in the Philippines, where her father was a wealthy
sugar and coconut plantation owner. But the life of the idle rich didn't suit
her.

   She went to work as a flight attendant, becoming, within two years,
the training manager for all Philippine Airlines' flight attendants. After
moving to the United States with her American husband, Mar Dell Casto,
she switched careers to become a travel agent. In 1973, she and a friend
opened Casto Travel with $1,500.

   When she first started, she says, few women were in the industry,
and the men were a "cliquish group. It was like a men's club." Still, good
relations generally rule among travel agencies, regardless of the operator's sex. "There is competition, but there is also respect," she says.

   Travel is a high-pressure business. "There are times when I want to
pull my hair," she exclaims. But Casto believes in living every moment to
the fullest. "I cannot stand negative people," she says. "You have to look
for a solution. If it has to be done, it can be done."

   Casto is known for her commitment to women in business. As part of
the company philosophy, she is very understanding of and compassion-
ate to single mothers and expecting mothers. Casto is the international
chairperson of the Committee of 200, a global organization of successful
entrepreneurial women, as well as a long-term board member.

   In 1985, she was named Woman of the Year by the San Francisco
Chamber of Commerce. In 1992, Casto received the Asian/Pacific American Heritage Award from former President George Bush. In December
1992, Junior Achievement elected her to be inducted into the Santa Clara
County Business Hall of Fame as one of five 1993 laureates.

Joanne Chappell

Name of Company:	Editions Limited West, Inc.
Location:	San Francisco
Date Founded:	1978
Description of Business:	Publishes limited edition art prints and art posters, which it sells on a worldwide basis to corporations, hotels, galleries, and collectors.
Description of *P*:	There is a vast need among all people in every culture to decorate their environments.
Description of *S*:	The print and poster market provides an ancillary channel for artists to earn supplemental income while providing visual benefits to the general public, most of whom cannot afford original art work.
Members of *E*:	Michael Ogura, director of Administration
Size of V:	The company is privately held but reports sales approaching $6 million.
Social Utility:	Chappell supports the AIDS Project and is a patron of numerous young artists.
Principal Source of Venture Capital:	$50,000 in loans

JOANNE CHAPPELL, raised by hardworking parents in a blue-collar family, dreamed of a life in which there would be more brightness and color than there was in the steel mill community where she grew up. Born in Hammond, Indiana, Chappell developed an avid interest in the arts in her early education and studied under Olga Schubkegel of the Bauhaus school. In 1960 she earned a BFA degree from the University of Indiana.

During the next ten years, while raising three children, Chappell taught art classes and developed and curated several art shows for nonprofit organizations.

In 1969, Chappell decided to capitalize on this experience by opening the first Editions Limited Gallery in Indianapolis. Over the next ten years she produced shows featuring such artists as Frank Motherwell, Picasso, Jim Dine, and Jasper Johns. The emphasis of Chappell's first gallery was on working with collectors and some local corporations, introducing them to various multiples and originals.

Chappell's husband's career was not moving along as swimmingly as was hers, and when it began to affect her ability to attract important collectors to her gallery, she says, "I had to leave him and my gallery behind, take my three children and my life and start over in a new city. It wasn't easy. I wasn't a young chicken anymore. But you do what you have to do."

She chose San Francisco because it was completely different, and with a business plan in her head she presented her ideas to some new friends, who loaned her the money to open Editions Limited West. She initially targeted her sales of fine art to the corporate market, a timely move in that it corresponded with the growth and development of nearby Silicon Valley. The gallery's customer list included Apple Computer, AT & T, Raychem, and many more.

Not satisfied with one product line and one marketing channel, Chappell entered the print and poster business in the early 1980s and began buying the publishing rights from some of America's (and Europe's) most highly regarded artists—Wayne Thiebaud, Frank Mother-well, Helen Frankenthaler, Peter Kitchell, and Frank Stella, among them. In short order, Editions Limited became the dominant fine art print and poster publisher in the West. One-third of its sales are to European corporate and hotel customers. If you are reading this book in an upscale hotel, the prints on the wall probably came from Editions Limited.

In 1992 Chappell was approached by an infomercial producer to begin selling prints and posters via cable television. "We sell more art in one hour via home shopping than we do in two weeks calling on the corporate market," Chappell says.

Always searching for new artists and new "artistic statements," Chappell has explored computer-generated abstract art as a new medium of expression. "The computer can do some amazing things, but I prefer dealing with artists," she says. And her stable of artists is loyal to her too. Many of them look to her as patron, publisher, critic, and, yes, even therapist.

Sandy Chilewich and Kathy Moskal

Name of Company:	HUE, Inc.
Location:	New York City
Date Founded:	1978
Description of Business:	Innovative fashion legwear design company known for its colorful line of hosiery and tights
Description of *P*:	In the ever-changing fashion world, hosiery has remained a simple staple commodity. However, as shorts got shorter, and as the miniskirt grew in popularity, women began to pay closer attention to their legs. Prior to HUE's introduction of a colorful assortment of hosiery, women could choose only from the basic colors of white, taupe, black, and nude.
Description of *S*:	HUE revolutionized women's legwear, changing it from a simple commodity to a "fashion accessory." HUE continues to offer innovative new colors and patterns in a full line of legware.
Members of *E*:	Sandy Chilewich and Kathy Moskal, co-founders/co-presidents
Size of *V*:	Gross sales in 1992 estimated at $35 million
Social Utility:	Supports various charities focusing on women's issues, as well as research on AIDS and other health crises (including DIFFA, Seventh on Sale, and the American Cancer Society).

Principal Source of
Venture Capital: Simon Chilewich (Sandy's father)

SANDY CHILEWICH, working as an independent jewelry maker and sculptor in New York, was not satisfied with her small-scale operation. "I just knew it wasn't going to be big," says Chilewich. Unknown to Chilewich at that time was neighbor KATHY MOSKAL, who had been a teacher for ten years and was dissatisfied with her career too. When these two minds met at a monthly tenant meeting, it was the beginning of a friendship and a partnership that would take them places that they had never dreamed of. It all began over a glass of wine. Kathy pulled out a pair of black Chinese slippers she had picked up in Chinatown and they both thought how nice it would be if the slippers came in different colors. That was all it took for this dynamic duo. Moskal remembers: "I had the Clorox and Sandy had the dye." They bleached and dyed a couple of pairs of shoes, and when they wore them to the next building meeting, they met with an overwhelming response. Everyone wanted to know where they got those shoes. When one tenant said, "If you make them I'll sell them for you," they both knew that they were on to something.

Chilewich, who had been trying to get her jewelry used in the editorial section of *Vogue*, decided to bring the shoes with her to an appointment she had at the magazine. Chilewich remembers: "It was like the whole floor stopped. They thought they were the greatest thing they had ever seen." When *Vogue* wanted an assortment of shoes in different sizes and in the same eccentric colors for their models to use the following Monday, Chilewich replied, "Sure, sure, sure, we can do that for you." "We spent all weekend trying to duplicate what we had just done," she continues, and Moskal adds, "We first had to go to Chinatown and find the right sizes and then figure out how to come up with the exact colors that we showed them. Eggplant, mustard, I mean it was hysterical. We took the shoes up to *Vogue* Monday morning still wet." Chilewich adds, "We sat there all morning with hairdryers. We just did whatever it took. The thing is that there was no separation between work and fun, we had a great time."

Vogue loved the shoes and when the staff got back to Moskal and Chilewich to find out who their main buyer was, in order to give that buyer a credit line in the next issue, they didn't have one at the time. "We told them we would get back to them and we immediately went to Bendel's and told them that our shoes were being featured in *Vogue* next month and asked if they were interested in buying some. They were and we had our first major buyer." The next month they had a two-page spread in *Vogue*, and as Chilewich remembers, "Everyone wanted the shoes. It just took off." Moskal reflects: "It was amazing. I think we forget how new this really was fifteen years ago. You couldn't find anything in twelve colors at that time. We got so much publicity. Everyone started asking us 'What else do you two do?' We would just tell them that we would get back to them, and run out to the stores and find anything that came in white cotton that we could dye. We found white gardening gloves in Chinatown, and suddenly we were doing gloves."

It was not until they got their hands on some nurse's white stockings that they really found their niche. The stockings took off and they were used by Perry Ellis in one of his first shows. But while their products were successful and very popular, they were not making much money at all. Chilewich remembers: "Everyone thought we were a lot bigger than we really were. We had all this publicity. All these beautiful displays. Meanwhile they had no idea that we were struggling. . . . there were so many technical and business obstacles that we had to overcome." "The first step," says Moskal, "was to focus on a single product."

In the first two years they had spread themselves thin, dyeing anything they could get their hands on. At the same time, the manufacturer of the shoes that they were dying began to dye its own shoes, and there was no way to compete with him. So they both decided to go to the mill that was producing the nurse's stockings that they were dyeing and see if they could buy directly from them. When they went down to this Southern mill, Moskal says, "We instantly fell in love, with the South, with the industry, with the mills, with the knitting. The whole thing intrigued us." "We were so optimistic and so excited to learn about the industry that the owner of this one mill that we went to, flattered by our interest, did anything he could to help us." The two would hang around the mill experimenting with the machines, asking lots of questions, and learning as much as they could about the industry. "We were very respectful and courteous and I think that they appreciated that. We were always honest and sincere. I think they just liked us," says Chilewich. They worked out an arrangement to buy the stockings directly from the mill and began to focus on the hosiery business. She attributes their success today to the early relationships that they built with the workers and the owners of the mill. Moskal agrees: "I think what we found was that so much in business relies on trust and personal relationships, and when we could not pay our bills, instead of having them come to us we came to them and offered a payment plan. If we couldn't make a payment, we would call them to tell them what we could pay them. We took full responsibility, and I think that gave them the feeling that they were always getting the straight story, so they trusted us and allowed us to slide a little."

Their integrity and honesty would eventually pay off. But before they could really see their company take off they had to learn by trial and error about running a company, about inventory, about markets, about spending, and about planning. With the help of an accountant and other financial people, they were able to move forward but they almost went bankrupt. Chilewich remembers: "Up until that point, it was like we were playing around. We had to make a real decision—do we want to be in this business or don't we? This was not a joke any longer." Moskal adds: "We really had to go through a psychological change. It's easy to fantasize about what you want and where you want to be, but to actually let yourself have that? Could we be successful women? Could we give that to ourselves?" Chilewich remembers: "We were exhausted, we were so tired. I went down to see my father and I started to cry, 'I'm tired, I'm going to quit, they think I should quit.' He just looked at me with this face that said 'Forget the tissues, gal; get this together and turn it around.' He was like . . . 'Just do it."

And that was exactly what they did in 1987. They made the psychological change they had to and that was all it took. From 1987, profits soared and sales grew year by year to a total of $35 million in 1992. Having achieved what they set out to do, they then allowed HUE to be bought out, and became a subsidiary of Leslie Fay Companies, Inc. "I think we both felt that a larger company would be able to take HUE to the next level. We were so busy running the company. We wanted to get back to doing the things that only we could do. To generate new areas of business and to come up with new concepts, that's what we loved to do," Moskal said. Sandy Chilewich and Kathy Moskal now serve as co-presidents of HUE International and continue to bring new, innovative ideas to HUE and to the fashion industry.

Their advice to young entrepreneurs? "Ask yourself, do you really have a good product?" "Be able to judge your feedback. Who are you asking [for feedback]?" "Be willing to adapt to the market. We went from slippers to socks to hosiery." "You need to have the confidence and the enthusiasm to see problems as challenges that need to be solved."

Sheila Cluff

Name of Company:	Fitness, Inc.
Location:	Ojai, California
Date Founded:	1959
Description of Business:	Offers aerobics, exercise, and fitness training at two spas, on cruises, in videos, and through books and other media.
Description of P:	Many people want to be entrepreneurs and corporate raiders in this age of entrepreneurship, but everyone cannot be one. Their option: to take over their bodies, slash the fat, spin off unnecessary weight, and become lean, fit, mega-effective women and men.
Description of S:	Cluff introduced "cardiovascular dance" to the world in the 1950s as an alternative to gym classes for high school girls.
Members of E:	Donald Cluff, co-founder Kimberly Cluff, Guest Relations Kathy Cluff, director, Advertising and Marketing
Size of V:	The company is privately held and does not have to publish financial statements. Sales are reported to be approximately $10 million per year.
Social Utility:	Sheila Cluff is actively involved in the Children's Home Center and the Juvenile Diabetes Foundation. She is also a sponsor of the local Senior Olympics.
Principal Source of Venture Capital:	$2,000 loan from her parents

SHEILA CLUFF has vision and energy—lots of energy. Creator and owner of sister spas, The Oaks at Ojai and The Palms at Palm Springs, in addition to being president and founder of Fitness, Inc., and Fit II, Cluff has been inspiring and invigorating people with her fitness expertise, spirit, and determination for over thirty-four years.

The world-renowned fitness expert is an inspiration because this fifty-six-year-old mother of four looks and lives the lifestyle she teaches. Cluff began her career as a Sonja Henie professional figure skater. A fitness pioneer long before the newly awakened health consciousness, Cluff introduced "cardiovascular dance" to the world in the 1950s.

The author of four books and leader of more than forty fitness and beauty cruises, Cluff personally helps participants attain individual power through healthful living. She travels the globe leading health tours so that others may learn how to lead more satisfying lives. After four decades of success, Cluff still takes the time to teach at least eight classes per week at her two popular California spas and to know her guests by name.

Drawing on her varied experiences as a professional figure skater, physical education teacher, professional model, fashion commentator, and TV exercise and talk show host, Cluff formulated a three-step program that incorporates healthful eating habits, exercise, and positive behavior reinforcement.

Exhibiting entrepreneurial spirit and foresight, Cluff knew that the budding of body knowledge and awareness would happen on the West Coast. And, in 1969, Cluff came to the Pacific Coast to help lead the way to a healthier, more fit future. Sensing that corporations were changing their priorities through realizing that a healthier employee was a more cost-effective employee, Cluff made the development and marketing of employee fitness plans to businesses her first endeavor.

Already the owner of a highly successful business, Cluff in 1976 bought a 1920s hotel in the resort town of Ojai, and The Oaks at Ojai was born. Under the guidance of Cluff, The Oaks flourished immediately, and continues to flourish, as one of the most popular fitness spas in the country. Cluff opened The Palms at Palm Springs in 1979, affording guests the same attention and amenities at affordable prices that had become hallmarks of The Oaks at Ojai.

In addition to teaching eight to ten classes a week at both The Oaks and The Palms, she has authored *Aerobic Body Contouring*, co-authored with Eleanor Brown *The Ultimate Recipe for Fitness*, publishes *Spa News*, a newsletter with a circulation of 55,000, writes several syndicated columns on fitness, has produced four fitness videos, and is constantly in demand as a speaker on both fitness and entrepreneurial endeavors.

Elizabeth R. Coker

Name of Company: Minco Technology Labs, Inc.

Location: Austin, Texas

Date Founded: 1981

Description of
Business: Designs, develops, and manufactures
                        customized computer systems that it sells to
                        the electronics, medical, and defense
                        industries.

Description of *P*:   The process industries require specialized com-
                        puter systems to operate complex equipment,
                        robotic systems, and assembly line controllers.

Description of *S*:   Coker is a stickler for quality, and in a market
                        where an entire plant can be shut down if a
                        defective chip is used in the computer that
                        controls a bottling line, quality is extremely
                        critical.

Members of *E*:   Don Potter, president
                        Rebecca Shackleford, chief financial officer
                        Mary Mooney, vice president, Sales
                        Beth Kohln, human resources officer

Size of V: The company is privately held, with sales of
                        approximately $12 million.

Social Utility: Coker and her husband are founders of their
                        church and are actively involved in all its
                        affairs. They are also actively involved in
                        the Special Olympics. To enable men and
                        women workers with parenting responsibilities
                        to bring their children to work, Coker started a
                        K–6 grade school at the company. Parents can
                        have lunch with their children every day.

Principal Source of
Venture Capital: A $30,000 second mortgage on her home plus
                          $70,000 raised from friends

ELIZABETH COKER was born and raised on a farm near Pulaski, Tennessee.
Her father got through the third grade, and her mother the eighth. "Dad
ran a sawmill. Mother loved to sew. She made all our clothes from feed
sacks that the cattle feed came in. We were poor, but we didn't know it.
We were a church-going family and we were taught to treat people
fairly," says Coker. She went to town for the first time when she was
twelve, and left high school at fifteen to get married. The marriage ended
four years later and Coker moved to Texas, where she enrolled in an
electronics course offered by Texas Instruments. Coker became the first
woman engineering technician at Texas Instruments in 1963. By 1967, she
was in charge of a new department that sold semiconductors to the
military, and in 1970 she became the first woman to travel on sales
assignments for Texas Instruments.

Coker left Texas Instruments in 1976 to co-found an electronics
manufacturing company in Northridge, California. As general manager,
she helped grow the company to $14 million in sales. But she left in 1981
to form Minco, bringing with her Mary Mooney, who had been a
colleague. When Mooney heard that Liz Coker was leaving, he asked,
"Where are *we* going?" Mooney and Coker have now worked together for
nearly thirty years. Minco began with just four employees, including her
son and daughter, but was profitable within three months. Minco's sales
in 1982 were $1.8 million. The company has since grown to sales of $12
million and now has 128 employees. Its customers include Hughes,
Raytheon, Teledyne, Texas Instruments, and other major corporations.
Minco has also produced three spin-offs: Austin Semiconductor, Inc.,
with seventy-four team members (Minco does not permit the use of the
word *employee*) and $7 million in sales; Technalysis, which develops and
sells medical equipment; and LCC, a sales representative organization.

Coker's fastidiousness about quality has earned the company numerous awards, including Subcontractor of the Year from Hughes and
Raytheon and five Administrators Awards of Excellence from the Small
Business Administration. Coker is the mother of two. Her son is Minco's
president and her daughter its chief financial officer. All teammates are
treated as if they are family, and with the new school being created at the
company, their children will be welcome as well.

Lisa A. Conte

Name of Company: Shaman Pharmaceuticals, Inc.

Location: San Carlos, California

Date Founded: 1989

Description of
Business:
Specializes in the discovery of drugs from tropical plants that have a history of folk use. Using ethnobotany (the study of how native peoples use plants) coupled with chemistry, the company believes that its pioneering drug discovery techniques are more cost-effective than conventional methods.

Description of *P*:
The world loses seventeen million hectares of rain forest—an area roughly equal to the size of Wisconsin—each year to deforestation. Shaman's approach to drug discovery helps to create an economic incentive to preserve rain forests.

Description of *S*:
Many important pharmaceuticals originated with plants: Quinine, L-dopa, pilocarpine (for glaucoma), digitoxin, aspirin, and taxol. But since the 1970s the pharmaceutical industry has moved away from plant-based drug discovery to the synthesis of new compounds using advanced biotechnology techniques. Thus, the door was left open for an entrepreneur to go into the world's rain forests with very little competition.

Member of *E*:
Richard D. Ring, executive vice president
Michael S. Tempesta, senior vice president, Research
Rozanne Rapozo, vice president, Finance

Size of V: The company has no revenues but is publicly
                              traded, and based on expectation of future
                              profits, its market valuation in early 1994 was
                              $117 million.

Social Utility: Shaman implements a conservancy project in
                              regions where it finds commercializable
                              products. The first active return of benefits
                              (and planned-for profits) was to Amazonian
                              Ecuador, where Shaman provided a doctor
                              who rendered his medical services to three
                              communities and treated thirty children during
                              a whooping-cough epidemic.

Principal Source of
Venture Capital: $4 million from Delphi Management Partners
                              and Technology Funding, Inc.

There are hundreds of drugs that have been derived from tropical plants,
including reserpine from the serpentine root for tranquilizers, diosgenin
from the Mexican yam for antifertility drugs, and vincrestine from the
rosy periwinkle for fighting cancer. Among the most indispensable
plant-based drugs are analgesics, antibiotics, heart drugs, anticancer
agents, enzymes, hormones, diuretics, antiparasite compounds, ulcer
cures, dentifrices, laxatives, dysentery treatments, and anticoagulants. It
is estimated that 25 percent of all prescription drugs in the United States
contain ingredients that are extracted from plants. Notwithstanding this
enormous contribution to health by the tropical plant, the pharmaceutical
industry has largely ignored this source because of its fascination with
biotechnology.

     Into this niche plunged LISA A. CONTE, thirty-four, who was perfectly
positioned for the opportunity. The idea came to her when she was a vice
president with Technology Funding, a San Francisco venture capital firm.
An article in a magazine on the destruction of the rain forest sparked the
notion of a national plant/drug collection system. Years earlier, Conte had
developed interest in native healers while traveling in the tropics. From
1985 to 1987, Conte had conducted risk and strategy audits for start-up
healthcare companies at Strategic Decisions Group, a management consulting firm. She has an AB degree in biochemistry from Dartmouth and
the University of California, and an MBA degree from Dartmouth.

     While conceiving her idea for what eventually became Shaman
Pharmaceuticals, Conte spent several months with ethnobotanists to test
her idea and ensure that her approach was rational. Many of these experts
are today members of the Shaman Scientific Strategy Team. The four
"achievers" whom Conte chose to join the new company had years of

experience with SmithKline, Genentech, and Virginia's Nature Conservancy.

To lay off the marketing risk onto established pharmaceutical companies with existing channels to health care providers, Conte struck strategic alliances with Eli Lilly & Co., Merck & Co., and Invermi della Beffa of Italy. Lilly and Invermi invested $8.5 million in Shaman, and Merck has agreed to provide, free of charge, in-vivo and in-vitro screening of Shaman's plant extracts for possible use in analgesics and diabetes. Merrick has first rights to negotiate licenses for compounds with interesting activity.

Conte expects the company's first product, Virend, to reach the market in 1994. An antiviral compound that has shown positive results against herpes I and II, Virend could capture a meaningful share of the $1.2 billion annual sales of acyclovir, the leading topical formulation, which has *not* been effective against genital herpes. The company has applied to the FDA to expand its Virend studies and to cover all AIDS patients with secondary herpes infections.

Because it is the company's mission to reinvest a significant percentage of its profits to maintain global plant biodiversity, the planet will be twice blessed if Shaman becomes a profitable company.

Jenny Craig

Name of Company:	Jenny Craig International, Inc.
Location:	Del Mar, California
Date Founded:	1983
Description of Business:	Operates the largest chain of weight loss centers in the world with more than 900 locations.
Description of *P*:	The overweight problem is like a Yeats poem—a series of widening gyres that expand inexorably. Not only do most people not know how to lose weight, they do not know the best diet for them, the most nutritious diet, the role of exercise, or how to keep weight off.
Description of *S*:	Jenny Craig brought *counseling* into the paradigm and proved its value as an important component in the diet-exercise-nutrition triad.
Members of *E*:	Sid Craig, chairman C. Joseph LaBonte, president and CEO Ellen Destray, chief operating officer
Size of V:	The company is publicly held and its market capitalization in early 1994 was $190.2 million.
Social Utility:	The Craigs wish to keep their charitable contributions confidential.
Principal Source of Venture Capital:	Personal revenues from prior business

Born during the Great Depression, JENNY CRAIG watched her parents struggle to make ends meet in a tough New Orleans economy. They encouraged her to get a dental hygienist degree, but when her mother became ill, Craig dropped out of school to work as a dental assistant. In

1954, she married her first husband and had two daughters. During her second pregnancy, Craig put on forty-five pounds.

She joined a fitness center in 1959, shed the weight, and joined the fitness center staff. Soon she was managing several centers, and in 1965 she opened her own. Three years later, Craig sold her fitness center and in 1970 moved to Los Angeles to supervise several health clubs that had been started by Sid Craig.

Romance didn't enter the picture for several years, as Craig was commuting from New Orleans and both people were still married to someone else. The Craigs were married in 1979, and in 1983 they sold their interest in the health club chain, and because they had signed two-year noncompete agreements, the couple left for Australia.

There they developed a comprehensive weight loss program consisting of nutritional guidance, counseling, and support. Other products and services, including a line of low-fat, low-sodium foods, would come later.

At the heart of the Jenny Craig weight loss program is the menu. Although it varies from person to person, the menu serves an important purpose. First, it temporarily takes away the need to make decisions about what to eat. Overweight people have difficulty in making appropriate food-related decisions. The menu trains them in new eating behaviors. By following the menus, they begin to train themselves in proper portion size. They also learn to eat foods that are low in sodium and low in fat, yet still taste good. Neither clients nor counselors are allowed to make changes in the menus without dietitian approval. Each day's menu is a nutritionally balanced unit and every food on the day's menu must be consumed. Menus are designed by the company's registered dietitians, and the counselors implement the menus as designed. If a client has a strong objection to a particular food, an entire new day's menu plan may be substituted, but not an individual food item. In this way, the client's nutritional needs are met.

During the second weekly visit, the client attends a lifestyle class. These classes were designed by a psychologist with a specialization in eating disorders, and consist of a meeting of from twelve to twenty clients and a lifestyle class facilitator. Facilitators are assisted by a series of sixteen videotapes in which experts in the fields of nutrition, exercise, physiology, psychology, and medicine discuss behavioral changes clients will need to make in order to successfully manage their weight. These tapes are followed by client discussion. A behavioral assignment is given at the end of each class and the client practices this assignment during the week.

Additionally, the clients may choose to make use of a set of sixteen audiotapes that reinforce the information covered in class each week.

Clients are encouraged to listen to one tape each week, three times a day, in order to facilitate their behavior changes.

When clients have achieved half of their desired weight loss, they begin planning their meals using their own food two days per week. They continue in this way until they reach their weight goal, at which time they begin the Permanent Stabilization Program, a one-year program consisting of the structured process of returning clients to planning all their own meals. Many clients fail on their own but, remembering their success at Jenny Craig, return in a year or two to begin anew.

The Craigs planned to be very large from the beginning. They opened nine centers in one year in Australia, grew that market to fifty, and returned the center of their operations to Los Angeles in the late 1980s. The company achieved its initial public offering in 1991, raising $66 million to repay loans used to build the chain.

The proof of the success of any business is word-of-mouth advertising. Approximately 40 percent of Jenny Craig's new clients are referred by a previous client.

Cecilia Danieli

Name of Company:	Danieli Officini Meccaniche SPA
Location:	Buttrio, Italy
Date Founded:	1962
Description of Business:	Builds steel mills, ports, railways, oil refineries, power stations, and waste treatment centers in Eastern Europe and the Third World.
Description of *P*:	The enormous needs of Eastern European countries after many decades of Communist rule, combined with the desire of Third World countries to build the necessary infrastructure to provide rudimentary conveniences to their citizens, offer an economic opportunity to construction firms with the courage to address these challenges.
Description of *S*:	Danieli has to make sure her company will be paid, which usually means arranging for financing through a Western intermediary, such as the World Bank. In addition, she has to locate, hire, train, and dispatch skilled people to remote areas of the globe. The task is awesome and many of Danieli's competitors find it too daunting to submit bids. This provides an uneven playing field in Danieli's favor.
Members of *E*:	Gianpietro Benedetti, chief executive officer
Size of V:	The company achieved a public market for its stock in 1984, and its capitalization in early 1994 was approximately $362 million.

| Social Utility: | Danieli & Cia. is run as a maternalistic organization in which loyal workers are considered and treated like family. |
| Principal Source of Venture Capital: | Project financing |

Dr. CECILIA DANIELI, or "La Dottoressa," as she is known to her employees, took over the managing directorship of Danieli & Cia. from her father, Luigi, in September 1980 after two years of heavy losses.

"If anybody had told me, back in 1964 when I was at university, that I would finish up managing all this, I would have said that they were mad," she says.[1]

"When I look at the names of our competitors, I giggle. I just can't believe it," confesses the mother of three.

Her competitors on paper number over 200, but direct rivals have fallen to a mere handful, including the Japanese trio Mitsubishi, Hitachi, and NKK, Germany's Krugg and Denag, and Britain's Davy Corporation. La Dottoressa shows up for the major bids in person—in Russia, China, Nigeria, Egypt. "I do it willingly," she says. "It is logical that a client who has paid several billions should want to see the face of the firm's representative."

While still a student in the early 1960s at Trieste University, Danieli became involved in the management of her sister's winery, producer of one of the best grappas in the region. When the call came from the family to come over to the project construction business, the switch seemed logical. The family needed her. She had skills. She knew the business indirectly as family members tend to.

But she did not know the turnaround business. In 1976, Danieli & Cia. was deeply in the red. People were leaving. A crisis was in full boil, and some managers were recommending that the business be shut down.

The breakthrough for the company came in 1978, when East Germany, probably out of political considerations, decided to strengthen its commercial ties with Italy. It needed a high-capacity turnkey steel meltshop plant, to be supplied to the Stahl- und Walzwerk, Brandenburg. "They chose us for the technology we could offer, but at the time, because of our small size, we could not take responsibility for a large turnkey plant. We asked several groups in Italy and abroad to share the project with us. Since, to put it mildly, we were not doing well then, they all

---

1. Gaia Servadio, "Italy's Woman of Steel," *Business*, January 1990, p. 57.

turned us down," Danieli remembers. Without many other options for new business, Danieli entered the plant-making business.

The success of the East German mill gave Danieli the confidence to build other steel minimills. As the steel-making industry downsized to smaller mills, Danieli was gaining in reputation for delivering turnkey projects to the industry at affordable prices.

Roanoke Electric in Virginia ordered a Danieli plant for packing rolled products that are continuously cut to length. It was the first plant of its kind to be installed in the United States. Another U.S. order, from Flasco Steel Corporation, followed this one for a 120-millimeter-per-second finishing block for wirerod, the first of its type to be sold by Europeans to the United States. Such has been the marketing thrust in the United States that Danieli can now claim 80 percent of the U.S. market for minimills.

Danieli scours the world for new processes that can transform steel into products with even higher added value. Techniques for building new electric furnaces and ladle furnaces for quality steels have been licensed from ASEA of Sweden; technology for making heavy drill collars from Breda Fucine of Italy; and increased capability for manufacturing metal-processing machinery from Britain's Hi-Draw Engineering. Danieli's own research and development department has patented an electromagnetic billet maker. The experimental phase lasted only two months and, as it concluded, four orders were taken in the United States, Italy, and Africa.

After pulling her family firm back from losses, Cecilia Danieli has done so well that 26 percent (four million) of its shares were floated on the Milan stock exchange, at 2,250 lire each, in May 1984. Half were bought by her own workers. In mid-1993, the valuation of the company reached $500 million. She remains reluctant to take credit or to be seen as the Danieli-savior. "I want to avoid a personalization. When the company was under my father's management things done were justified by the times and by my father's personality.

"The social base has been broadened; I do not want the personality of Luigi Danieli, the father, to be followed by that of Cecilia Danieli, the daughter. I am the trainer of a team, and you must take in the whole team."[2]

The remarkable thing is that she regards herself as unremarkable. "For me," she says, "this job is not heavy. As for the responsibility, I think that one becomes accustomed to everything." She has scarcely noticed

2. Ibid.

that the company has moved from sales of 30 billion lire in the mid-1970s to 150 billion in 1972.

She has never regarded being a woman as a difficulty, and even concedes that the glamour that has captivated the world is at times an advantage. "If nothing else, I am recognizable when I enter a room."

Being a woman, it might be argued, makes her more adaptable. Her family is local, it comes from Friuli, with some injection of blood from Val Sugana and Lombardy. Friuli is a highly civilized area, which reaps the fruit of centuries of wise administration by Venice and, later, the Austrian empire.

La Dottoressa spends free weekends studying at the Istituto Adriano Olivetti (ISTAO), an institute of economics in the Marche, in central Italy, the main function of which is to study and assist the projects of small and medium-size industries. She is on the ISTAO board, and relishes the position. "It is important to withdraw into thinking at times," she declares, "to look at things from a distance, in the abstract."

With nothing to lose in 1980, Danieli developed the habit of direct contact with heads of state to make certain they knew the name Danieli & Cia. "I find relationships with politicians easy. One rings up the minister and, three or four days later, something happens. Not only now that we are what we are, also ten years ago, when nobody knew us."

She is proud of her team and points out: "We have more women at the top levels than most other firms." The average age of the Danieli management is forty-one. "I suppose that, for Italy, we are young birds. In the U.S. we would be ripe for retirement!" Decisions are taken swiftly. "Our staff is organized so that decisions can be taken independently by the specific department."

When she tours the factory, she is cheered by the workers. How many CEOs can say that has happened to them?

Jan Davidson

Name of Company:	Davidson and Associates, Inc.
Location:	Torrance, California
Date Founded:	1982
Description of Business:	Davidson and Associates, Inc. is the leading publisher of educational software in the world based on retail shelf space occupied and market share data. The company currently publishes thirty-seven titles, among them *MathBlaster*, which has sold more than one million copies since its introduction in 1983.
Description of *P*:	The need to make the learning process pleasureful at an early age in order to engender and make habit-forming the desire to self-teach
Description of *S*:	Davidson designs, develops, and markets educational software for home and school use targeted at the pre-K to twelfth grade age groups.
Members of *E*:	Jan Davidson, president Robert Davidson, chief executive officer and chairman
Size of V:	The company's 16,400,000 shares of common stock were trading at $16.75 on NASDAQ in mid-1993, giving the company a market value of $275 million.
Social Utility:	Answer a child's math question and you have fed him a meal. Teach him math and you have given him the tools to garden for life.
Principal Source of Venture Capital:	Founders' sweat equity

JAN DAVIDSON may be a teacher at heart, but she has also shown that she is an honor roll student herself when it comes to business. After spending more than twelve years teaching high school and college students, she unknowingly started to become a student herself. During the mid-1970s, when Proposition 13 hit California, school districts that relied heavily upon local property taxes for their budgets were forced to close early. Students were being let out of school at noon because of the lack of funds available. Jan Davidson knew that she had to do something and founded a nonprofit organization called Upward Bound, which gave college-bound kids supplemental educational courses in math, reading, SAT preparation, speed reading, and computer literacy.

Always interested in making herself more effective as a teacher, Davidson saw the new personal computer that Apple Computer had released as a means of making students more interested in what they were learning. Having no knowledge of computers and having never taken a computer class before, Jan Davidson sat down and began to learn how to program the computer to meet her students' educational needs. "They had a book on *Applesoft* and I just followed the directions," says Davidson. Her first program, appropriately called *Speed Reader*, was designed to teach speed reading. That was followed by *Word Attack* and *MathBlaster*. *MathBlaster*, a video-arcade-style game in which you solve math equations to shoot aliens out of the sky, has been her most successful program, selling over a million copies. When Apple found out about the three programs Davidson had created, they decided to list her programs in the mail-order catalog they were running at the time. However, when Apple decided to discontinue its catalog business and concentrate its efforts on hardware, Davidson initially looked to a software publisher.

When Davidson decided to meet the prospective publisher for lunch in San Clemente, halfway between Torrance and San Diego, little did she know that the restaurant they had chosen to meet at had two locations, one off the highway just north of San Clemente and one just south of San Clemente. While the publishers were waiting at the southern branch, Davidson and her husband waited at the northern branch. She considers her husband her "business confidant," who, she says, always encouraged her. While the couple waited for the publishers, Robert Davidson made his pitch to her to publish the software herself because, unlike the technical publishers, she really understood education. He also used the fact that the publishers apparently were being irresponsible in not showing up for the meeting. Jan Davidson decided that if she could find a distributor she would publish her own programs. She decided to pitch her software to a distributor called Softsel, now known as Merisel, and they ended up buying 100 copies of her software.

The education/entertainment software market is brutally competitive. It was and, to a large extent, still is a new and constantly developing market, in which software packages can be rendered obsolete without warning by hardware changes. Davidson and Associates has continued to develop, publish, and distribute award-winning, educationally sound, and high-quality software for home and school use since its inception in 1982. Davidson says, "We've made some good decisions and some really bad decisions but I guess we made more good decisions than bad ones." She claims that it was her willingness to be open and to learn new things all the time that led to her success. "We had to be extremely flexible, extremely responsive to the marketplace, and willing to change on the drop of a dime." The whole experience has been pleasant, according to Davidson. While she says that "every day has its challenges," she finds it "intoxicating. It has been one big learning experience." She recalls a sign that she had in her classroom that said "If you're not making at least ten mistakes a day you aren't trying hard enough." "I'm achieving that," laughs Davidson.

When her company became too large, Davidson decided to conduct a search for a manager so that she could leverage her strengths. Her search ended at home when she realized that her husband was the perfect man for the job. It took a bit of coaxing but he joined forces with his wife in 1989. Jan Davidson is the first to admit: "I always hire people who are much smarter than me who have completely different strengths than I do. I just do what I know best and let them do what they do best. I'm a good team builder."

Patricia Defibaugh

Name of Company:	Aloette Cosmetics, Inc.
Location:	West Chester, Pennsylvania
Date Founded:	1977
Description of Business:	Designs, develops, and manufactures skin-care products and cosmetics, which it sells through the party-plan method.
Description of P:	The principal economic justification of the party-plan method of marketing is that the customer pays up front, thus reducing the cost of carrying inventory and receivables. Moreover, "beauty" is a subject that many women prefer to discuss on their own turf, where there is greater intimacy and privacy, than over a cosmetics counter in a department store.
Description of S:	Defibaugh, with great insight, modified the basic party-plan formula initiated by Tupperware and Mary Kay Cosmetics. Her company sells franchises throughout the United States and Canada, and the franchisees in turn hire and train downline beauty consultants. The incentive to build value thus becomes instructive among the franchisees, some of whom earn more than the company's founder—upward of $1 million per year.
Members of E:	John Defibaugh, co-founder, since retired
Size of V:	The company achieved an initial public offering for its common stock in 1986. Consistently ranked by *Forbes* as one of its "200 Best Small Companies in America," Aloette Cosmetics' capitalization in late 1993 was $15 million.

Social Utility:	The company has created opportunities for more than 5,000 women to succeed in their own businesses. Ms. Defibaugh also supports the Adam Walsh Child Resource Center.
Principal Source of Venture Capital:	$500,000 of personal savings plus a mortgage on the Defibaugh's home

PATRICIA DEFIBAUGH is the product of a strict Mennonite background who was raised to be a "Donna-Reed-type" mother and homemaker, always supportive of her husband's endeavors. She remembers: "Growing up in the sixties, the only options seemed to be marriage, become a teacher, secretary, or a nurse. It was real difficult to break through what was normal." When her first marriage ended in divorce, Defibaugh and her daughter were left financially devastated. She took a part-time job in 1970 as a receptionist in a beauty salon, where she earned $60 a week. "There were no role models for women at that time," Defibaugh says.

As a model, she attended a cosmetics show given by The Magic of Aloe in 1973, and the company's sales reps persuaded her to sell The Magic of Aloe products at home parties. Because there was no upfront inventory purchase requirement, Defibaugh took a shot at it, and thereby found her niche.

In 1974, "Tricia" married John Defibaugh, who saw the enormous skills that his wife had, and he convinced her that they could start their own company. With another Philadelphia couple, the Defibaughs launched Aloe Charm in 1975. The venture succeeded, but the partnership soured, and the Defibaughs sold their interest two years later.

Within a month, the Defibaughs conceived of a new business plan and launched Aloette Cosmetics, with franchising at the heart of it. They invested $500,000 of their own money and borrowed on their home. Tricia and John worked eighteen-hour days. Tricia wrote a 345-page training manual for the consultants while simultaneously developing a 125-unit product line with chemists. First year sales were $500,000. They doubled the following year and grew to $15 million in 1993.

Defibaugh says it was hard, but she comments: "It's not what you get dealt in life, but how you respond to it." She says that people should find what they are good at, be comfortable doing it, and keep doing it. "Be prepared to incorporate your job into your lifestyle," she adds.

"Committed to making others successful and recreating success," Aloette does exactly that. By training women and nurturing an entrepreneurial spirit within them, Defibaugh has enabled thousands of women to incorporate their work with their personal life. On the average, an Aloette beauty consultant will spend 8:00 A.M. to 1:00 P.M. on the phone at home setting up shows and helping current clients, leaving her most of the afternoon to spend time running errands and taking care of her own life. In the evening, the consultants sell their products through home shows. While those women have been learning about cosmetics and being effective consultants, Defibaugh has had to learn about running a business and has proven herself to be an over-achieving business-woman. She can swing an axe at overhead when it is essential.

As the clouds of recession roiled over the country in 1990, Defibaugh looked for ways to slash costs. Aloette acquired three of its suppliers to eliminate their overhead factors in its cost structure: Dallas-based skin-care line manufacturer Superior Products, bought for $2.8 million; Ontario, Canada, glamour-line producer Spectrum Cosmetics Laboratories, for $600,000; and Chemetics Laboratories, the Dallas-based supplier of aloe vera, for $50,000.

Aloette, now fully integrated and with operating costs pared to the bone, is poised for substantial growth. Tricia may never get to stay home and bake bread for her husband the way Donna Reed did.

Anita Dimondstein and Joan Cooper

Name of Company:	Biobottoms
Location:	Petaluma, California
Date Founded:	1981
Description of Business:	Mail order catalog of natural-fiber children's clothing and accessories
Description of *P:*	Cotton diapers required pins and tricky folding. The only diaper covers that were available were coated nylon or plastic and created an airless bacteria environment that could lead to diaper rash. Disposables were expensive and wasteful.
Description of *S:*	Marketed Japanese-made wool diaper covers with pin-free closures.
Members of *E:*	Joan Cooper and Anita Dimondstein, co-founders
Size of *V:*	1992 revenues were $17.1 million.
Social Utility:	Committed to helping those in need, Cooper and Dimondstein send excess clothing to various child-aid groups and donate funds to environmental groups and socially responsible business organizations.
Principal Source of Venture Capital:	$3,000 from each of the co-founders' savings plus $500,000 capital infusion in 1988

When ANITA DIMONDSTEIN and JOAN COOPER, two former college roommates from the University of Pennsylvania, decided to invest $6,000 of their own money into a diaper-cover venture with absolutely no prior business experience, people told them that they were crazy. But, as the saying goes, "Mothers know best," and they proved it so. Learning from their own frustrations as parents, they knew that they could not find a diaper cover that would not leave a rash on their own children's sensitive bottoms. When they saw a baby wearing a soft wool diaper-cover with Velcro-type closures, they quickly asked where the proud mother had located this diaper cover. When they learned that she had bought it in Japan, they immediately contacted the Japanese manufacturer and began to distribute the diaper cover in the United States. It was exactly what they were looking for. The machine-washable, soft, woolen, natural cover would not irritate the skin and the use of Velcro-type fastening eliminated the use of sharp pins. When they sought the opinion of others, they were not discouraged by the negative feedback that they received. They were told that no one used cloth diapers and the product was too expensive. Nevertheless, Dimondstein and Cooper believed in the new product because they had both been searching for a similar product for their own toddlers. It filled a personal need.

They started to market the wool diaper cover through alternative-culture magazines and sold their product through the mail, using Dimondstein's home as headquarters for their company. That was in 1981. By 1984 they had developed a large-enough client base that they could send out their own mail order catalog and they mailed 20,000 copies to their loyal customers. In addition, in 1984, in response to their customers' request for other natural-fiber clothing, they introduced a line of children's clothing and other accessories, and sent out a separate catalog to 20,000 of their customers. Nine years later, the founders estimate that they will send out approximately 8.5 million copies of their 56-page color catalog.

Today Biobottoms has a full line of natural-fiber children's clothing and have also made available cotton/polyester covers along with the original soft woolen ones. According to the founders, they really had to educate the public about the benefits of cotton diapering. They cite some alarming statistics about the impact on the environment of using nonbiodegradable disposable diapers. For instance, 18 billion plastic diapers are buried in landfills each year, making up 30 percent of the total nonbiodegradable materials buried in landfills, each one taking 500 years to fully biodegrade. Every disposable diaper ever used is still buried on the planet, except for those that have been incinerated. With statistics like that, and with the steady growth of environmental consciousness, it did not take long for the concept of diapering with cloth to catch on. Dimondstein and Cooper learned as the business grew, seeking information from experienced businesspeople, their bankers, direct mail industry gurus, and even competitors. They have shown the power of the entrepreneurial spirit and have proven that successful entrepreneurship is a discipline that one can learn. It is not in the genes. Furthermore, they have used their talents for the greater good of the environment not only through their products but also through direct action within their own community. The company recycles internally, limits packaging, and encourages employees to think and act socially responsible.

Tomima Edmark

Name of Company:	The TOPSYTAIL Company
Location:	Dallas
Date Founded:	1989
Description of Business:	Designs, develops, produces, and markets TOPSYTAIL, a patented plastic loop supported by a knitting needle that helps women braid their ponytails.
Description of *P*:	The difficulty involved in braiding a ponytail: The process is cumbersome and usually requires a knowledgeable friend.
Description of *S*:	A serendipitous device involving a plastic loop that fits into the top of a knitting needle. Cost: 22 cents; selling price: $10 and up.
Members of *E*:	Edmark's housekeeper
Size of V:	The company is privately held, with estimated annual sales of $40 million.
Social Utility:	Edmark works with dyslexic children.
Principal Source of Venture Capital:	Edmark invested a $15,000 advance she received from a book on kissing.

What factors spark the birth of an entrepreneur? There are three: dissatisfaction, insight, and energy. Dissatisfaction is an everyday occurrence; something we read or do upsets us and we grumble about it. Insight is the recognition that a solution exists for the problem that upset us. Energy is the drive to do something about it.

Some of us are dissatisfied and curse the things that bother us. Others have the insight to identify both the problems and their solutions. But only entrepreneurs conceive the *means* of delivering solutions to problems in a consistent, intelligent manner, and rapidly, before the competition can raise a battalion.

TOMIMA EDMARK was dissatisfied that she could not braid her ponytail with ease. She wasn't all that excited about her $80,000 a year job selling mainframes for IBM; thus, the notion of leaving her job was hatching in her fertile mind as well. For after-hours amusement, Edmark wrote *Kissing: Everything You Ever Wanted to Know*, published by Fireside/Simon & Schuster in 1991 with a first printing of 37,500 copies. It is now in its second printing, and a sequel, *365 Ways to Kiss Your Love*, was released in 1993.

For $5,000, Edmark developed a solution to her problem, which she named TOPSYTAIL, and patented it. Edmark had a mold produced for $9,000 and took it to a plastics maker, who agreed to produce as many products as she wanted for 50 cents apiece.

Then she called on hair brush and comb manufacturers to market it for her. They laughed her out of their offices. The same thing has happened to every inventor from Gail Borden (condensed milk) to Chester Carlson (xerography), and the turndowns become turn-ons. They produce energy and conviction.

Edmark began advertising in small hairstyle magazines, and as the orders came in, she stuffed envelopes at night after work. By 1991, she was selling 200 per month at $10 apiece. While in New York for IBM, Edmark stopped in at *Glamour* magazine headquarters, which featured TOPSYTAIL in its February 1992 issue. Three weeks later, orders grew to 400 a week, and Edmark enlisted her cleaning lady to help stuff envelopes.

Shortly thereafter, IBM eliminated her job and three-fourths of the Dallas mainframe office. "It was really a load off my mind," Edmark told *Forbes*.[1]

With a $25,000 early retirement windfall, the thirty-five-year-old lit out on the sales trail, something she knew a fair amount about. She demonstrated TOPSYTAIL at beauty salons and at trade shows and then connected with T.V. Products, Inc., a New Jersey-based company that promotes kitchen gadgets and sunglasses on television. T.V. Products assumed the full responsibility for advertising. Edmark appeared in all commercials. In the first six months that T.V. Products ran commercials

---

1. R. Lee Sullivan, "Unemployment Insurance," *Forbes*, August 2, 1993, p. 134.

for TOPSYTAIL on television, it sold 3.6 million units at $15 apiece. Five million TOPSYTAILS have been sold to date, producing revenues of more than $50 million.

With money in the bank, Edmark is fending off pirates and working on product development. She is conceiving a line of hair jewelry and she has signed a deal with Tyco Toys to develop a TOPSYTAIL doll.

How did the spark of opportunities reach the kindling of insight and set Edmark's heart racing into the fanatical role of entrepreneur? While watching the movie *When Harry Met Sally*, Edmark admired the unusual twist in the long hair of Meg Ryan. She went home and tried to replicate the twist, but could not. So, she decided to invent a tool to do it. Why so confident? "As a dyslexic person I was used to seeing things in reverse, which is pretty much what the TOPSYTAIL is. . . . Inventing was part of my family life," she explained. While she was growing up in Seattle, her father, a surgeon and inventor of a successful artificial heart valve, would often leave the valves in the refrigerator. One of her five brothers invented a modular storage unit for compact discs called the High Rise. Her own first attempt was a rubber band on the end of a toothbrush and jerry-rigged circular knitting needle. Phenomenal successes like this one come around all the time. They are almost always developed by entrepreneurs. The suits lack the ingredients: dissatisfaction, insight, and energy.

Ruth Fertel

Name of Company:	Ruth's Chris Steak House
Location:	New Orleans
Description of Business:	Upscale restaurant chain specializing in steaks
Description of P:	Nothing could ever be more certain than the consumer demand for a good steak and a baked potato cooked and served in a family-style environment.
Description of S:	Ruth Fertel provided customers with what they wanted: a large cut of steak and a good feeling that they were enjoying it in the warmth and friendship of a working mother of two.
Members of E:	Ruth Fertel, founder
Size of V:	Gross annual sales from thirty-nine restaurants are around $100 million. Publicly held restaurant chains currently trade for more than annual sales.
Social Utility:	Ruth Fertel has donated her steaks to feed thousands of people when disaster struck.
Principal Source of Venture Capital:	A $22,000 loan from a friend who was a banker, of which $18,000 went to purchase her first restaurant and $4,000 was used as working capital.

"Something good always comes out of something bad," says RUTH FERTEL, founder of Ruth's Chris Steak House, and rightly so. She is someone who has stared adversity in the face and come out on top. Always a competitor, Fertel has had the desire to win ever since she was a child. "I think I got my competitive spirit from my older brother. I was always trying to better him. I always wanted to win." In addition, her father was a competitor himself in the world of sales. "Father always won many awards. He was a real overachiever. He always pushed us to do things to the best of our abilities." With a degree in chemistry and a minor in physics, Ruth Fertel left her brief teaching career to raise a family. Fourteen years later, she found herself with two young boys and no career, living on child-support payments from her divorced husband. Fertel, recognizing the need for more money, got a job making drapes at home so she could be there to raise her two boys. Not having a proper drafting table, Fertel made the drapes on the floor on her hands and knees. This did not last very long, Fertel explains: "My knees just plain gave out." Fertel then got a job working in a medical lab at Tulane Medical Center, but after working there for a couple of years she realized that she was not making enough money to be able to send her sons to college. So, in 1965, after seeing an ad in the paper for a steak house for sale, Ruth Fertel found her calling. Having no experience in restaurants or in buying or cooking steak, she made the decision to buy and operate what was then called Chris Steak House. When she approached a banker friend and told him of her plan to mortgage the house and get an $18,000 loan for the restaurant, she remembers, "He told me I was going to lose my house. I told him that I knew I wasn't, so please make me this loan. He did and gave me an extra $4,000 for expenses." She adds, "I was so naive that I only asked for what the restaurant was going to cost. . . . But I never thought for a minute that I would not succeed. I never thought it. I just knew I would make it."

Fertel says "I never thought of myself as a woman in business, I never felt any negativity towards me or what I was doing. . . . I think people really try to help someone they see is working very hard. I used to butcher the meat, wait on the tables, run the register, and do the books. I was there from 9:00 A.M. till closing, which was usually around midnight to 1:00 A.M. People would always bring in new customers to bring in new business for me. . . . Because 95 percent of my customers were men, I think being a woman actually helped me. They all wanted to help the little old lady who was butchering their steaks and working real hard to raise her two boys." Within the first six months of opening her restaurant, disaster hit when Hurricane Betsy devastated southern Louisiana. Fertel reflects: "The lights were out for a week, we had no electricity. I knew my meat was going to spoil, so I cut it and cooked it all up myself and brought it to the local parish to be passed around. I knew that most of these people had not had a good warm meal in over a week." Fertel admits that she was worried about getting back on her feet after having taken a major loss on her meat. However, she believes that "something good always comes out of something bad." She immediately replenished her stock and her business began to boom. "Because New Orleans was so devastated, the telephone, utility, and construction workers were working around the clock and they all had unlimited expense accounts; they all heard about the little old lady's steak house and business began to boom. . . . The archbishop even declared a special dispensation for people who could not eat meat on Fridays because of the shortage of food and supplies. Up until then, I was closed every Friday." Out of this whole experience came a loyal customer base and steady growth in the following years.

A few years later, Fertel met with disaster once again. A fire completely burned down her original restaurant. With a little help from a carpenter she was able to reconstruct a building down the road that was three times the size of her original place. She says, "I was turning people away at that time, I was always busy, and there were always long lines. I only had sixty seats. The new place now had 160 seats and I was able to do more business." "Something good always comes out of something bad."

The transition from being the owner of a single steak house to the head of a major corporation claiming thirty-nine steak houses bringing in $100 million in annual revenues has been a slow learning experience. "I learned by doing it. I always consulted with my staff and got their feedback. Whenever I found that things were getting too busy, I expanded." Fertel says that it's all about "going with your gut and doing what your gut tells you to do because most of the time it's right." That's prime advice from one tough woman who has met sizzling success feeding America top-quality U.S. steak.

Debbi Fields

Name of Company:	Mrs. Fields Cookies, Inc.
Location:	Park City, Utah
Date Founded:	1977
Description of Business:	The company owns and operates a chain of more than 700 cookie stores throughout the United States, Europe, and the Far East.
Description of *P:*	John Naisbitt's "high tech/high touch" principle was at work in the rise of chocolate chip cookie chains in the late 1970s.[1] The more people are isolated from each other by the introduction of technology into their lives, the greater their need for human contact in shopping malls, movie theaters, and restaurants, as well as their need for simple things that remind them of less technological times. The chocolate chip cookie says it all. Americans spend a couple of million dollars on chocolate chip cookies every year.
Description of *S:*	Mrs. Fields Cookies reaches the public through co-owned and franchised stores, shopping malls, and free-standing locations. Store managers and team members are expected to care about maintaining superior product quality as well as have fun with the

1. John Naisbitt, *Megatrends* (New York: Warner Books, 1982), pp. 35–40.

	customers. Because of the company's desire to serve only fresh cookies, cookies not sold within two hours are donated to a national food bank and Second Harvest, so that the customer receives only *fresh* cookies.
Members of *E:*	Debbi Fields, chairman Larry Hodges, president, CEO, COO
Size of V:	Privately held, the company is not required to disclose any financial information and chooses to keep this information private.
Social Utility:	The company has created more than 5,000 jobs. Debbi Fields, a thirty-seven-year-old mother of five daughters, will continue to be an inspiration to thousands of young mothers seeking to become active in the business world as well as in home life.
Principal Source of Venture Capital:	The company was launched with a $50,000 bank loan.

DEBBI FIELDS borrowed $50,000 from a bank in 1977 to open a cookie store in Palo Alto, California. Fields had developed an ultra-chocolatey cookie and felt that people would pay for the experience of enjoying a freshly baked, warmed-from-the-oven cookie whenever they wanted one. At first, no one came into the store, so Fields went outside and handed out cookies to passersby. Within a week, the store was profitable, and Fields never looked back. Her success formula: "I use nothing but the best ingredients, like real butter, pure vanilla, and lots of rich chocolate. My cookies are always freshly baked. I price cookies so that you cannot make them at home for any less. And I still give cookies away."[2]

According to the Small Business Administration, about 1,600 bakeries in the United States are owned by women, as are another 800 food-related businesses. But Fields is the only woman bakery entrepreneur; the others are small-business women.

"It's important to me that our customers get a good feeling every time they buy and eat a Mrs. Fields Cookie. Two things we never compromise on are customer service and quality. Without superior customer service, it doesn't matter how good your product is, you are not going to keep that customer."

2. Micki Siegel, "Cookies Are Good Fortunes," *Good Housekeeping*, September 1983.

Fields is smart. She knows the ease of entry into her market, so she makes the business seem complex in the sense of requiring "heart" to keep out Nabisco Brands, Inc., Pillsbury Company, Hershey Foods Corporation, and the other food processors whom she, Famous Amos, and David's Cookies have scooped.

At some point, the number of cookie stores will approach market saturation, and Mrs. Fields Cookies will either diversify into other markets or be acquired. How high is up for this smartly run company? Can a high-touch business become as large as one that is high-tech? Easily.

Valerie Freeman

Name of Company:	The Imprimis Group, Inc.
Location:	Dallas
Date Founded:	1982
Description of Business:	Imprimis (formerly Wordtemps) is a computer-oriented temporary and permanent placement agency that offers a full line of staffing services.
Description of P:	During the early 1980s personal computers had made their way into businesses and there was a strong demand for computer-literate employees. At the same time, Valerie Freeman was teaching the students who were needed for these jobs.
Description of S:	By making a strategic move from teacher to president of her own personnel service, Valerie Freeman was able to capitalize on the demand for computer-literate employees. She had been training them and already knew what businesses were looking for.
Members of E:	Valerie Freeman, president
Size of V:	Estimated total revenues in 1993 were $17 million.
Social Utility:	Imprimis is responsible for finding employment for over 1,000 temporary employees a day as well as seventy full-time staff members.
Principal Source of Venture Capital:	$1,000 from personal savings

After nine years of teaching others about business and computers in the Dallas Community College district, VALERIE FREEMAN decided it was time for a change. When the business department at her college entered the age of personal computers, Freeman was not intimidated by the computers, as were many of her colleagues. She was quick to learn about the new personal computers and acquired the skills needed to teach the first word processing course at her college. Freeman also made inquiries at local businesses to get a better sense of what skills her students would need once they left school. Little did she realize that she was laying the groundwork for her multimillion-dollar placement and staffing company. But while she was teaching her students marketable computer skills that she knew businesses were in need of, she was also looking for a new career option. Although she loved teaching, she did not feel that she was being challenged enough. By the time she had nurtured her entire department into the age of computers she was poised to make her move.

When other employers did not seem to be interested in what she had to offer, Freeman decided to take a chance on herself. Up until this point, Freeman had never thought about starting her own company. However, the opportunity she was looking for was right in front of her eyes. She had already been providing an employment service to local businesses that were calling to find out if she had students who could perform certain tasks. So, in 1982, she and a partner split the cost of $2,000 in rent and office supplies and started Freeman & Associates. Within seven months, because of differences in style and philosophy, Freeman and her partner went their separate ways. Freeman says that she had modest aspirations when she first started and was only looking to make as much as she did as a teacher.

Yet, without knowing it, she held the keys to a multimillion-dollar service business. First, she already had numerous contacts from being a business instructor. This gave her access to an enormous client base. Second, she was one of the few people at that time who understood computer concepts and their applications in business. This gave her an educational edge over the rest of the employment services. Most important, she was a teacher and knew how to communicate her know-how to trainees who were computer-shy and computer-illiterate. This was essential, especially in the early 1980s when the PC began to make its way into businesses and home offices.

While Freeman & Associates started off placing computer-literate individuals in full-time positions, within a year Freeman had started a second company, called Wordtemps, which focused on placing temporary help. This was the move that catapulted the former teacher into the

CEO's chair of a multimillion-dollar company. Not only was she a good teacher; she was a good student as well. Asking a lot of questions and not being afraid to make mistakes, Freeman enrolled in her own crash course in business management. "It was very lonely out there. There were no role models or resources for women who wanted to start their own business, as there are today," says Freeman. Nevertheless, by enlisting the help of advisers, attending seminars, and reading whatever she could get her hands on, she passed the course with flying colors. By paying attention to the market and staying ahead of the rapidly changing computer trends, Freeman has remained a leader in her field.

In 1986, after her father-in-law could not find a job, she recognized the need to place older workers in full- and part-time jobs and therefore started a third company, called Primetimers. Primetimers focuses on people who may have retired early but find that they want to work again. Although Freeman's is not the only agency that provides this service, hers is one of only a few and remains on the cutting edge of the concept of employing older workers. As the baby boomers age, the market and potential for services like Primetimers can only get better.

Today, Freeman has consolidated her services under the name of The Imprimis Group, which is divided into four divisions: Imprimis Staffing Solutions, which provides temporary personnel and other staffing services in the office and computer areas; Primetimers, which provides office staffing services using the experience of older workers; Art Squad, which provides on- and off-site staffing in the graphic design and desktop publishing areas; and ACE (Accelerated Computer Education) Centers, which provides on- and off-site computer training and training facilities for management services.

Lois Geraci-Ernst

Name of Company:	Advertising to Women, Inc.
Location:	New York City
Date Founded:	1975
Description of Business:	Advertising agency focusing on the development and marketing of products for women
Description of *P*:	Although women buy over 80 percent of all consumer products, only 8 percent of the decision-making process in advertising firms is influenced by women.
Description of *S*:	Advertising to Women is the first full-service agency totally devoted to understanding the needs and motivations of women and how to communicate with them.
Members of *E*:	Lois Geraci-Ernst, chief executive officer
Size of *V*:	Total billings for 1992 are estimated at $35 million.
Social Utility:	Lois Geraci-Ernst is one of the founders of the Committee of 200, an organization consisting of the top 200 women business owners. Advertising to Women has funded the development of three hotels for the homeless using a direct mail campaign.
Principal Source of Venture Capital:	$20,000 in life savings

LOIS GERACI-ERNST had no interest in business. Having graduated from Elmira College summa cum laude and Phi Beta Kappa and after earning a

Master's degree from Duke University, she says she "wanted to write the great American drama." In fact, she even scorned business, especially advertising. Her unyielding passion for creativity led her to pursue a career as a writer. She wrote poetry, short stories, plays, and music while she worked in on- and off-Broadway theater. She sent her materials to various magazines and publications in an attempt to be published. However, when the lights went out in her apartment one night while she was writing, she knew that she had to find a job that would pay the bills. She picked up the want ads and found a woman who was looking for a Phi Beta Kappa. She ended up taking the job, working under the "greatest copywriter in the world, Bernice Fitzgivvons," who served as her mentor. Geraci-Ernst says that she "beat the dullness out of me. She was a taskmaster who would not tolerate mediocrity." From there she reluctantly moved into advertising working for Interpublic's Marschalk Company, where she became senior vice president of Interpublic and served as the creative director for the Marschalk Company. The whole time she was there she was thinking, "I've got to get out of here. I can't work in this kind of ha ha . . . bim, bam, bop . . . jingles and rhyme business. I just had so much contempt for it."

One day she got a chance to work on a perfume campaign for Coty. The company was trying to rescue one of its fragrances called Emeraude. Among various ideas submitted by her co-workers and herself was the slogan she entered at the last minute: "If you want him to be more than a man, try being more of a woman." It met with overwhelming success and ran for twelve straight years. Lois Geraci-Ernst says that that slogan marked a turning point for her. "I thought that if I could do something that I was proud of I could stay in the business. *The New Yorker* magazine, which had rejected all of my stories, did a front-page Talk of the Town lead on it. I said to myself, I finally got into *The New Yorker*; how can I lose in this business? What I was most thrilled about was the emotional truth to the ad, and the fact that everyone could understand it. . . . From that time on I promised myself that I would only do emotionally true things, truth about the product, truth about how it relates to people's lives, truth about people's feelings." She was given affirmation that she could do her own kind of advertising, advertising she could believe in. The experience cast a whole new light on advertising for her. This was the beginning of a long list of award-winning, record-breaking, and revolutionizing advertising campaigns that this would-be writer would produce over the years.

While she was at Foote Cone and Belding she came up with one of her most famous slogans; this one for Clairol: "You're not getting older, you're just getting better." She says that when her co-workers heard the ad, they told her that she could not mention age and that she would be laughed out of the room. But that did not stop her. She says, "I started with the feelings of the people. It was like writing a personal letter to someone who had a problem or was missing out on some wonderful joy in life." She explained to her superiors where the ad was coming from and they loved it. That was in 1973.

By 1975, Lois Geraci-Ernst decided to go out on her own and opened up her very own advertising agency. She worked seven days and seven nights a week for over eight years before she could take weekends off. She says that she had no idea how to run a business and that if she had really known what she would have to do to be successful she might never have started it. "I just held my nose and jumped." Her hard work has paid off, not only for herself and her clients but for all the women she has touched with her campaigns. She is the winner of numerous creative awards, from the Triple Threat Creative Award given by the International Film and TV Festival, to the Andys and Clios. Her favorite awards are the Effies, which are given not only for creativity but also for effectiveness in the market-place. She has won many Gold and Grand Effies. One of her most effective ad campaigns was for Enjoli perfume, which brought the product into the top five selling fragrances for eight years. The words: "I can bring home the bacon, fry it up in a pan, . . . and never let you forget you're a man" captured the heart of the young, empowered woman of the eighties. She is also responsible for reviving many products. She doubled the sales of Jean Naté after taking over the marketing and advertising for the slipping fragrance. She has been so effective that her ad campaign for Silkience shampoo, which increased sales by $150 million in one year, is being used as a case study at Harvard Business School. The list of brand names she has launched goes on and on. Advertising to Women not only comes up with the advertising for a product but sometimes creates the product as well. One of her most recent and well-known products is the Easy Spirit pump that "looks like a pump" but "feels like a sneaker," with an ad featuring women playing basketball in the shoes. This campaign helped generate over $300 million in new sales for the U.S. Shoe Corporation.

Today Lois Geraci-Ernst is still coming up with new products in her think tank, which she calls her "greenhouse." It is in the greenhouse that the seeds are planted for such great successes as the Easy Spirit pump and Silkience shampoo.

Sandy Gooch

Name of Company:	Mrs. Gooch's Natural Food Markets
Location:	Sherman Oaks, California
Date Founded:	1977
Description of Business:	One of the largest-volume natural-food retail stores in the United States
Description of *P*:	As science revealed the importance of exercise and nutrition, people began to watch what they were putting into their bodies. During the mid-1970s there were few stores dedicated to providing the health-minded consumer with natural, wholesome foods.
Description of *S*:	Mrs. Gooch's has set the standard for natural food outlets, carrying only products that are without harmful chemical additives, harmful preservative agents, artificial flavorings, artificial colorings, artificial sweeteners, refined white sugar, refined white flour, caffeine, chocolate, hydrogenated oil, isolated synthetic MSG, irradiation, or bovine growth hormones.
Members of *E*:	Sandy Gooch, founder Dan Volland and John Moorman, partners
Size of *V*:	Gross sales estimated at $90 million
Social Utility:	Not only does Sandy Gooch help Americans to lead healthier lives by providing them with the most natural and wholesome foods available on the market today; she is also responsible for educating the public about the importance of eating healthful foods, offering a variety of services and information.

Principal Source of
Venture Capital: Her teacher's retirement fund and life savings

SANDY GOOCH has put food to the test. In any one of her seven markets you will not find a single product that contains harmful chemical additives or preservatives, artificial flavoring or coloring, refined white sugar or flour, alcohol, caffeine, hydrogenated oil, MSG, chocolate, or irradiated foods. To qualify for a spot on the shelves of Mrs. Gooch's Natural Food Markets, they must first pass this strict product code. Aside from the basic food reports made available to wholesale food stores, Mrs. Gooch makes every supplier guarantee the quality of his products and furnish additional laboratory analyses and signed affidavits upon request. However, this does not mean that all the food on her shelves is necessarily good for you. It may have high fat content or cholesterol and may not have the best nutritional value. However, you can be sure that the hamburger meat you buy will not contain any growth hormones. Mrs. Gooch sees one's fat intake and calorie consumption as the responsibility of the consumer, probably because that information is generally attainable. It is the hidden, potentially harmful chemicals and additives that she worries about because consumers may not be aware of them. She suggests to consumers that if you cannot pronounce it, you probably should not be eating it.

Sandy Gooch's high standard of product quality and purity is the result of a near-death experience she had. In 1974, this former teacher was given tetracycline to cure an eye infection. Mysteriously, Sandy Gooch became ill and was hospitalized immediately. While she was in the hospital she took a sip of a popular diet soda and became so dizzy that she thought she was going to die. She says a shot of Benadryl saved her life. Her father, who was a biochemist, traced the cause of her seizure to a complicated chemical reaction. What was explained to Mrs. Gooch was that she was allergic to tetracycline and that the brominated vegetable oil in the soda she drank inhibited the ability of the natural antihistamines in her body to fight the allergic reaction to the tetracycline.

After recovering, Mrs. Gooch began to find out as much as she could about the foods she ate. She found that most of the food she was eating contained harmful chemicals and additives that were making her body work overtime to purge these toxins from her system. She also found that a natural-food diet would permit her body to function properly. The problem was that she could not find a store that had an adequate stock of natural foods. At that time, Mrs. Gooch was also being asked to share her experience with various groups. After talking to many people, she recognized the need for a comprehensive natural-food market that carried everything for the health-minded consumer.

In 1977, with the help of Dan Volland, a manager of a natural-foods store, Mrs. Gooch opened her first store in West Los Angeles. One year later, John Moorman joined forces with Volland and Gooch, bringing his astute management and leadership skills to the company. With the help of Volland's knowledge of natural foods and Moorman's business skills, Mrs. Gooch was able to make the market of her dreams a reality. Seventeen years later, Mrs. Gooch had grown her business to seven markets grossing a total of $90 million a year, at which point (late 1993) she sold the chain to a rapidly growing competitor for an undisclosed price.

Mrs. Gooch says, "I believe the stores are successful not only because of our vast experience and commitment, but because they fill a tremendous need that has existed for some time. I always felt that if a product were good and presented honestly in an atmosphere of integrity, it would succeed on its own merits. I have been delighted to find this is true."

Andrea Grossman

Name of Company: Mrs. Grossman's Paper Company

Location: Novato, California

Date Founded: 1979

Description of
Business: Designs, develops, manufactures, and markets "Stickers by the Yard," which it sells to gift, stationery, toy, and craft stores throughout the United States.

Description of P: The celebratory nature of people and their continual need for gift giving creates an enormous, elastic market, which can become as large as the need to celebrate.

Description of S: What Grossman discovered was the simple sticker, an add-on to an already beautifully wrapped package that carries an extra message "that sometimes people prefer not to put into words." In fact, Mrs. Grossman's stickers are so expressive of people's feelings that the company frequently receives letters from people who say that they saved the wrapping but gave away the gift.

Members of E: Calvin Goodman, consultant to the arts
John Burton Clausen, director
Mary Liz Curtin, Donna Dodson, Bonnie Loizois
Jason Grossman, who recently brought manufacturing in-house after persuading his trepidatious mother of the need to vertically integrate

Size of V:	The company is privately held but reports sales in excess of $10 million per year.
Social Utility:	Grossman is very active in her church and in dealing with neighborhood issues.
Principal Source of Venture Capital:	$10,000 in personal savings

Nietzsche wrote that "It takes chaos to create a shooting star," and for Mrs. Grossman's Paper Company it took a crisis to create the heart sticker. ANDREA GROSSMAN, a talented artist, had been a graphic designer, selling her skills to others and being paid a fee for her services. She did very well at it throughout the 1960s and 1970s, and when her son was born she took some time off to raise him.

When he was six years old, Grossman looked for more graphic design work and was offered a very large job doing all the work for a certain corporation. When it folded and left her bills unpaid, she owed a lot of money to subcontractors and vendors. Grossman was in crisis and she sought solutions through prayer.

"I prayed for guidance in how to use my talents, to help my family, to help others, and finally to express my talents," she says. "Prayer led me to find a very old book full of beautiful woodcuts of nature. It was an old seed catalog from 1895 and the woodcuts were in the public domain, so I could photograph them without paying a royalty."

This put Grossman into the stationery business in which she sold a line of craft paper with beautiful, woodsy photographs on them. A stationery store customer asked her if she knew where to find some heart stickers. "Because she was a fairly big customer," Grossman explains, "I put some time into trying to find her a roll of heart stickers." But she couldn't, so she decided to make them herself.

"It's not as easy as it looks," says Grossman. "You need special dies and special printers. It's quite technical and, of course, that's probably why nobody had ever done it."

Today, Mrs. Grossman's Paper Company produces a line of heart stickers as well as 200 images made into stickers on rolls. Some of the images never change, but at least one-fifth are refreshed each year. The company does not rely on the trendy children's market, but instead produces whimsical and sincere stickers that express gratitude for nature and the beautiful things in life.

To come up with a continual flow of good ideas, Grossman holds frequent meetings with groups of her employees and asks them, "What is our mission? What do we stand for? What image do we want to convey?"

Through this process, the employees generate a river of ideas, which Grossman is able to visualize and then convert into new sticker images. "We're truly a family here. That's how I run things," she says, speaking of the company's seventy-five employees. But it is a growing family of thousands of customers categorized into forty generic retail types, with a different line for each, such as college bookstores, hospital gift stores, florists, and so on. The advent of the computer makes it possible to manage so many inventory items and so large a customer base.

Did she ever think it would get to be such a large business? "Well," Grossman replies, "it would be larger if we didn't have so many competitors. But they come and go, mostly go, and we continue to roll along enjoying what we're doing more each day."

Vinita Gupta

Name of Company:	Digital Link
Location:	Sunnyvale, California
Date Founded:	1985
Description of Business:	Digital Link designs, manufactures, and markets data communications products for Wide Area Networks (WANs).
Description of *P*:	Large companies with many geographically dispersed locations that need a centralized data base for such things as inventory management, engineering developments, and electronic financial transactions must have their information transferred quickly.
Description of *S*:	Using T1, T2, and T3 lines, Digital Link serves the high-speed data connectivity market, transferring computer data up to 3,000 times faster than regular phone lines.
Members of *E*:	Benjamin Wilson Berry, vice president Marketing Richard Holder, vice president Operations Stanley Kazmierczak, CFO, vice president Finance Daniel Palmer, vice president Engineering
Size of *V*:	1993 sales reaching $25 million
Social Utility:	Digital Link has created more than 130 jobs. Vinita Gupta is a model not only for women entrepreneurs but for all Indian women, as she has broken away from the traditional cultural role Indian women play, proving that Indian women can make it in the modern world.

Principal Source of
Venture Capital: $100,000 in personal savings

VINITA GUPTA grew up in India. Because her father was a civil engineer for the government she moved from city to city throughout India whenever her father's services were needed elsewhere. Although her mother was educated, she stayed at home to raise her three daughters. Raising three daughters in India is not as simple as it sounds. Daughters are valuable for one thing: to be married off. Prestige and the family name are associated with the men in the family, primarily the eldest son. There is incredible pressure on wives to have at least one son, if not many more. Undaunted by the traditional cultural roles defined for her daughters, Vinita Gupta's mother encouraged all three daughters to get a good education and instilled in all of them the birthright that they were capable of doing anything they wanted to do. Vinita says: "I think that she wanted to prove to everyone that she did not need a son . . . that her daughters were capable of making it." As an honors math student, Vinita Gupta pursued a career in electrical engineering. She completed her B.S. in electronics and communications engineering at the University of Roorkee, Roorkee, India, and earned her Master's degree the following year at the University of California, Los Angeles, in electrical engineering.

She spent the next twelve years working as an engineering manager and design engineer for two major telecommunications companies. As design engineer, she developed and patented a new product called the Solid State Relay. However, Gupta says, "I got edgy. I was not growing professionally and I knew I had to quit. I could not remain in middle management in a major company." The first problem was the company was not growing. Second, she explains, "I felt that my contributions were not being recognized." However, "I never felt that being an Indian or being a woman held me back. I did not think that anyone was discriminating against me. It was that the company was too process-oriented rather than results-oriented. Everyone was worried about covering their behind."

When Vinita Gupta decided to leave her middle-management position, she quickly drew up plans for her new business. With the help of a co-worker, who also quit the company, she incorporated Digital Link in 1985. They both invested their own money totaling $100,000. Her partner worked on developing new products while she worked on marketing and selling the products. However, after eight months, when the company did not reach the expected sales volumes they had projected, her partner got nervous and left. Gupta, now all alone, was faced with a major decision. Her husband had always been supportive of her career and when she was left hanging by her partner, he encouraged her not to give up. Gupta says, "He told me I could do it." For the next eight months Gupta worked month by month trying to keep her business afloat. "I could have gone out of business at any time. I hired my first employee to handle the office while I peddled my product. Every employee I hired was a risk. If there was no sales that month there was no paycheck." She worked very hard, putting in about sixty hours a week. However, "It wasn't the work that was the hard part," says Gupta. "It was not knowing if the hours I was putting in were going to get me anything."

Her hard work eventually paid off. Her management skills and her ability to find highly qualified and skilled people to join her company attracted outside venture capital three years later. Up until that point, she was doing everything. She managed to bring the company to approximately $4 million in sales. But it was not until she put together a senior-level management team that business began to take off. Today Gupta's Digital Link has eight offices nationwide, an office in Germany, and an office in London. Although privately held, Gupta says 1993 sales are approaching $25 million.

On business, Gupta says, "Every stage of business has new challenges. You have to continue to learn and grow personally and professionally. There is always constant excitement and enjoyment. The thing you have to remember (about running your own company) is that you can't blame anyone else for your mistakes."

Phyllis Haeger

Name of Company:	Haeger & Associates, Inc.
Location:	Chicago
Date Founded:	1978
Description of Business:	The company manages associations for trade and industry groups. Its specialty is trade groups of women in business.
Description of *P*:	Many industry associations and trade groups lack the leadership or the imagination to develop and implement interesting and revenue-producing programs.
Description of *S*:	Haeger not only built one of the largest and most successful association management companies; she also founded or co-founded some of the most significant and relevant organizations for women entrepreneurs, including the Committee of 200.
Members of *E*:	Bill Smith, mentor Lydia Lewis, Patricia Doherty, and Susan Davis, partners in founding the women's organization
Size of *V*:	Haeger & Associates has revenues of approximately $10 million. It was recently sold, and its founder acts as a consultant to the new owner.
Social Utility:	Haeger's life has been devoted to encouraging, pulling, pushing, and funding young women to finish college, earn a living, and/or start a new business. She has generated grants from the Carnegie Foundation and others for several

hundred young women to obtain college
degrees and to earn college credits. When not
working for the good of women, Haeger puts
her energies into the Brookfield Zoo.

Principal Source of
Venture Capital: Personal savings

Let us now praise PHYLLIS HAEGER, a legitimate American hero. She founded the Committee of 200 (now 325 members strong). And she co-founded the National Association of Women Business Owners, an organization that has provided college degrees and credits for tens of thousands of young women.

The word *hero* defines someone who has achieved an authentic degree of greatness, someone who has intentionally taken a large step, one far beyond the capacities of most persons, in solving problems that affect a large number of people. A hero brings about something that is unlikely to happen by the mere force of events, by the trends or tendencies of the times. That is, something that is unlikely to occur without her intervention. Haeger is distinguishable in the first instance by the fact that her intervention made the highly improbable happen.

Haeger is not a publicity seeker. In fact, she did not wish to be profiled in this book. In her shy and involuntarily confined personality, she has developed an independence of outlook, with a strong, self-possessed, energetic, and hopeful attitude toward life. She has built groups of followers, such as the Committee of 200, by convincing uniquely powerful women that her view of the future could become their reality. Joining with Haeger has enriched their lives and enhanced their belief in themselves and their entrepreneurial missions, their dignity, and their strength. You have only to ask a member of the Committee of 200 if this organization occupies a meaningful place in his or her life to understand fully the heroic role of Phyllis Haeger.

It was 1982, and Haeger asked herself, "What can I do to get women to help women, to raise money from women to be used to help women who could not otherwise get it?" The idea that came to this manager of associations was to form an association. "I thought I might be able to convince 200 women business owners to write a $1,000 check. As it turned out, many more than 200 women signed up and sent their checks," Haeger said.

"For the first meeting of the Committee of 200 I put together what I thought was the kind of program the members wanted—management gurus such as John Naisbitt. The women didn't care about that. They just wanted to talk to as many other women as they could get to about *how they got started*. Why they became entrepreneurs. How they were doing at it." What they wanted was a forum for entrepreneurial women, a place to come together and discuss the entrepreneurial process in its particularized character, as it applies to women.

Phyllis Haeger, more than any feminist leader or writer or any other prominent American woman in government, business, or the arts, legitimized the woman entrepreneur.

Jean Hails

Name of Company:	Hails Construction Company
Location:	Atlanta
Date Founded:	1973
Description of Business:	The company is a leading commercial construction company in the Atlanta metropolitan area.
Description of *P*:	Hails is the survivor's survivor. She has taken every shot the economy can give plus three husbands, and stands like a statue, smiling and proud, head and shoulders above the competition.
Description of *S*:	Atlanta grew fast and far during the go-go 1980s and arguably became one of the most overbuilt cities in the country. Because it was debt-free, Hails Construction Company has survived while other construction companies have fallen by the wayside.
Members of *E*:	Roger Watson, executive vice president Bob Turner, a Houston builder who has supported Hails throughout the years
Size of *V*:	The company is privately held. Its sales are approximately $15 million a year.
Social Utility:	Hails has traveled to every state in the Union speaking to industry groups and to her favorite audience, young women executives. She also served on the Presidential Commission on Women Business Ownership.

Principal Source of
Venture Capital: $10,000 raised from selling a house, an income
                            tax return, and friends

JEAN HAILS picked up her uncanny business skills from her mother, who ran
a grocery store and served as postmistress in Huntland, Tennessee,
population 500, located between Beans Creek and Elora. The family lived
next to the store, and Jean's father ran a farm and was a coal miner who
went into the mines and brought back coal that he sold in town. Jean
worked in the store, learned about credit, which her mother frequently
extended, and watched the customers.

Although her parents wanted her to go to college, Jean Hails went to
work in the mortgage business right after high school for the lofty salary
of $40 per week. She stayed at her first job for six years and during that
time married her childhood sweetheart and had a daughter.

When she was twenty-five, Hails became manager of the Ingles
Mortgage Company in Huntsville, Alabama, just as NASA was turning
the area into a boomtown. Her first marriage ended "because he was
more of a good friend than a husband," and Hails married a second time,
on the rebound. "But let's forget about him," Hails says. "Then I met Tom
Hails. It was 1973. He had been in the construction business, and his
business had failed. We decided to move to Atlanta and start a construction business. Atlanta was becoming a major metropolitan area. We were
successful right from the beginning, and the business grew by leaps and
bounds.

"Tom and I got married in 1981, and a few years later, he decided he
wanted to sail his sailboat around the world. So, I agreed to buy him out.

"The divorce lasted nearly four years, one of the longest on record. It
went to trial, and that lasted three-and-one-half weeks. Clearly, Tom
wasn't excited about the buyout offer I made."

Right after the trauma of a "public" divorce, the construction business hit the wall. "Builders were falling like flies," recalls Hails. "But I
knew about debt and how it can be your worst nightmare when times are
tough; so the company never borrowed. And we'll be around when the
economy of Atlanta picks back up again."

Hails was the first woman president of the Association of Builders
and Contractors, the 20,000-member industry trade group, a position she
held for three years. The job was hands-on, involving lobbying in
Washington and numerous speaking engagements across the country.
This got Hails interested in politics, in which she has been active in the
Republican party for several years.

Lillian B. Handy

Name of Company:	TRESP Associates, Inc.
Location:	Alexandria, Virginia
Date Founded:	1981
Description of Business:	High-technology consulting firm
Description of *P*:	The Federal government and its hundreds of agencies frequently lack the expertise to carry out the functions assigned to them by Congress. Therein lies the problem that has created the community of consultants that circumnavigate the nation's capital.
Description of *S*:	To succeed in the high-tech consulting business, the consultant's reputation for consistently high quality and fairly priced work must be impeccable. Without that reputation, there are no follow-on jobs. TRESP soon won that reputation.
Members of *E*:	Kenneth J. Jones, executive vice president and chief operating officer
Size of *V*:	The company's revenues reached approximately $14 million in 1993. Assuming TRESP earns at least a 10 percent profit, the company would easily be worth $7–8 million to an acquirer or in the public market.
Social Utility:	TRESP conducts science and technology institutes; maintains a partnership with nearby Hammond Junior High School in Alexandria; and supports a range of national and regional causes.

Principal Source of
Venture Capital: Her American Express card

LILLIAN B. HANDY earned all the promotions and pay raises that were made available to her. But she never got a chance to become vice president of the company she worked for. Although she was doing the work of a vice president, she never received credit in her pay envelope. Rather than wait for the recognition and credit to come to her, Handy went out and got it on her own. In the process, she built a highly successful business, one that will endure for years to come.

"I'm not the technical person," Handy readily points out. Her strongest asset, she says, is "my management capability. Technical people usually don't make good managers. Likewise, managers don't often make good technical people. It's very difficult to combine the two."[1] A company will fail most often, she adds, "because they don't manage."

The youngest of seven brothers and sisters, Handy grew up emulating one of her sisters, a social worker who had moved from the family's native Baltimore to Los Angeles. Handy attended Morgan State University, following in the footsteps of her older sisters, all of whom also attended the historically black institution in Baltimore on scholarships and earned straight A's—all, that is, except Lillian. "I didn't apply myself," she admits. "By the time I got to school, everyone knew my name through my sisters, and I got a lot of my grades ahead of time. I got comfortable and lazy with it."

Handy remembers her father, who worked as a laborer for Westinghouse and retired in 1975, as pushing his children to do well. The family was raised strictly Catholic (one of her two brothers later joined the priesthood; the other brother is an attorney). Going to church on Sundays was not a choice in the Handy family, which was one of the largest in the congregation; it was "mandatory," she says. "The only excuse for not going to church was if one of us were sick, and then you had to stay in bed all day."

At Morgan State, Handy majored in sociology, then went to work after graduation as a caseworker for the Baltimore Social Services Department. Exactly one year later, she quit her job, packed her bags, and moved to California.

Settling in Los Angeles, she went to work for the L.A. Job Corps Center as a counselor during the evenings, and took classes at UCLA

1. Jeanie M. Barnett, "Unlimited Ceiling," *Minority Business Entrepreneur*, Vol. 7, No. 5, September–October 1990.

during the day. Her next job, with the Watts Labor Community Action Committee, had Handy working at a training center 45 miles outside the city. It was there that she made her switch to the private sector, when a group of consultants from Manpower Assistance Projects in Washington, D.C., lured her back to the East with the promise of a job. Handy left California for Washington, only to wind up taking a job with a different consulting firm, which was fulfilling a contract with the Department of Housing and Urban Development to develop model city projects around the country. The very next week, Handy was off to Columbus, Ohio, to evaluate a training program, and she maintained a rigorous travel schedule for the next eight months. When the contract ended, Handy went to work with the Leadership Institute for Community Development as a traveling trainer of community action agency directors.

Moving from one job to the next, Handy quickly learned the hazards of the consulting business: living from contract to contract. Looking for something more stable, she accepted a position at Ernst & Young's consulting division as an associate and from there was promoted to manager. She met her mentor, Jack Neal, who later left the big firm to work for a smaller company. When Handy realized she wasn't going to see another move up, she let Neal talk her into coming to work with him.

"When the buyout happened, I knew I was doomed," Handy says. "I wasn't a technical person and I was doing their marketing and writing proposals. My salary was higher than my boss's—it would depend on me to tell him what to do next, and how to do it—and that became a drawback." Handy says she "got the message," and after leaving for a vacation, she decided not to go back. In mid-1981, Handy formed TRESP and worked out of her home.

"I never considered it was going to be as involved as it was so early on," says Handy about her first contracts. "It happened very quickly." During the first two years, however, she did not draw a salary: "Everything went back into the development of TRESP."

TRESP's clients read like a Who's Who of cutting-edge technology. Here is a sampling:

* For IBM, the company supports the Federal Aviation Administration's Advanced Automation Systems in Rockville, Maryland.
* For Oak Ridge National Laboratories, TRESP has seventy staffers supporting the applications development, telecommunications management, and facilities operation for the Lab's Energy Systems Group.

* For the Office of the Secretary of Defense, TRESP manages the Defense Applied Information Technology Center, where it tests and prototypes information technologies utilizing VAX 11/780, SUN workstations, and a variety of sophisticated computer systems.

What creates that special moment in time when a seemingly content corporate employee suddenly steps into a telephone booth and in a wink of an eye steps out wearing an entrepreneur's cap and uniform? It's the combination of dissatisfaction, energy, and insight. Handy had been held back and knew she could do better. She had the energy to build her own company. And she knew the problems that she was peculiarly and uniquely situated to solve. Stir these three ingredients together with Handy's background, especially her father's confidence in her, and a stunningly successful woman entrepreneur is the end result.

Nancy Heller

Name of Company:	Nancy Heller, Inc.
Location:	Los Angeles
Date Founded:	1971
Description of Business:	Produces casual women's apparel, which it sells through eleven franchised Nancy Heller retail stores. It also designs apparel for Disney World and for an Italian apparel marketer under the Malo Tricot label.
Description of P:	Heller has demonstrated throughout her twenty-two-year career in the apparel industry an uncanny ability to design clothing that the market is seeking.
Description of S:	Heller launched her company by putting rhinestones on undershirts, which became an instant hit and the young designer's launchpad.
Members of E:	Art Snyder, president
Size of V:	The company is privately held; its revenues are reported at the $34 million annual level.
Social Utility:	Heller devotes her time, and contributes funds, to the AIDS Project Los Angeles and to helping elect responsible California politicians.
Principal Source of Venture Capital:	$3,000 in personal savings

"I've always worked," said NANCY HELLER. "That's all I ever wanted to do. When I was a child, my father took me to work in his coat factory, and I have worked in the garment business ever since."

Heller went to high school under a work-study program that permitted her to work four hours a day. Upon graduating, she got a job as a showroom girl at Don's Sophisticates, a Los Angeles women's apparel manufacturer.

"At night, I designed clothes. My first designs were rock 'n roll clothes—leathers and costume jewelry. I called up Cher and Diana Ross and sold them. That's how I got started," Heller explains.

"Then one day I got this idea of putting rhinestones on undershirts. I bought a dozen size 16 men's undershirts and a box of glittering rhinestones and sewed them on. I took them to Herbert Fink on Rodeo Drive and he sold them as fast as I could make them."

Heller then contacted Geraldine Stutz, who ran Henri Bendel. She ordered them in carloads. *Women's Wear Daily* featured the rhinestoned undershirt in a cover story, and in ten months Heller had sold 80,000 undershirts out of her apartment. A legend was born.

Still in her twenties, Heller needed a second act. She built a design and manufacturing company selling primarily upscale T-shirts and cashmere sweaters to department stores and specialty shops throughout the country. Heller shuns publicity and keeps a low profile. "I would rather be in my office making clothes than out there PR-ing."

Now she is into her third act, as she refers to it: opening a chain of Nancy Heller stores. The primary franchisee is Saks Fifth Avenue. "But the storefronts say 'Nancy Heller for Saks Fifth Avenue.' " The stores are popping up on the major fashion streets throughout the country—Rodeo Drive, Michigan Avenue, Madison Avenue. Heller's manufacturers are her business partners. They produce her designs under contract, and, after inspecting them for quality control, drop-ship them to the franchisees. Heller developed a sales training manual for the retail clerks, and she persuaded her husband, Art Snyder, an architect, to join her in running the operations.

Never one to be satisfied with one marketing channel, Heller also designed the Nancy Heller line for Disney World and an upscale cashmere sweater line for Malo Tricot, an Italian apparel firm. She is also designing a line of linens for the Nancy Heller stores.

Always working. Ever creative. The queen of the rhinestoned undershirt is on the rise again.

Laura Henderson

Name of Company:	Prospect Associates
Location:	Rockville, Maryland
Date Founded:	1979
Description of Business:	The company is a research and information-gathering firm that produces reports in the health care and biomedical fields, which it publishes for government agencies and industry.
Description of *P*:	When the National Institutes of Health want to publish information about a drug or the outbreak of a new disease, they turn to the private sector of think tanks that operate along the Beltway.
Description of *S*:	Prospect Associates is known for the high quality and accuracy of its research, its speed of delivery, and the high level of readability of its reports.
Members of *E*:	John Alciati, executive vice president William Rudd, a colleague John McShulkis, "who saw in me a potential I never saw in myself"
Size of *V*:	The company is privately held but reports its revenues at more than $10 million.
Social Utility:	Prospect Associates has set up a community-service steering committee, aimed at making volunteer opportunities more available to its employees. Committed to serving its community, Prospect has started various food, clothing, and holiday toy drives; has an

adopt-a-school tutoring program with a local
elementary school; and has an in-house
recycling program (they've cleaned up a local
public park). During the Persian Gulf War,
Prospect employees donated items to put in
care packages for service men and women
through "Operation Something From Home."
Prospect also conducts two blood drives each
year.

Principal Source of
Venture Capital: $35,000 in personal savings

LAURA HENDERSON has built one of the most respected health communications and biomedical research firms in the country. The company integrates the scientific discipline of medical research with the art of communication. The gathering and publishing of information has created some of the world's great fortunes, and publishing entrepreneurs today represent more than 20 percent of the *Forbes* 400 wealthiest Americans.

Ever since Johann Gutenberg invented the printing press in the 1450s, inventive entrepreneurs have been discovering unique purposes to which the printed word could be put. The first important use of Gutenberg's invention was how-to-do-it books, which spread knowledge about craft techniques in particular. This put the responsibility for accuracy on the authors and led to the agreement on materials and principles for various crafts.

With the advent of xerography and desktop publishing software on easy-to-operate personal computers, everyone can be a publisher. But when accuracy of information is critical, companies such as Prospect Associates rise to the top. Maintaining its role as the leader in health and biomedical reports is a difficult challenge.

Henderson has accomplished this through innovative management and interdisciplinary teamwork. Her managers are entrepreneurs, responsible for specific intellectual areas, all of which are critical for public health.

Her most difficult assignment is to blend scientific research disciplines, on the one hand, with the art of communicating, on the other. Proof of her success can be seen not only in Prospect Associates' healthy financial statement but in Henderson's and the company's numerous awards. In 1993 she received a Social Responsibility Award from the George Washington University School of Business and Public Management. In 1991 she was named Women in Business Advocate of the Year. She also serves as chair of the National Foundation for Women Business Owners.

Henderson was born in Albemarle, North Carolina, and devoured biographies of courageous women and men as a child. This instilled in her a missionary zeal to make the world a better place. But how? At Duke University, Henderson was a civil rights activist. In her first job, she worked for an international organization fighting the world hunger crisis. "I bounced around after that, then landed a job at SysteMetrix near Washington, D.C., in a division that did work for NIH. The owners didn't support this division, and this made me angry. I told them how I felt. And they paid me to leave. Fifteen people left with me," Henderson says, with a knowing chuckle. The entrepreneurial itch had been scratched years ago by Henderson's maternal grandmother, whom she describes as "somewhat of a feminist." "We spent a lot of time together in the summers, mainly in deep philosophical discussions. She felt strongly that I should stretch my wings to the fullest."

Prospect Associates' major client is the National Institutes of Health, for which it developed a cholesterol screening, education, and control program called "Take Heart." Another program, "Eater's Choice," teaches about cholesterol, diet, and health. The company won awards for its report *Preventing Heart Disease and Stroke* and its booklet *The Diabetes Dictionary. Thoughtware*, published by the company, covers every major area of health care concern from AIDS to Alzheimer's disease.

Not satisfied with these impressive accomplishments, Henderson has become one of the nation's most outspoken speakers in pressing the rights of women business owners.

Leslie Hindman

Name of Company:	Leslie Hindman Auctioneers
Location:	Chicago
Date Founded:	1982
Description of Business:	Auctioneer of fine art
Description of *P*:	The Midwest was virtually an untapped market for the auctioning of fine art. Many beautiful pieces remained in estates because of the inconvenience of having to send them to New York or Los Angeles to be sold by the big auction houses.
Description of *S*:	Hindman Auctioneers has brought a fresh, friendly, and more personalized service to collectors and dealers, encouraging their clients to unveil their prized treasures in Chicago.
Members of *E*:	Leslie Hindman, president
Size of *V*:	1992 gross sales are estimated at $14 million.
Social Utility:	Leslie Hindman has held numerous auctions in support of various organizations, including the Pediatric AIDS Foundation and the Chicago House.
Principal Source of Venture Capital:	$250,000 raised through private investors

Although LESLIE HINDMAN grew up in the wealthy suburbs of Chicago, is the daughter of the owner of a $400 million company, and attended Pine Manor College on a two-year program in Boston for young women, she has proved to be a lot more than Daddy's little girl. After summering in France, her parents urged her to go to their alma mater, Indiana University, to earn her college degree. Aside from the art, French, and literature classes she was taking, after a year and a half she decided school was not for her and dropped out—to her parents' horror. Within a few months, her parents decided to send her off with $500, telling her that if she wanted to continue her schooling she could pay for it herself. Instead of sitting in the waiting room waiting for someone to rescue her, she rose to the occasion and got a job performing secretarial tasks at Merrill Lynch. She quickly moved on to find a job at an art gallery even though they told her that she would never get that kind of a job without a degree in art or history. Within four months she moved on to Sotheby's Chicago office as an assistant director and later became office manager. But after four years she was bored, and quit.

At age 27 she seemed to have a natural knack for what she was doing and people began to suggest that she open her own auction house. The idea seemed ludicrous at first. She could not imagine anyone taking her seriously, let alone helping her finance the project. She decided to make an inquiry anyway and asked some of the older people whom she respected if they thought it was a good idea. She met with a favorable response. However, when she finally decided to give it a shot and asked her father for a loan, he told her that she should get married and start having babies! Undaunted by her father's rejection, Hindman, with the help of an accountant friend, drew up a thirty-page business plan and began to ask corporate leaders for their investment. Hindman did not want the help of anyone she knew in case her project did not work out. Within a short time, she secured approximately $250,000 in private investments and was able to open her 8,000-square-foot auction house, which held its first auction in 1982. But it was not until 1985 that she turned a profit and things began to take off. The formative years were extremely difficult and took a lot of hard work. She relied on the help of good friends and worked around the clock. She says that her usual days would start early in the morning, during which she did everything from looking at potential sales items to cataloging the items, and end around midnight. Initially, she ran into problems collecting money owed her and almost went under. However, she learned how to be a businesswoman and get what she wanted accomplished. Hindman relied on young, energetic, and friendly staff, who made her dream a reality.

Today Leslie Hindman Auctioneers sits comfortably in a 20,000-square-foot building and is considered the most highly regarded auction house in Chicago. Hindman has hired branch office representatives in nine other cities and commands a staff of more than sixty employees. The house holds twelve auctions a year. Its most famous sale was of an unknown Van Gogh painting that sold for $1.43 million in March 1992. In addition to Hindman Auctioneers, Leslie Hindman has two other successful ventures: Salvage One, the Midwest's largest source of architectural artifacts, and the Chicago Antiques Center, Chicago's first midtown retail antiques center.

Caroline Hirsch

Name of Company: Caroline's Comedy Club & Pinky Ring Productions

Location: New York City

Date Founded: 1981

Description of Business: Upscale comedy clubs

Description of *P*: As they say, "Laughter is the best medicine." With the rise of stand-up comedians during the early 1980s, comedy clubs became the hippest night life scene in big cities such as New York and Los Angeles.

Description of *S*: Having a knack for recognizing talent, Caroline Hirsch signed up such comedy greats as Jay Leno, Jerry Seinfeld, Pee Wee Herman, and Sandra Bernhardt when they were just getting their careers started.

Members of *E*: Caroline Hirsch, founder and president

Size of V: Privately held, Caroline's chose not to reveal company revenues.

Social Utility: For more than ten years Caroline Hirsch has not only brought laughter into the lives of millions of New Yorkers; she has also played an active role in her community. She serves as president of the Association for the Help of Retarded Children and is a member of the Friars Club. Committed to the women's movement, she sits on the board of the Ms. Foundation.

Principal Source of Venture Capital: Private funding through personal savings and friends

CAROLINE HIRSCH is no joke. She has proved herself to be a first-class entrepreneur as she continues to prosper in some of the toughest times her industry has seen. She has displayed her business savvy, acute marketing ability, and courage in her ability to adapt to a changing market. Clubs have been around for years. Some of them, such as The Improvisation, have filed for Chapter 11. Another one, Catch a Rising Star, has closed six of its seven clubs. But none of this stopped Hirsch from opening a new club in midtown Manhattan in 1992.

Caroline's Comedy Club started out in New York's trendy Chelsea district in 1981 as a cabaret. When Hirsch had problems filling the bill for cabaret acts, she decided to move into comedy. Having a keen sense for talent, she signed future comedy greats such as Billy Crystal and Steven Wright. As stars were being born at Caroline's, she began to make a name for herself. In 1987 she opened up her second Manhattan club in New York's South Street Seaport. That year the club pulled in approximately $4 million in sales. Not wanting the clubs to take away from each other, she converted the Chelsea club into a Cajun restaurant and club. As cable television began to grow, producers started bringing comedians into the homes of television viewers. Caroline was quick to jump into the cable scene by signing a contract with the Arts & Entertainment Network in 1989 to produce "Caroline's Comedy Hour." Her production company, Pinky Ring Productions, is also responsible for producing comedy shorts for Comedy Central, another cable-TV network.

In 1992, when the lease on her Chelsea restaurant had run out, Hirsch decided to close it down and to move her Seaport club to midtown, near Times Square and the theater district. The strategic moves that Caroline has made reveal an astute manager and marketer. She obviously cares about the people she serves and the comedians who perform. When cable-TV started producing comedy shows, she followed suit with her own show. When her Seaport Club, which relied heavily on the Wall Street crowd for weekday business, began to slide owing to economic pressures on Wall Street, she moved. Another contributing factor was weather. When it rained, no one would be hanging out at the Seaport. Consequently, she moved to where theater-goers and tourists congregate and opened her new club in an area accessible to high-rollers and entertainment lovers who wanted a change of pace. By centrally locating the club, she also made it easier for uptown New Yorkers to get a few laughs.

Her marketing strategy includes everything from inviting local hotel concierges to a free show, in the hope that they will recommend the club to their guests, to direct advertising in hotel magazines. In addition, she works with comedians in setting up television and radio interviews to help them draw bigger crowds. Caroline says, "When you have your own business, you take pride in the business, and it makes you want to do whatever it takes to make it work." She certainly has done just that. She has spent close to $2 million creating the beautiful interior of her latest Broadway club and continues to sign on big-name comedians every week for her club and her television show. Appropriately dubbed the "queen of comedy," Caroline Hirsch has earned her rank as one of the 100 greatest entrepreneurs of our day.

Nancy Hoffman

Name of Company:	Nancy Hoffman Gallery
Location:	New York City
Date Founded:	1972
Description of Business:	Art gallery specializing in contemporary art
Description of *P*:	In the late 1960s and early 1970s, most art galleries were located in uptown Manhattan on or north of 57th Street. The need for larger wall and floor space, the presence of a growing number of emerging artists, and the need for proximity to their studios in SoHo created a climate for a new area of galleries to arise in SoHo (South of Houston Street). While the galleries uptown were considered high-priced, galleries in SoHo, showing younger artists, were more affordable.
Description of *S*:	Opened in 1972 in New York's SoHo district, the Nancy Hoffman Gallery showed a combination of undiscovered artists along with contemporary artists whose work was emerging or already known.
Members of *E*:	Nancy Hoffman, owner and president
Size of V:	The company is privately held.
Social Utility:	Visitors walk through the Nancy Hoffman Gallery, free of charge, viewing art in a variety of media that is life-enhancing and affirming. Part of Hoffman's mission is to educate the public about the art in the gallery.
Principal Source of Venture Capital:	$100,000 borrowed through private sources

NANCY HOFFMAN has loved the world of art ever since she was a young girl growing up near New York City. "From the time I was a teenager, I would go to museums and galleries. Art always interested me." Graduating from Barnard College in 1966 with a degree in art history, Hoffman spent the next six years gaining experience in the art world at a museum of Asian art and at a contemporary art gallery in uptown Manhattan. As a result of taking a business course taught jointly by university professors and corporate executives, Hoffman learned the essentials of finance, accounting, and management. She knew how to put together a business plan and prospectus. "It was a great course; I learned how to do it all!" Armed with several years of gallery experience and information from the course "How to Run Your Own Small Business," Nancy Hoffman drew up plans to open her own gallery. "I put together a business plan and found myself a lawyer. When I showed him my prospectus, he said, 'Who put this together for you?,' surprised that I had done it, assuming that some male professional might have helped me."

With $100,000 borrowed from private sources, she rented space in the downtown SoHo area of Manhattan in an old landmark building that needed extensive renovation. "The place was a mess when I got it; everything had to be changed. It had been a heavy-duty sheet metal manufacturing factory." With a lot of hard work and the support of friends, she was able to open in 1972, garnering a great review for her opening show from *The New York Times*. From its inception, the Nancy Hoffman Gallery took off. Within six months her enterprise was in the black, breaking even months before she had anticipated. Hoffman reflects: "It was challenging and difficult at first. I was working around the clock, seven days a week. The gallery was my whole life. Twenty years later, it continues to be a challenge, as it has been each decade."

Hoffman's unique contribution to the art world is defined by the artists she has discovered, supported, and shown over the years, as well as by her consistency and loyalty to her "stable" (the group of artists represented by the gallery). Among the artists are Don Eddy, Carolyn Brady, Joseph Raffael, Rafael Ferrer, Viola Frey, Juan Gonzalez, and John Okulick. In 1992, the Nancy Hoffman Gallery celebrated its twentieth anniversary. Her success can be attributed to her positive outlook, her sense of integrity, and her commitment to the artists. Hoffman is the first to admit that her gallery is a business. "I am in business and I'm in business to stay in business." However, the art work that she shows in her gallery is not selected on the basis of what she feels the public wants or what will sell. Her decision is based on a commitment to the work itself, "to the unique, original statement of the work, its quality and potential for evolution."

Nancy Hoffman continues to be known for her ongoing commitment to her artists, some of whom have been represented by her since the gallery opened in 1972. Hoffman says that she looks to the "conviction, beliefs, and philosophy of each artist to see whether I respond to the underlying content of the work. Part of my response has to do with manifest content, that is, subject matter, gesture, color, composition, technique in painting, drawing, and sculpture. . . . Part of my response is how the work relates to the environment and art history." She continues: "It is not black and white, it is not as simple as likes or dislikes, it is much deeper than that. I look to the richness of the work, what meets the eye as well as what motivates the artist's expression. I have remained true to my sensibilities over the years rather than blowing with the wind of what is fashionable in art." Satisfying her need to communicate with people, Hoffman adds that the work she shows is "life-enhancing," not "violent or nihilistic." "I am a positive person, a quality that is reflected in the art work shown at the gallery." Having a true sense of integrity, Hoffman says: "It's what you put out into the world that is important. If I could not build a business that was true to my vision, I would not want to have started my own business. With hard work, luck, stamina, business savvy, and energy, I have been able to enjoy the creation and building of a business. I continue to enjoy the discoveries of each day."

Maria Elena Ibanez

Name of Company: International High Technology, Inc.
Location: Miami
Date Founded: 1991
Description of
Business: International distributor of personal computers
                   and computer-related products to Africa, the
                   Middle East, Russia, and Eastern Europe
Description of *P*: In most Third World countries the computer
                   systems that are being used are archaic. There
                   is a need for new hardware and for the
                   knowledge of how the new hardware works
                   and of how it can benefit business.
Description of *S*: Using her finely tuned marketing skills, acquired
                   during her start-up of International Micro
                   Systems, a company that Ibanez founded in
                   1979 and eventually sold in 1988, and her
                   profound knowledge of computers and
                   applications, Ibanez began to set up seminars
                   throughout various Third World countries,
                   showing business owners the need for new
                   computer systems and how these systems
                   could make them more money.
Members of *E*:   Maria Elena Ibanez, president
Size of *V*:   1993 revenues are projected at $15 million.
Social Utility: Maria Elena Ibanez has volunteered endless
                   hours speaking to members of the Hispanic
                   community and to women around the world,
                   encouraging entrepreneurship and social
                   advancement.

Principal Source of
Venture Capital: Personal savings

MARIA ELENA IBANEZ has been a rebel since she was a young girl growing up in Colombia. Daughter of a successful fruit juice exporter, Ibanez had the access to a good education that most young girls did not have in Colombia. However, the strict Catholic school she attended did not interest this young girl and as a consequence she found herself always in trouble. "I would never conform to the rules," says Ibanez. "I think that showed that I was an entrepreneur from the beginning. . . . I remember when I was eight years old, I was very sure of myself. The nuns always wanted me to go to mass and pray. I hated it. So one day I told one of the nuns: 'Listen, nun, I don't think that we should pray the rosary and repeat the same prayer fifty times to the Virgin. If the Virgin is smart, she will hear me the first time.' "

Ibanez stayed in school, but when she was suspended at the age of fifteen, her father convinced her to take a computer course offered by Boris Computers, a local manufacturer of computers that needed programmers to develop software in Spanish. "My father told me that I was not going to stay home and watch TV. It was almost my punishment." But when she went to this course, she was fascinated. "It was so interesting to see something different like the binary system. When the instructor said 1 + 1 is 10, I immediately became interested." The rest of the people in the course were over thirty-five and thought it was too confusing and eventually quit. Ibanez loved it and became the only person in Barranquilla, Colombia (population one million) who completed the course and knew how to program in assembly language. Ibanez continued going to school, but after school she would program accounting packages in Spanish for the Boris computer systems. At age 16, she was going to her father's friends' businesses and selling the software she had developed. This was just the beginning for this computer jock. Being a woman in Latin America did not seem to bother Ibanez. "My father was good for me; he always pushed my education. In my mind it was never an issue that I was a woman. I think because I had this attitude I never felt the discrimination. Also, since I started programming, people did not have a choice, I was the only one who could do it. So they could not discriminate against me. It was me or nobody else." She sold her software for a high price and saved a lot of money.

When she came to the United States in 1973, she did not speak any English at all. She moved to Miami and continued her education at Florida International University, where she majored in computer science. "I was one of two women in that major. I spent all of my time in the lab working with computers. I did not know any English, so I stayed away from courses I had to write in. I took only computer and math courses until I could learn English." Because she still had a hard time understanding the professors, she developed a plan to learn English quickly. "I enrolled in a crash course in English and made it a point to learn 50 new words a day. I would read the paper each day and write down the first 50 words that I did not understand on index cards and would review them all day. In about three or four months I was able to understand everybody." She adds, however, "Not too many people could understand me." She continues: "I had a lot of trouble with verbs. Being a mathematician, I developed a technique to learn as many verbs as I could in a short period of time. If I could learn all the verbs in the present tense, I could learn 900 verbs instead of 300 in all three tenses. And if I just added 'ed,' I hit 80 percent of the verbs right. That meant that I was speaking correctly 80 percent of the time. That was good enough for me." Within four months she was fluent and could communicate with people in English. She eventually graduated in 1978 with high honors and a degree in computer science and went to work as a troubleshooter for the school's computer lab, where she had spent most of her time as a student. "I was a nerd. I was always in the computer lab whether I had work or not. I loved it, though, so I put a lot of time into learning everything about computers." It did not take her long to realize that she was not going to get anywhere working for the university. "My boss was making nothing and he had been there for twenty years." Ibanez is the first to admit that her first motivation is to make money. "I like a high standard of living."

With the development of the personal computer came a cheaper and more powerful machine. The cost of a PC was a fraction of the cost of the big computer systems they had in Colombia. Realizing this, Ibanez says, "I saw an opportunity to become a distributor of personal computers to Colombia. I knew the Colombian market." She proceeded to find a small manufacturer and became their distributor. "I began to call all of the people I had done programs for in Colombia and right away I was selling computers." Having no business experience at all, Ibanez had quite a bit to learn. "I knew about accounting and I knew a little bit about exporting from my father, but I did not know anything about marketing, sales, or finance." I figured if I could study computer science and get straight A's, then I could study anything on my own. I was always very confident." Ibanez says she gets this confidence from her mother, who would always tell her, "Don't complain. Fix it yourself. Crying will not do you any good;

no one will fix things for you." Ibanez proceeded to consume book after book, learning as much as she could about marketing and sales. "If you can read, you can learn," says Ibanez.

Before she made the switch to hardware, Ibanez was producing accounting software in Spanish. She pulled in $60,000 in the first month. But soon after, sales began to decrease, so she spent her money advertising in a major computer magazine, following the advice of one of the books she had read. Unfortunately, she did not realize until after most of her money was gone that there were no copyright laws in Latin America and that people were buying and selling pirated copies of her software without her knowledge. This did not stop Ibanez. She scraped together whatever money she had left, spent two days calling every computer manufacturer, and ended up with a distributorship for five computer companies. She now had the product but did not have the clients, so she traveled to Latin America, stopping at all major cities and cold-calling from her hotel rooms. "I ended up stealing the yellow pages from every hotel room I stayed in. It was the best source book I could get my hands on. I began to call companies with the biggest ads that I thought would be interested in my services." She ended up coming back home with $100,000 in orders and was able to get back on her feet in three months. Her father had warned her not to go because she was so beautiful and that no one would take a woman seriously. Being a rebel and an entrepreneur at heart, she says she "bought the ugliest suits I could buy, I wore no jewelry, and dressed like an old lady. I even bought myself a pair of glasses." However, Ibanez maintains that it was her profound technical knowledge of computers that enabled her to attract business.

That was the beginning of International Micro Systems (IMS), a company that was ranked 55 among the top 500 fastest-growing companies in the United States in 1987. In 1988, with sales at about $10 million, Ibanez sold IMS to a larger computer company when it made her an offer she could not refuse. "They offered me more money than I could make in ten years." Ibanez says she thought that this was what she wanted and decided to become a beach bum. "I gave all of my business suits to a lawyer friend and filled my closets with bathing suits and shorts." But this did not last very long. She found herself very restless and decided to go back into business. Having signed a noncompete agreement with the buyer of her company, Ibanez had to seek out different markets. She turned her focus on Africa and the Middle East and began the same process of marketing computers in these Third World countries. People once again told her that she was crazy and once again she has proved them wrong. Ibanez feels that being a woman doing business in cultures that repress women has been outweighed by her technical know-how and her natural ability. "Discrimination does not exist if you do not think about it. If you are good at what you do and you know what you are talking about, it does not make a difference who you are." Her 1993 sales are estimated at $15 million. Today she is expanding into Russia. "The harder they say it will be, the more interested I am. It means that there is little to no competition."

Sandra Dixon Jiles

Name of Company:	UBM, Inc.
Location:	Chicago
Date Founded:	1975
Description of Business:	The company is a construction management firm specializing in commercial buildings in Chicago.
Description of P:	The construction business requires marketing, engineering, and architectural skills, job costing, a network of skilled craftsmen to draw on, and timing.
Description of S:	Jiles pooled her management talents with those of an engineer and a marketing person to fill a need for project management.
Members of E:	Paul King, Sham Dahbadghad
Size of V:	The company is privately held, with revenues of $16 million.
Social Utility:	Jiles devotes her spare time to mentoring programs at her church, and her time and money to the United Negro College Fund.
Principal Source of Venture Capital:	Customer financing from the first job

SANDRA DIXON JILES wasted no time getting into business. Upon receiving her Master's degree in business administration from Roosevelt University, she founded the predecessor of UBM, Inc., with two partners, each of whom brought something different to the company. Paul King said he could bring in the work. Sham Dahbadghad said he could design and engineer the jobs. Jiles said she could hire the people to do the work, and manage everyone profitably. It was their first venture, and if eighteen years is the measure of continuous success, the threesome has turned its plans into reality.

Capture the moment in your mind: three university friends, then in caps and gowns, graduation celebrations, excitement, and then, in the next scene, they huddle over cups of coffee: Sham is talking, Sandra is taking notes, then Sandra is talking, Paul chimes in, then Sham adds something, then Paul draws boxes and arrows, then they laugh and embrace—and United Builders Management Company is formed. There is no money to incorporate; thus the business remains a loose affiliation for three years until the "Inc." can be paid for.

It took guts, which replaced business experience. It took insight, which stood in for strategic planning. It took the ability to cooperate—not an easy thing for strong-willed, twenty-two-year-old entrepreneurs to do. But the UBM partnership has held together and prospered.

"Start-up capital?" Jiles laughs at the question. "We had no money. Out start-up capital came from our first job. Progress payments kept us going. We lived very inexpensively."

Today, UBM employs fifty professionals—engineers, architects, programmers—and seventy-five craftsmen on various jobs. It bids on construction jobs that involve concrete, its specialty. Its clients have included the City of Chicago, the Capital Development Board of Illinois, the Gateway Foundation, Waste Management Corp., and Federal Express, among others.

Jiles' entrepreneurial urge came from her father. "He owned a fruit cart. He had a grocery store. He was always in business for himself. He stressed education to my three sisters and me, and each one of us has a master's degree. One sister went into special education; the second went into affirmative action work, the third is an artist. I am the only business-woman.

"But I always liked numbers as a child," she explains. "When we played Monopoly, I was the banker. I liked accounting, and when I graduated, luckily I met two men I could get along with whose skills complemented mine. And I guess they needed what I could do because they made me president."

Like other women entrepreneurs, Jiles postponed having a family until her company was up and running. She is now married and has two sons, eleven, thirteen.

Donna Karan

Name of Company:	Donna Karan New York—DKNY
Location:	New York City
Date Founded:	1984
Description of Business:	International fashion company that designs and manufactures apparel for men and women
Description of *P*:	As Karan puts it: "That I'm a woman makes me want to nurture others, fulfill needs, and solve problems. How can I make life easier? How can dressing be simplified so we can get on with our lives? How to add comfort and luxury? What travels? And what will accentuate the positive and delete the negative?"
Description of *S*:	DKNY was created to answer these questions and is known today for its use of black cashmere, stretch fabrics, body suits, unitards, and sensuous silhouettes that wrap the body. To complete the whole image, DKNY provides its customers with all the accessories for dress from head to toe.
Members of *E*:	Stephen Weiss (husband)
Size of *V*:	Gross sales estimated at $275 million in 1992
Social Utility:	Karan is actively involved in AIDS awareness and education, and has held benefits and fund raisers for AIDS programs including the Pediatric AIDS Foundation. She is also a member of DIFFA (Design Industries Foundation for AIDS).
Principal Source of Venture Capital:	Personal Savings

"Everything I do is a matter of heart, body, and soul," says DONNA KARAN, designer and chief executive officer of the international fashion empire that bears her name. "For me, designing is a personal expression of who I am—wife, mother, friend, and businessperson—the many roles women everywhere are trying to balance. But before I can be anything else, I'm a woman—with all the complications, feelings, and emotions." In fact, Karan credits her feminine instincts for the success of her company, which she founded with her husband, Stephen Weiss.

Karen feels that clothes should function like a modern security blanket. They need to be user friendly, luxurious, and all about comfort, ease, and sensuality. And in addition to the emotional aspect, they have to work within a person's lifestyle. That means being flexible enough to cross climates, and versatile enough to go day-into-evening.

"I'm designing for an international man and woman, a person who never knows where a day is going to take them," says Karan. "That's why New York is on the label. It sets the pace, the attitude." From the beginning, DKNY has never been just about clothes. DKNY hosiery, shoes, intimates, eyewear, belts, and jewelry have been created to fulfill Karan's woman from head to toe.

Ever since she was a young girl, Karan was always interested in fashion. By the time she graduated from high school, she had already designed and made her first collection for a fashion show. Karan was born into fashion on Long Island, New York. Not only was her father, Gabby Faske (who died when Karan was three), a haberdasher, but her mother, Helen, was a showroom model and fashion sales rep. Even Karan's stepfather, Harold Flaxman, was in the fashion business.

Karan pursued her love for the fashion industry at New York's Parsons School of Design. When she was hired by Anne Klein for a summer job following her second year at Parsons, it was the beginning of a relationship that would change Karan's life. Karan continued to work for Anne Klein as an associate designer for three years, and was named successor after Anne Klein died in 1974. Karan had the skills she needed and worked diligently to continue the excellence of the Anne Klein Collection. A year later, she teamed up with Louis Dell'Olio, a fellow classmate from Parsons, and together they designed the Anne Klein Collection. After a few years, Karan began to develop a style of her own. In 1982, she introduced Anne Klein II, bringing the concept of bridge and lifestyle dressing into the fashion industry. This was just the beginning.

Two more years passed before she decided to go out on her own. In 1984, with the help and encouragement of her husband, Stephen Weiss (an accomplished sculptor), they opened Donna Karan New York.

Working out of their front living room, Donna Karan and Stephen Weiss began creating one of the greatest fashion statements the industry has ever seen. By the fall of 1985, Donna Karan introduced the fashion world to the first of many Donna Karan New York collections, which was met with overwhelming success. In fact, that same year, Donna Karan was named Designer of the Year by the Council of Fashion Designers of America. This was just the beginning. In 1986, she was honored for her influence in head-to-toe dressing. In 1987, she received a joint award with the Arnell/Bickford Agency for their hosiery campaign. In 1990, she was once again named Designer of the Year. In 1992, she was named Menswear Designer of the Year.

Karan has introduced everything from eyewear to footwear. Still, Karan says: "There's so much to be done. DKNY underwear, swimwear, home furnishings. . . . The designs are already in my head; it's just a matter of getting them executed."

Georgette Klinger

Name of Company:	Georgette Klinger, Inc.
Location:	New York City
Date Founded:	1940
Description of Business:	Manufactures men's and women's skin care products
Description of *P*:	In the late 1930s, women really did not have many options in skin care products. Furthermore, skin care "specialists" were using harmful X rays to cure acne.
Description of *S*:	Georgette Klinger recognized the need for customized treatment of each individual's skin and created an entire line of skin care products with over thirty different types of cleansers.
Members of *E*:	Kathryn Klinger, president
Size of *V*:	1992 sales exceeded $20 million.
Social Utility:	Klinger was a pioneer in enlisting aid for New York's homeless. She is an avid supporter of the American Health Foundation, Cleveland Amory's Save the Animals organization, and many musical groups including the Metropolitan Opera Guild and the National Symphony.
Principal Source of Venture Capital:	$20,000 bank loan

GEORGETTE KLINGER was born in Czechoslovakia. She remembers that from an early age, she insisted on finding her own solutions to problems in spite of the fact that, because she was the only girl in a family of four, her brothers had the protective urge to help her grow up. Her relentless pursuit of knowledge combined with her genuine humanitarian instinct has been the guiding force in both her personal and professional life. When she was in her teens, Georgette Klinger suffered from persistent acne after "foolishly experimenting with untried makeup." She dogged the footsteps of doctors and scientists until she found a cure for herself. With a firsthand understanding of the suffering caused by complexion difficulties, Ms. Klinger devoted herself to becoming an expert on skin care.

She began her own curriculum of beauty science studies in a series of courses with leading professors of dermatology and biology in Prague, Budapest, Vienna, and Zurich. Her research, meticulously compiled, prompted her to develop her own theories. The Klinger methods of treatment and skin care were already clear in her mind when she arrived in New York with her family. Prior to coming to the United States, she opened her first salon in 1921 in the Czech city of Brno. She decided to work with a male doctor to give her salon more prestige. While she says that he was a good businessman, he also "took money for the sake of taking money. He prescribed treatments that were not necessary. He was very greedy." That was not her only problem. Her mother-in-law thought it was "ridiculous" that she was working. How could the wife of a lawyer be working? "How would that look?" asked her in-laws. It did not matter to Ms. Klinger. She continued her pursuit to perfect the treatment of the skin.

In 1939, when Hitler began to conquer Europe, Klinger's family fled to the United States. She was horrified to discover that the skin "specialists" were using X rays to treat acne. Klinger says the United States was "very, very, very behind Europe" in its treatment of the skin and in its taste in fashion. Klinger says that the main problem was that "to be a skin care specialist, you had to have a hair dressing license at that time. They [the United States] had no idea how to treat the skin. X rays were burning holes in people's skin!" Ms. Klinger managed to secure a $20,000 loan from a bank after she told the loan officer, "Take a look at the women around you!" She explained the need for new treatments and persuaded the officer to loan her the money. The first Georgette Klinger Salon opened in 1940, next door to the building the salon now occupies at 501 Madison Avenue. In 1970, she expanded her empire, opening her second salon in Beverly Hills under the direction of her daughter Kathryn, who is now president of the company. Two years later, Georgette Klinger established "Klinger for Men," her treatments and preparations for men, anticipating a trend that has grown in recent years. Now, Ms. Klinger oversees and monitors her eight salons in Beverly Hills, Dallas, Chicago,

Washington, D.C., Bal Harbor, Palm Beach, and the two original salons in New York City. She also has created the Georgette Klinger Laboratories, where her preparations are made fresh daily to her exact specifications. Her research continues in the field of skin care. Ms. Klinger's salons provide skin care consultation and her specialized line of skin care products. In addition, all of her salons offer exercise and nutritional consultation, as well as consultation in hair and scalp conditioning and styling.

Ms. Klinger's achievements go beyond those of her professional life. Besides being an active philanthropist on behalf of those causes that are close to her heart, Ms. Klinger was named Woman of Vision by the Eye Research Institute in 1981 and was awarded the 1983 Spirit of Achievement Award by the Albert Einstein College of Medicine for outstanding achievement in the field of skin care. Most recently, Ms. Klinger has been sought out by various groups devoted to the advancement of professional women. She has spoken before the Women's Forum of New York, the Harvard Business School, and many other organizations. To be included among women of such eminent achievement, commitment, and intelligence is the source of great satisfaction to Georgette Klinger.

In her personal life, Georgette Klinger immerses herself in activities and surroundings that reflect her exquisite sense of beauty. She lives in a large Manhattan apartment with an impressive collection of antique porcelain, jade, antique dinnerware of museum quality, and her poodles. Her love of music comes first as far as relaxation and pleasure. One of her precious possessions is her piano; she is an accomplished musician.

Above all, Georgette Klinger's most profound pleasure is her family; she has made them the unquestionable top priority throughout her life. She enjoys a warm, loving relationship with her daughter, Kathryn, and in 1984 was blessed with her first grandchild, Trevor.

Georgette Klinger's instinct for caring carries over into all aspects of her life. Although it seems impossible, Mrs. Klinger appears to know every one of her clients at the salon—and there are sometimes more than 200 a day! Her intense concern with a young client whose acne is acute but obviously clearing up fabulously is countered by her satisfaction when an elderly client confides that "everybody tells me that I look twenty years younger." As Klinger puts it: "There are givers and there are takers. . . . I am a giver." Ms. Klinger says to the young entrepreneur: "Nothing is easy. Expect a struggle. Do your very best and do it with love. Do not do it for the money. It all takes time. The only one who can help you is yourself. It's all about heart and knowledge. Always be willing to give to the people you serve."

Gail Koff

Name of Company:	Jacoby & Meyers, Inc.
Location:	New York City
Date Founded:	1976
Description of Business:	Owns and operates a chain of 110 storefront legal clinics in New York, New Jersey, Connecticut, Pennsylvania, Arizona, and California.
Description of *P*:	Legal services were once available only to the middle and upper classes, leaving commercially and physically injured poorer people without representation in the confusing maze of the civil and criminal justice system.
Description of *S*:	Offers affordable legal assistance in convenient locations.
Members of *E*:	Leonard Jacoby and Stephen Meyers, partners
Size of *V*:	The company is privately held, with estimated revenues well into eight figures.
Social Utility:	Koff serves on community service boards that further the causes of women entrepreneurs and of legal assistance to the working class.
Principal Source of Venture Capital:	Warburg Pincus Venture Partners

GAIL KOFF, lawyer, entrepreneur, author, lecturer, and mother, runs a national law firm with more than 600 employees. Koff's involvement with Leonard Jacoby and Stephen Meyers began in 1976 at a conference she had organized on the availability of legal services to working-class and middle-income people. This meeting led to a partnership that today has become one of the country's fastest-growing law firms, consisting of 110 offices and 302 attorneys who provide legal services to more than a million people.

Jacoby & Meyers is the firm that pioneered the concept of retailing legal services through neighborhood offices, and has received national acclaim as an innovator in people-oriented legal assistance. Koff is the official spokesperson for the firm and is primarily responsible for the development and expansion of new markets throughout the country.

Koff is a charter member of the prestigious Committee of 200 for women entrepreneurs, is chairperson of the board of the Office of Economic Opportunity's Legal Services Project (which she helped found in 1969), and is on the board of directors of more than half a dozen philanthropic and professional committees and groups, including the powerful Executive Committee of the Association of the Bar of New York, on which she serves with Chairman Cyrus Vance, among others. In addition, Koff serves on the Bar's Special Committee for Lawyer Advertising and Special Committee of Lawyers' Pro Bono Obligations.

Since its beginnings, Jacoby & Meyers has served to fulfill the legal needs of a large class of people often ignored by traditional law firms. At that time, the American Bar Association estimated that nearly 70 percent of the population did not have adequate access to the legal system. Koff and her partners developed the "legal clinic" concept that has driven the firm to national prominence.

The premise behind this concept is that the average person needed greater accessibility to the legal system for personal legal services involved in divorce, personal injury suits, bankruptcy, criminal liability, the making of wills, and real estate transactions. A high-volume standardized system was envisioned to provide quality legal services to middle-income Americans at reasonable fees.

The Jacoby & Meyers concept required restructuring the traditional general-practice law firm. Lower fees could be achieved by increasing client volume and office efficiency. Jacoby & Meyers located branch offices in urban and suburban neighborhoods, often in storefronts and high-traffic areas. Now people did not have to travel far from their home or work to get legal help.

A streamlined office management system was developed to ensure uniform quality and efficiency in each neighborhood location. Units for handling cases requiring special experience, such as bankruptcy, criminal, and personal injury cases, were implemented in addition to the general services performed in branch offices. Jacoby & Meyers clients received the best of both worlds. They got the individual attention and care of a small law office coupled with the legal resources and expertise of a large law firm. Jacoby & Meyers' attorneys were equally satisfied; they received a continuous and diverse caseload together with the satisfaction of managing a law office.

Central to the Jacoby & Meyers concept has been its effort to demystify the legal profession. Lawyers, their services, and fees must be held accountable to the general public. In 1977, court decisions in *Jacoby & Meyers v. California State Bar*, before the California Supreme Court, and the *Bates and O'Steen v. State Bar of Arizona* case before the U.S. Supreme Court allowed attorneys to advertise for the first time. Jacoby & Meyers has since spread the message about its unique services.

Jacoby & Meyers was the first law firm to advertise its services. Public response has been overwhelmingly positive. The firm has won many awards for its advertising campaigns, and its commercials are often looked to as models for attorney advertising. The message was simple: "If you're rich you can afford any attorney. If you're poor free legal aid is available, but you're in the middle. Jacoby & Meyers can help. For $25 you can speak with an attorney about your case and you'll receive a written estimate of the fees involved."

In January 1985, the Federal Trade Commission released a seven-year study entitled *Improving Consumer Access to Legal Services: The Case for Removing Restrictions on Truthful Advertising*. It concluded: "Legal clinics, once viewed with skepticism or hostility by many members of the profession, have proved to be viable methods of delivering legal services to consumers. . . . Advertising of legal services, as is generally true for goods and other services, tends to lead to lower prices, stimulates competition, and may enable millions of Americans to find an affordable attorney who can help them resolve legal problems."

In addition, an early study published by the American Bar Foundation concluded that, "despite charging lower prices, [Jacoby & Meyers] does not provide a lower quality of service. In fact, on some measures of quality, [their] services are demonstrably better than those of traditional firms providing the same services." In this study, Jacoby & Meyers was rated superior to competitive traditional firms on the scores of promptness, interest and concern for clients, honesty, explaining matters fully to clients, keeping clients informed of progress, paying attention to what clients have to say, and charging fair and reasonable fees.

Today, Jacoby & Meyers' growing national network of branch offices provides legal services to well over 10,000 people during an average month. When Koff, Jacoby, and Meyers conceived the concept eighteen years ago, it was considered revolutionary. Now, it is seen as the future for the delivery of personal legal services.

Kay Koplovitz

Name of Company:	USA Cable Network (formerly MSG)
Location:	New York City
Date Founded:	1977
Description of Business:	A premier cable network
Description of *P*:	Although cable television was available during the 1970s, it served primarily as a means of receiving normal air stations in areas that were mountainous or had high interference. The possibilities of using cable as a means of transmitting entertainment, news, and sports had not been explored.
Description of *S*:	Kay Koplovitz joined forces with UA-Columbia to launch the first basic cable network in America: MSG (Madison Square Garden) Sports.
Members of *E*:	Kay Koplovitz, president and chief executive officer
Size of *V*:	1992 sales are estimated at $400 million.
Social Utility:	In 1990, the company was the leader of an industrywide antidrug initiative in cooperation with the Partnership for a Drug Free America.
Principal Source of Venture Capital:	Convinced partnership of MSG and UA-Columbia to move forward and invest in her ideas.

KAY KOPLOVITZ has been interested in satellites since the age of twelve, when she avidly read accounts of the launching of Sputnik. Interestingly enough, when she attended the University of Wisconsin, she was pursuing a premed major until she heard a lecture by Arthur Clarke, author of *2001*. In his lecture, Clarke discussed the potential impact of satellite technology on communications. Koplovitz immediately changed majors and ended up writing her thesis on Clarke's prophecy. After graduating from the University of Wisconsin as a Phi Beta Kappa, she completed a Master's degree in communications from the University of Michigan. She then went to work in the public relations department of COMSAT (Communications Satellite Corporation). Koplovitz was next hired by UA-Columbia Satellite Services, where she served as vice president and executive director. An entrepreneur at heart, Koplovitz decided to move on and open her own communications management and public relations firm.

In 1977, four years after working for UA-Columbia, Koplovitz joined forces with UA-Columbia to launch the first advertiser-supported basic cable network in America, MSG Sports. In 1980, MSG Sports became the USA Network. Since its inception, Koplovitz has served as its president and CEO. Koplovitz has been and continues to be a pioneer in her industry, blazing a trail for other independent cable networks. She was the first to negotiate national cable rights for major league sports (Major League Baseball, NBA, NHL, and World League) and in 1981 she began twenty-four-hour programming. In 1985 she signed licensing agreements with several movie studios for rebroadcasting rights to more than 100 titles. In 1987, MCA and Paramount bought out Time Inc.'s share in USA, making the three equal partners. In addition, later that year, USA acquired the exclusive rights to ninety-two episodes of the hit TV program "Miami Vice." This was considered a milestone in cable TV by industry analysts, for it represented the first time an independent cable network had acquired the rights to a hit television show. Up to that point, the major networks would sell the rights to groups of stations usually not affiliated with the major networks. Today rerun acquisition is a major source of revenue for independent cable stations. That was just the beginning for Koplovitz. After "Miami Vice," USA acquired the rights to "Murder She Wrote" and the Home Box Office (HBO) hit series "The Hitchhiker," which was the first pay-television program ever to be sold to a basic cable network. Koplovitz did not stop there, however; the list of firsts continued.

In 1989, she was able to secure the exclusive rights to twenty-six Touchstone Pictures movies, marking the first time a basic cable station gained the rights to a package of motion pictures from a single studio. The following year Koplovitz acquired the rights to forty-three more movies from MCA and Paramount Pictures. Her most recent venture was the launching of the Sci-Fi Channel, which was offered to the second-largest audience in cable television's history.

Koplovitz continues to blaze a trail and remains on the cutting edge of the cable television industry. She has been married for more than twenty-two years to William Koplovitz, Jr., a lawyer in New York City, and enjoys camping and hiking when she has the time. Koplovitz is considered the most powerful woman in television and continues to be an effective leader and pioneer in the cable television industry.

Sandra L. Kurtzig

Name of Company: The ASK Group, Inc.

Location: Los Altos, California

Date Founded: 1974

Description of
Business: Designs, develops, and produces MRP turnkey systems: software that is marketed along with minicomputers to industrial corporations to assist them in improving manufacturing productivity through optimizing inventories, reducing operating expenses, and improving customer service.

Description of *P*:   Industrial computer users began purchasing computers for the plant and warehouse, but they lacked the in-house software capability to generate the desired efficiencies and cost savings. Computer manufacturers focused on financial and information systems applications. Thus, a niche was created for independent software companies. ASK Computer Systems sales in 1992 reached $400 million.

Description of *S*:   Kurtzig designed software modules for the factory and warehouse, integrated them into a well-known minicomputer, the Hewlett-Packard 3000 series, and began selling and installing software, with the customer's need in mind. With customer input, the modules became a complete manufacturing information system called MANMAN, and further refinements have included a network and microcomputer system for smaller users.

Members of E:	Pier Carlo Falotti, president and chief executive officer
	Leslie E. Wright, executive vice president
	Eric Carlson, president, ASK Computer Systems
	David Sohm, president, Data 3
Size of V:	The approximately 2.3 million shares of common stock outstanding traded in a range of $9.50–$28.13 per share in 1993 for an average valuation of $483 million.
Social Utility:	Kurtzig has demonstrated the ability of a woman to succeed in a male-dominated business. ASK has created 2,400 jobs in ninety-one offices in fifteen countries, and its investors have earned an average of more than 25 percent return on equity since 1981.
Principal Source of Venture Capital:	Kurtzig's personal savings of $2,000

SANDRA L. KURTZIG was trained in math, engineering, and computer systems marketing, but in 1972, wanting to start a family, she quit her job at General Electric. Feeling the need to work part-time, she took $2,000 of her savings and started a contract programming business in a spare bedroom of her California apartment. "My part-time job was taking up to twenty hours a day. I had the other four to start my family."[1] Her first program was one that let weekly newspapers keep track of their newspaper carriers.

She recruited several bright computer and engineering graduates and directed them to write applications to solve the problems of local manufacturers. Manufacturers' needs were well known to Kurtzig. She says, "When you spend a fortune buying expensive equipment and end up following some manufacturer's programming book one-two-three-four, it gets frustrating. You want someone to come up with easy answers, and the big companies are not aggressive or creative enough to supply them. The big companies put in the computers and open the doors for the new, aggressive companies to nibble away at the business. In general, the small companies are better at this business because the employees feel they can make a difference."[2]

Kurtzig has always been cash-conscious. Initially, she stashed all her

1. Lisa Gubernik, "A Most Successful Part-Time Job," *Forbes*, Fall 1983, p. 198.
2. Joel Kotkin, "New Money," *TWA Ambassador*, April 1982, p. 48.

business funds in a shoe box in her closet. If there was more money in the shoe box at the end of the month than at the beginning, her company made a profit. The Silicon Valley venture capitalists would not contribute to her shoe box, so Kurtzig had to launch ASK on retained earnings alone.

Friendly executives at a nearby Hewlett-Packard plant permitted Kurtzig and her programmers to use one of the company's series 3000 minicomputers at night to try to develop a manufacturing inventory control program. The group slept in sleeping bags at the company, and by 1978 it had a salable product. The breakthrough was the result of putting useful, easy-to-use software on a well-known, highly reliable computer. ASK's sales soared.

Without money for a sales force, marketing, advertisements, or brochures, ASK built its customer base by selling systems to "big corporate clients like Hewlett-Packard and Hughes on our personality, our ideas, our energy, our hard work, and our commitment to their success."[3] On the subject of rebounding from market setbacks, Kurtzig says: "A confused marketplace is an opportunity for a smart company. When a recession hit in 1981 and potential customers put us on hold, we brainstormed an answer that locked those customers into ASK. You always have to think about breaking things—patterns, products, and processes—in order to grow."[4] From $1.9 million in 1980, the company achieved revenues of $189 million in 1989, the year Kurtzig resigned from the company.

This was also the year Kurtzig returned to ASK. Her sixteen-year-old son, Andy, had developed an interest in the stock market that year. Andy pointed out to Kurtzig that with the stock having fallen, ASK's market value was less than its revenues. Andy thought the company might be taken over by a raider and encouraged Kurtzig to go back in and fix it up. She did just that and remained there for four more years.

Unable to interest many investors in her stock when ASK was privately owned, Kurtzig is today one of the wealthiest self-made women in America. The Small Business Administration reports that businesses founded by women are increasing at the current rate of 55 percent per annum versus 17 percent per annum for men. In fact, more women own their own businesses in 1993 than work for the 500 largest corporations. Success stories like this one surely help the shoe box manufacturers.

3. Sandra L. Kurtzig, *CEO: Building a $400 Million Company From the Ground Up* (New York: W. W. Norton, 1991), jacket.
4. Ibid.

Lin W. Lan

Name of Company:	Pacific Pioneer Insurance Company
Location:	Artesia, California
Date Founded:	1980
Description of Business:	A property and casualty insurance underwriter
Description of *P*:	Lan observed the need among Asian-American business owners for purchasing insurance from someone with a shared experience whom they could trust.
Description of *S*:	Lan built from scratch the first woman-owned, California-domiciled insurance company to meet those needs.
Members of *E*:	David Einhorn, chief financial officer
Size of *V*:	The company is privately held, with annual gross premiums of $30 million. If it were publicly held, Pacific Pioneer would be valued at more than $18 million.
Social Utility:	Lan gives her time and resources to the Women and Children Center in Whittier, California, and she is on the board of numerous community service organizations, including the Taiwanese American Citizens League.
Principal Source of Venture Capital:	Personal savings; offers of venture capital funds have been rejected.

"I don't do that well with partners," admits insurance mogul LIN W. LAN. "That has nothing to do with the people who want to be my partner, but it has to do with my background.

"For many years I was an obedient housewife," Lan explains. "Every morning I would wake up and turn on the shower for my husband. Then I would put out his suit, shirt, socks, underwear, tie, and shoes. I would even light his cigarette, and I don't even smoke.

"Then I would make his and the children's breakfast and send them off to work and school. That was my life. But I always knew there was more. But to go out and get it, I had to leave my husband. That was the last partner I had. I'm not looking for another one."

Needing to support her children, Lan got a job as an insurance rater with Travelers Insurance Company and simultaneously began attending evening classes at the local college. Five years later, she graduated with the Chartered Property and Casualty Underwriter degree.

In 1980, Lan left the comfortable vice president's position at Union Federal Savings & Loan, where she managed the insurance brokerage and insurance loan servicing operation, to form her first company, Unico Insurance Agency.

For the next twelve years, she built up a large agency serving the Asian-American business community in southern California, while also adding a risk management subsidiary. Her route had many serious obstacles. Most people would have given up during the conspiratorial litigation, investigations, and libelous attacks on her character she had to put up with, but Lan hung in and defeated her detractors.

In 1992, she purchased the California-licensed Enterprise Insurance Company and an Oklahoma-licensed underwriter and merged them with Unico to form the Pacific Pioneer Insurance Company.

To help raise the $6 million in capital needed to purchase these underwriters, many venture capitalists and private investors were interested in joining hands with Lan. However, Lan decided to invest her own savings and to borrow the balance of the purchase price because she felt that she needed full control of a new company in its early stages to ensure growth in the direction that she chose to follow. She was willing to take on the entire financial risk to own 100 percent of the enterprise. No partners for this woman entrepreneur need apply.

Kimberle Levin

Name of Company:	JVC Technologies, Inc.
Location:	Wayne, Pennsylvania
Date Founded:	1987
Description of Business:	The company designs, develops, and integrates various disparate computers within an organization into a network that permits each of the computers to communicate with each other.
Description of *P*:	Many corporations and government agencies have ordered hundreds, even thousands, of different computer models over the years, and they face the choice of replacing them with compatible computers or hiring a systems integrator to lash them into a network.
Description of *S*:	Levin saw the opportunity to become the largest network design and engineering company in the region, notwithstanding "that I didn't know anything about computer networks at the time. I'm driven by challenges," he says.
Members of *E*:	John Cellini, co-founder and partner
Size of V:	The company's sales are approximately $10 million per year and growing. Investment bankers have been seen parking their cellular-phone-equipped rental cars at the company's Wayne, Pennsylvania offices.
Social Utility:	Levin speaks to young people about the entrepreneurial process.
Principal Source of Venture Capital:	Levin persuaded the first client to pay one-third of the contract up front. "We still ask for progress payments," says Levin.

KIMBERLE LEVIN, twenty-nine, barely made it through high school, but became valedictorian of her class at a one-year business school. Arthur Andersen, the giant accounting firm, hired her as a secretary. She excelled, graduating to executive secretary in five years. "The personal computer was coming into its age, and I knew that in one way or another, I had found my future. I didn't know how or why, but I started to soak up computer programs like a sponge. I began to teach Lotus to new recruits," says Levin.

Levin left to have a baby, and two weeks later she joined a construction engineering company, whose CEO, Mark Geller, gave Levin overall responsibility to manage operations while he brought in business, diversified into related businesses, and created complex, interwoven transactions for Levin to understand, unwind, and simplify. "Mark was the best mentor I could have asked for. He gave me all the responsibility I could handle," she said.

As Geller's empire in the east was winding down, Levin began talking to John Cellini, a computer technician who was servicing the company's computers. "He's not a 'tech weenie'," Levin said. "We chose networking as the business we would go into because it was the emerging technology. We figured John would do the installations and I would do sales and manage the business. Six years later, he and I are interchangeable parts."

JVC Technologies began with no capital. It persuaded its first client to pay one-third up front, one-third in thirty days, and one-third upon final installation. "We were on C.O.D. with our suppliers, so I learned how to live on float real fast. John and I made our second client presentation shortly thereafter. It was to a hospital. We told them our payment terms, and the hospital administrator said, 'We can't do that.'

"I felt a lump grow in my throat. Then she said, 'Why don't we pay you 50 percent today, and you can invoice us for the other half?' "

Cellini and Levin could barely contain their joy. They had cash flow. They could hire people, open an office, pay for equipment. JVC had a foundation for growth.

What Levin enjoys the most is management. She has introduced the concept of cooperation to her seventeen employees, and sprinkled it with games and celebratory events.

"We have barbecues on Friday, and the five prima donnas in the sales department have to cook for all of us," she says.

JVC Technologies has become very important to its suppliers and to its clients. It's the novel integrator in the Midatlantic region. "A network is a network," says Levin. "And we know networks."

Harriet Gerber Lewis

Name of Company:	Gerber Plumbing Fixtures Corp.
Location:	Lincolnwood, Illinois
Date Founded:	1932
Description of Business:	Produces and markets plumbing fixtures.
Description of *P*:	Lewis was called upon to run the family-owned business upon the untimely death of her father in 1953.
Description of *S*:	From the time she was fourteen, Harriet Lewis was trained in the plumbing fixtures business by her father, Max, who took her on sales trips and introduced her to customers. When the time came for her to take control, she was prepared.
Members of *E*:	Al Korman, financial adviser Robert Luker, board member Alan Lewis, chief executive officer Ila Lewis, vice president, Marketing
Size of *V*:	The company is privately owned and has sales of more than $90 million per year. If the company were publicly held, and its profitability in the range of that of its publicly held competitors, the company's valuation might be approximately $50 to $70 million.
Social Utility:	Lewis has won practically every conceivable award for charitable work and community service. She was the first woman to receive the Rosenwald Award, one of Chicago's most coveted awards, and the first woman to head the Jewish United Fund in Chicago. She was

active in the creation of the U.S. Holocaust Museum. "I don't do things to achieve awards," says Lewis, "but because I believe the things I do are right."

Principal Source of
Venture Capital: The company was founded by Max Gerber, a Polish immigrant, with personal savings.

My research into the characteristics of successful women entrepreneurs produced a number of findings. Among them is the fact that most of the women interviewed said they were encouraged by their fathers—or a male mentor—relatively early in their lives to believe that they could succeed in *any* field they selected, and that they should not settle for living with a husband and supporting that husband's career. "My father took me all over," said HARRIET GERBER LEWIS. "We called on customers together. He took me to trade shows. I got to know the business, the families who were our customers, and because he was charitable, I learned that from him as well."

Gerber Plumbing Fixtures Corp. is a three-generation business. It began in 1925 with a single store, which has been maintained up to the present at the same location on Milwaukee Road in Chicago. "The store, which is primarily a wholesaler, supports twenty-six employees and their families," says Lewis. In 1932, Max Gerber began manufacturing plumbing fixtures, and at the time of his death, in 1953, the company had sales of $7 million. Harriet was tapped to run the business, and her brother, five years her junior, came along shortly thereafter. He died in 1983. Harriet Lewis grew the business to $90 million "with the help of several very fine people." Her daughter Ila and son Alan now hold key senior positions in the company, but according to Ila, "Mother remains involved in all key decisions, such as capital expenditures."

Lewis says, "My grandson, who is twenty-two, wants to come into the company. But I told him to work somewhere else first to prove what he is and to find out who he is." Should he join Gerber Plumbing, it will become a fourth-generation family-owned business, a rarity in American industry. Many of the company's 900 employees are third generation as well.

Gerber Plumbing Fixtures operates five plants in Indiana, Alabama, and New Jersey. The industry has many giants, including Kohler and Masco, which makes it even more unusual that a family-owned and operated business has thrived for sixty-one years. "We have never tried to be fancy," Lewis says. "Basic fixtures are our business. You can't catch every trend, and we never tried to." To what does she attribute the company's success? "We know our customers very well. Many of them are family-owned businesses in their third generation as well." A solid foundation of trust has been poured out like concrete over the last sixty-one years, and it has been carefully built up with years of honest transactions, quality products, and attention to detail. Today, the relationship between Gerber Plumbing Fixtures and its customers is indestructible.

When asked about the research I had done on successful women entrepreneurs and their fathers, Harriet Lewis responded: "Fathers and daughters get along better than fathers and sons. Your theory doesn't surprise me at all."

Carole Little

Name of Company:	Carole Little, Inc.
Date Founded:	1975
Location:	Los Angeles
Description of Business:	Women's fashion and design company known for its use of colorful rayon/crepe prints
Description of *P*:	Carole saw a fashion need that was not being met. She was unable to find clothes in the colors, textures, and materials she desired at a price she could afford. The company's enormous growth over the last nineteen years is proof that there were many women who felt the same way.
Description of *S*:	The Carole Little label assures women affordable and functional yet fashionable clothes to meet their professional and leisure wardrobe needs.
Members of *E*:	Leonard Rabinowitz, co-founder
Size of *V*:	1993 total retail sales were approximately $600 million.
Social Utility:	Carole Little sits on the board of directors for the California American Women's Economic Development and The Trusteeship. She also supports the Cedars Sinai Medical Center, AIDS Project Los Angeles, and Parsons School of Design in New York and Los Angeles, where she is a guest design teacher.
Principal Source of Venture Capital:	$20,000 loan

Behind the CAROLE LITTLE label is a woman who exemplifies what perseverance, talent, and imagination can be. She is involved in every level of designing her collection. From the original concept's inspiration, to the textile design and color, to the fitting and merchandising, Carole maintains artistic control over her six lines. "I am inspired by the world I live in, from my friends and the people I see in restaurants, on the streets, at the theater, and in my travels around the United States and Europe. Different environments and decors fascinate me. My inspiration is everywhere." Known for her signature of colorful rayon/crepe prints, it is interesting to note that Carole Little dresses mostly in black. Little explains, "Color is the first thing I consider when I design a line. I usually dress in black because my design world only deals in color. If *I* wear color, it detracts from my creative process."

Carole Little has always loved design and fashion. After attending UCLA as an English major, she discovered her true passion: design. She left college to attend L.A. Trade Tech to learn to design and make patterns. "The course was so compelling that I immediately knew that I would not be happy doing anything else. After finishing school, I worked for two years and then met my current partner, Leonard Rabinowitz. With a borrowed $20,000, we decided to start our own business. That was approximately nineteen years ago, and I still love it as much as ever." With Leonard Rabinowitz's corporate expertise and Carole Little's inventive designs, one of the most formidable partnerships in the industry was formed. In 1975, Carole Little started with seven employees—under the name Carole Little for Saint Tropez West. Now the company has grown to over 850 employees in 3,100 stores and has showrooms in New York, Los Angeles, Dallas, and Chicago. Today, Carole Little, Inc. boasts six lines, including two new lines: Street Wear, an urban denim-based line, and CL II, designed exclusively for larger sizes. With annual retail sales over $600 million and with Carole Little, Inc.'s exceptional growth in the recent years, the company is poised to reach over $1 billion in annual retail sales within the next five years.

To aspiring designers, Carole Little says, "Go to a good design school and learn the mechanics of your craft. Understand sketching, pattern making, and how fabrics drape and sew. Many schools will help you with an apprenticeship job or job placement. Job success starts with basic ability, but after that, it requires much persistence and hard work. Fashion is a fascinating career no longer limited strictly by rules and trends. However, it is a business, and one of the biggest challenges is developing an understanding of your customer and her needs." As it is a business, Carole Little concludes, "Learn your market and know your competition. Acknowledge your weak areas as well as your strengths, and hire the most knowledgeable staff you can afford. This will be your wisest investment."

Anne Machado

Name of Company:	Creative Staffing Inc.
Location:	Miami
Date Founded:	1985
Description of Business:	A job-staffing service that offers temporary, temporary to permanent, and permanent help to companies in need of highly skilled clerical, manufacturing, and technical personnel. In addition, Creative Staffing offers consulting services and contract staffing to its clients.
Description of P:	During the mid-1980s, Miami experienced a surge in start-up companies. With the new growth came the need for skilled workers.
Description of S:	Creative Staffing helped fill the needed positions and cashed in on the temporary-help explosion. Machado says, "I was in the right industry at the right place at the right time." Today Machado is on the cutting edge of her industry, moving into what industry specialists call "contract staffing."
Members of E:	Anne Machado, president
Size of V:	Revenues of $10 million in 1992
Social Utility:	Creative staffing employs over 7,000 temps (in data base) and twenty-six permanent employees. In addition, Anne Machado has an outstanding record in community service and a strong social conscience.
Principal Source of Venture Capital:	Personal savings of $100,000

When ANNE MACHADO was fired from her last job, it wasn't because she was late all the time, lazy, or unproductive. She was simply "too entrepreneurial," according to her boss. From the beginning, Machado always seemed to be one step ahead of the rest. After finishing college, following in the footsteps of her father, who was a principal at the local high school, Machado went for her teaching certificate. This usually takes students two years to complete, but Machado earned hers in one year. When the school board decided to send her to complete her teaching degree on a scholarship, Machado decided that she really did not want to be a teacher and set off for Europe to "go find herself." What she found was a temp agency in London that landed her a job setting up teams of people for an international consulting firm. "That's where I got into the personnel side of business and realized that that's what I wanted to do." After two years, Machado moved to Miami. Friends who owned a British travel agency that was based in London and New York asked her to open a branch in Miami. She did, and a year later the company went bankrupt.

Without a job, Machado found herself standing in the unemployment line. "I was standing there reading the classifieds and I saw 'Sales Rep for Kelly Girl,' and it was the only job under sales that did not require you to be bilingual." She applied, got the job, and spent six months with Kelly before she moved on to American Temporary Services, which would eventually be bought out by ADIA. Machado worked seven-and-a-half years for American/ADIA, five of which she spent as the area vice president. During her stay with ADIA, Machado ran five offices and opened up five more offices in five years. "It was like opening five new businesses and making them successful. It was a huge job and today the same job is now divided between three people. I learned a lot. I learned how to open offices, negotiate leases, all the skills that I needed to be successful. It was trial by fire. I also learned about turnover. They had about 100 percent turnover a year. Today I only have about 3 percent. I learned all the things that made ADIA successful and I also learned about all the things that were detrimental to ADIA." Machado found herself butting heads with upper management constantly. The Swiss-owned company, with its U.S. headquarters in San Francisco, made things "very difficult," according to Machado. "They kept trying to tell me how to run Florida from San Francisco. I told them you had to be here. It's not like anywhere else. I had five distinctly different markets. We had a tri-ethnic community. . . . They thought that they could run all the territories the exact same way." Machado tried to convince them to change their policies, to no avail. Machado was eventually fired.

It did not take long for Machado to get back on her feet. She had all the practical experience she needed to manage and operate her own business, having opened ten new offices for ADIA. After talking it over with her mentor from American Temporary, she decided to open her own business. "I thought it was going to be a low-key operation. I would come home at six, cook dinner, and spend time with my kids for a change." It turned out to be very much bigger. "By the end of my first year," she reports, "I had made almost as much money as I had made in twelve years in the business working for other people. By the second year, I had paid more in taxes than I had made in my entire life. I had no idea that I was sitting on such a gold mine. "It's all about risk taking," says Machado. "There are the talkers and the risk takers. I think that people are willing to take a risk when they feel deep in their gut that they have nothing to lose. Everyone said, 'Oh, my God, I can't believe that you did all this.' I can't believe that I wouldn't do it. . . . I can't stand mediocrity. To me, to be average is too boring for words!"

Machado enjoys being her own boss. "As long as I make the payments to the bank, I can do anything I want." She believes that being a woman has helped her develop a management style that works: "I think that women have more of a social conscience and are more concerned about the happiness and job satisfaction of their employees. They also understand that women are the only people in our society who can have the babies and still bear a lot of responsibility for the child rearing and the care of the home. And to do that and have a full-time career and be advancing in the career is a constant case of choices." Machado has used her feminine insight in developing policies for her own company. For example, "Instead of having people making up excuses and lying about being sick, I allow my employees to use their sick day on days when their child is sick. We have a very caring, nurturing, and flexible work style at the office. We have happier employees. No one is coming in with a knot in their stomach or an ulcer. Most of the things that put stress on people in their jobs are artificial barriers to success. Our goal is to make people feel good about coming into work. People are here because their emotional needs are met." She sums up her achievement: "Our customer does not do business with us because we are the cheapest or because we necessarily have the best temporaries. They do business with us because they like the relationship. They like the way it feels to do business with us." Machado continues to gain more and more clients. Creative Staffing made the *Inc.* list of the 500 fastest-growing companies in 1992 and continues to expand at a phenomenal rate.

Lucy Mackall

Name of Company:	Have A Heart, Inc.
Location:	Cambridge, Massachusetts
Date Founded:	1977
Description of Business:	Owns, operates, and franchises retail stores that sell shoelaces, T-shirts, canvas bags, and knickknacks decorated with hearts.
Description of *P*:	The need was there all along—products for teenage girls who wear crazy clothes, roller skate, and like bizarre, bright-colored, fun things.
Description of *S*:	Mackall spotted the niche and designs her merchandise strictly for her market. Can it be replicated? Possibly, but Mackall ships over 7 million pair of heart shoelaces a year, so we could say that she's captured the market's heart.
Members of *E*:	Reynold M. Sachs, husband and business adviser
Size of V:	The company is privately held and does not have to publish its financial results.
Social Utility:	Lucy Mackall plays an active role in her local community. She is a Brownie leader and a member of the PTA. She is also speaking at the twenty-fifth anniversary of her college.
Principal Source of Venture Capital:	Cash flow from Lucy's Canvas, Mackall's previous business

A 1969 graduate of Wheaton College, LUCY MACKALL was building architectural models and waiting on tables in 1974 in Boston when a friend asked her to start a business. "I thought about it carefully for two seconds and said 'yes,' " says Mackall.

Her friend knitted sweaters and Mackall's contribution was hand-sewn canvas log carriers. The business failed, but the retailing bug bit Mackall. She went looking for a storefront in order to sell her second idea: brightly colored tote bags with hearts on them. Most tote bags were fairly drab affairs back then.

She needed $3,000 to get started, so Mackall went to the bank and explained her need for a loan. The banker, a conservative New England male, heard her out and responded: "Okay, Lucy. I'll make you the loan, but I will have to take your keys."

Mackall burst into tears, but reluctantly opened her bag and tossed her car keys across the mahogany desk. Alarmed, the banker jumped up from his desk and came around to comfort the sobbing entrepreneur. "I don't want your car, Lucy," he said. "The bank needs to use it as collateral for the loan."

Business was good and costs were low, mostly because Mackall did all the sewing herself. Still, it wasn't until she opened a second store in Boston's well-known Faneuil Hall Marketplace that the operation really turned the corner. The increased exposure helped Mackall do $200,000 worth of business the first year at the new location and enabled her to pay back the $3,000 she had borrowed.

In 1977, she opened her fifth store, this one called Have A Heart, which Mackall says was the first one in the country to specialize in products bearing a heart motif. The stock ranges from mugs and glasses to stationery and clothing, but all the items have one thing in common: hearts—either painted on or incorporated into the item's shape. Initially, Mackall had to scour all sorts of shops to assemble her inventory, picking up one item here, another there. As the fad caught on, she was able to arrange for manufacturers to produce merchandise directly for her store. She was also able to expand her operation by selling franchises; currently, she has fourteen of them scattered across the country. Another indication of her success was the striking number of nearly identical shops that popped up in various locations. If imitation is the sincerest form of flattery, then Lucy Mackall certainly has a lot of admirers.

But Mackall still wasn't making her mark financially. In late 1979, she was at a trade show looking for grommets and other supplies she needed for her canvas-bag business. There she ran into an exhibitor who had a machine that could put images on shoelaces. She ordered some laces with hearts on them, figuring they'd be a natural for her shops, and she started wholesaling them as well. But the turning point came at the National

Stationery Show in 1981. "People just went nuts over the laces," recalls Mackall. "In one month, our peak sales were over $1 million." By the end of the year, she had shipped four million pairs to over 6,500 outlets in the United States, Europe, Japan, and South Africa. Today, the laces come adorned not only with hearts but with frogs, unicorns, sailboats, rainbows, ice cream cones, and many others as well.

Have A Heart grew with the aid of talented people holding down responsible positions. "They're mostly women," says Mackall. "Oh, we have a few male employees, mostly in the shipping department."

As the "number of men who are intimidated by me" grew smaller, Mackall married—"guess who, another entrepreneur"—and has two small children. Husband Reynold Sachs, who sold his interest in a telecommunications company, now presides as touchstone for Mackall's heartfelt ideas.

Mary Madden

Name of Company:	Information America, Inc.
Location:	Atlanta
Date Founded:	1982
Description of Business:	Provides on-line, real-time public record information—e.g., suits, judgments, liens—to attorneys and commercial bankers.
Description of *P*:	Madden asked herself the question: What do people in business need to know every day in their business lives that is not presently being provided to them? Her friend, Buck Goldstein, took her down to the courthouse and said, "Mary, look at all these lawyers searching for information." She said, "Buck, that's the market I have been looking for."
Description of *S*:	An inexpensive, easy-to-access service that provides public information to anyone with a personal computer and a modem.
Members of *E*:	Buck Goldstein, co-founder
Size of *V*:	The company's sales are $18 million per annum
Social Utility:	Madden doesn't publicly disclose her charitable contributions.
Principal Source of Venture Capital:	$325,000 raised in a first-round private placement with friends

MARY MADDEN had just had her first child and was thinking about the possibility of divorcing her husband when she felt bored with her job. "I had been doing the same thing for twelve years—automating public libraries—and although the challenges were still there, I felt that there must be something more important that I could do with my life." Madden has a B.S. degree in mathematics and an M.S. degree in library automation, and she went straight to the New York Public Library out of graduate school. She performed the same tasks with newer and more efficient computers with a succession of computer companies, then went out on her own as a consultant to libraries. The insight for Information America came partially out of a need to be independent and partially because the companies that should have jumped into the on-line information service for lawyers and bankers (Dun & Bradstreet, R. L. Polk, R. R. Donnelly) were asleep at the switch.

"I grew up in South Shore in Chicago, and my father, who died when I was eight, was an architect and had his own firm. My mother was not very communicative, but she told a friend of hers that I was capable of doing great things. Her friend told me, and that gave me great inspiration."

It has been said that entrepreneurs are people who overcome an innate insecurity by starting businesses. That may be the case with Madden. She has done three rounds of venture capital financing, the third with Massey Burch Ventures for $7 million, and taken her company public. A small competitor entered her market, and she removed it by buying it.

Her launch pad was the insight that in chaos lies opportunity. When Madden visited her friend Burton Goldstein at the Fulton County Courthouse one day back in 1982, she was amazed at the lack of organization of data and the ensuing chaos. She noticed that many of the courthouse records were on computer paper. Thus, there had to be a hand copy of the data. Both Goldstein and Madden realized that if they could buy the data on magnetic tape and download the information onto a computer, they could create an online service for lawyers that would give them access to courthouse records. Most of the work had already been done. With Madden's computer experience and Goldstein's legal background, they were able to form Information America.

Information America is broadening its data base to include assisting lenders in locating the assets of their borrowers who are in troubled situations. The hope is that the bankers might be able to recapture their loans by improved asset identification. The company now employs 220 people of whom 60 percent are women. Madden has created personal wealth by capturing and organizing a paperwork-strewn market.

Carol Mann

Name of Company:	Triage, Inc.
Location:	Willow Grove, Pennsylvania
Date Founded:	1988
Description of Business:	A workout and turnaround consulting firm
Description of *P*:	Most business owners and managers are unable to deal with crises, and rather than treat the resuscitation of their businesses as systematic processes, they call in bankruptcy counsel, with the result that assets are usually sold off to pay creditors and their businesses, with many employees, are left in financial ruin. Into this morass boldly steps a new breed of business "therapists" known as workout and turnaround consultants, of whom Carol Mann is among the best.
Description of *S*:	A capable workout consultant can analyze the source of a company's problem, stop the creditors from forcing the company into bankruptcy, and initiate a turnaround plan within a few hours on-site. The most troublesome companies to turn around, however, are family-owned businesses in which each member, no matter how weak, has his or her territory to protect. It is these kinds of companies that have become Mann's stock in trade.
Members of *E*:	Founder, Carol Mann
Size of V:	Triage is a privately held company that is not required to publish financial statements.

Social Utility: Saving jobs, shoring up troubled companies, and
                                   putting a finger in the dike that holds back the
                                   rising tide of litigation contributes to the
                                   country's socioeconomic health on an equal
                                   footing with entrepreneurs who start new
                                   businesses.

Principal Source of
Venture Capital: $5,000 in personal savings

As a twenty-five-year-old, CAROL MANN had been working in her husband's family business for a couple of years. She had taken over the responsibilities of sales manager and decided that she needed to know more about the business and the electronic equipment the company manufactured and distributed. As a result, she enrolled in a tool and die school. Little did she know that when she tied on the toolmaker's apron, she was actually beginning a new career.

The company was a distributor of specialized electronic assembly equipment manufactured in Japan, Germany, and Switzerland. Started twenty years earlier by Mann's husband, the company collapsed with the value of the dollar and suffered massive losses in the mid-1980s. Much of the company's inventory, which had been bought on apparently advantageous credit terms, now cost more than it could be sold for.

Despite the mounting losses, Mann's husband was unable or unwilling to limit his extravagant lifestyle, which dragged the company deeper into debt. And when Mann and her husband went to the bank to try to extend their credit line in order to pay off creditors and reposition the company, the banker said, "Carol, we need you to guarantee the loan along with your husband."

Carol responded, "If you need my guarantee, you have a bad loan because I don't have any assets." With that, the banker called the loan, and demanded eight cents of every dollar deposited beginning that day, and requested that another president be found.

When Mann's husband, who had become an emotional wreck, refused to deal with the crisis, Mann took over and her career was born.

Mann acted quickly. She restructured the debt, reduced the workforce, sold off a research and development project, restructured the sales organizations, put the salesmen on straight commission, tightened credit requirements for customers, brought in a telemarketing expert to collect receivables, and, most impressively, returned the company to positive cash flow in a mere seven months.

Mann became aware of her business acumen, her skill in making efficient, accurate decisions, her ability to act decisively, and her intuitive feel for dealing with business and financial crises. Moreover, she liked the challenges and the opportunities they provided for achievement.

Mann began a workout consulting practice in 1988 devoted to helping family-owned, middle-market companies weather crises ranging from the unexpected loss of a major customer to the death of a partner to an impending bankruptcy filing. Mann described her typical day at the time as one that might involve "meeting with the business owner to map out strategy for downsizing operations, then personally delivering the bad news to employees, to a meeting with the bank to increase credibility, to a meeting with the owners to coach them on the activities for the next day. Because these companies are family-dominated, I wind up meeting with husbands and wives," Mann added. For companies seeking protection from creditors under Chapter 11 of the Federal Bankruptcy Code, Mann may move into the company's offices and provide transition support.

Mann found that she needed to provide emotional support as well. Fortunately, she was good at this too. "When a corporate giant declares Chapter 11, it has a team in place to deal with the details. In small businesses, this job falls upon the shoulders of the owners, who, in most cases, are already reeling under the emotional strain of being forced into Chapter 11," she explained.

It is the interim management situations that Mann enjoyed the most. "When I can run the company, I am able to control the situation, follow through on my analyses and diagnoses, and bring about the changes needed with less hassle and frustration," she observed.

I spotted Mann's talent for quick action when she was called on to help a troubled North Carolina chair manufacturer. Mann expected to spend a couple of days analyzing the situation; instead, she found that she had to go straight to the bank to prevent them from shutting the company down so that she would have an opportunity to begin her assignment. I observed in an earlier book that "Mann demonstrated in thirty minutes at the bank some of the extraordinary ways in which experienced workout consultants earn their money. If turning around a default notice into a standstill agreement and then engineering a workout . . . isn't the equivalent of a heart transplant or a triple bypass surgery that restores the life of the patient, then I don't know what it is."[1]

---

1. A. David Silver, *The Bankruptcy Workout and Turnaround Market Sourcebook* (New York: HarperCollins, 1990), p. 113.

Since 1990, Mann has handled a balanced variety of assignments, and she has taken advantage of the opportunities to broaden her experience and knowledge and develop her skills. She has performed evaluations of the risk-worthiness of companies as diverse as hotels and printers for banks that must decide whether to extend lines of credit and make loans; she has provided shorter-term support and consulting services for companies in crisis situations—a fabric retailer, a woolen manufacturer, a distributor of durable medical equipment, a steel fabricator, a forms printer, and a cellular telephone company; and she has provided interim management for many concerns, including a $5 million holding company owned by physicians with interests in real estate and operating companies as diverse as an automobile dealership, a metal fabricator, and a taxi cab company.

Mann plans to raise capital to launch a venture capital fund to buy ownership in some of her fallen angels.

Lois Vana Marshall

Name of Company:	The Marshall Group
Location:	Salinas, California
Date Founded:	1969
Description of Business:	The company is an international executive search firm specializing in franchising nationally and internationally.
Description of P:	Companies looking to expand internationally may not understand the local business, legal, or cultural customs, and sometimes the seemingly inconsequential remark can cost them valuable business opportunities.
Description of S:	Lois Vana Marshall's searches provide businesses with executives who understand the prospective country's customs and give businesses the extra edge in ensuring a successful international venture.
Members of E:	Lois Vana Marshall, founder
Size of V:	Privately held, The Marshall Group chooses to keep its financial information private.
Social Utility:	Lois Marshall is active in her local school district and is a loyal supporter of the March of Dimes.
Principal Source of Venture Capital:	$6,000 bank loan

The distinguished Harvard psychologist Carol Gilligan, one of the greatest students of the psychology of women, says that women are ideally suited to observing the potential in human connection. Gilligan may have had LOIS VANA MARSHALL in mind when she made that observation, for Marshall has risen to the top of the business world by seeing the potential in human connection and in making connections. She has grown her business, The Marshall Group, by selling area franchises and cloning executive search consultants in her image. Moreover, her business is placing executives, primarily male, in businesses in which they can blossom. Today The Marshall Group is focusing on the international franchise market.

The advice "When in Rome . . ." has new meaning as more and more U.S. franchisors put their international expansion programs in place. And it is especially relevant when it comes to selecting executives to manage operations in Europe, Canada, Australia, and the Pacific Rim nations. Business, legal, and cultural differences between American and overseas markets usually make it impossible to directly transplant a U.S. franchise executive to foreign soil. Without a thorough knowledge of overseas business environments, the most adept managers can trip over unfamiliar stumbling blocks. Lois Marshall has been successfully placing top foreign executives in foreign countries for U.S. businesses for years.

Marshall was raised by a strong, pioneering mother who was devoted, attentive, well-intentioned, and ambitious for her daughter. Marshall says, "My mother always encouraged me. She told me never to look back and correct my own mistakes. She really gave me a passion for success. . . . She is a woman of integrity and character." This was all the support that Marshall needed to step out into the business world.

Without a college education, she went to work for the local telephone company as an operator and worked her way up to the engineering department while she took courses at night. Marshall next took a direct sales position at one of the local radio stations but was disappointed at its treatment of women because, she explains, "We were expected to solicit ourselves." With the strength and integrity of her mother, she did not put up with her bosses very long. All positions she held required a college-level education; however, being a good networker and a good people person, she was able to convince the companies she worked for that she had what it took.

At age twenty-one, when most people are just graduating from college and are looking for their first job in the "real world," Marshall already had four years of business experience behind her. She found herself in Vancouver, British Columbia, looking for a job through various search companies. As a candidate, Marshall says, "I was treated very poorly. They were all very unprofessional." Vancouver had been hit by hard economic times, the market was deflated, and there were many disgruntled workers and employers. Marshall recognized the need for a friendly, effective, and professional service. Refusing to put up with the lack of professionalism she encountered, she decided to start her own consulting company. With no prior entrepreneurial experience, she figured that the start-up costs would be low and that she could learn the business easily. She was right and began her consulting firm helping the local oil, gas, timber, and mining industries. "It was difficult at first," says Marshall; "there was a real old-boy network in Vancouver." However, by maintaining the highest professional demeanor and remaining true to her word, she was able to become very successful in the search business. As time went on she moved back to the states and continued to grow and prosper by focusing on franchise systems. Today The Marshall Group has expanded into the international franchise market and specializes in helping both U.S. and foreign businesses secure valuable overseas markets.

Gilda Marx

Name of Company:	Gilda Marx Industries, Inc.
Location:	Los Angeles
Date Founded:	1977
Description of Business:	Designs, develops, produces, and markets bodywear and activewear for wellness, exercise, and aerobic activities.
Description of P:	Prior to the wellness wave that broke on U.S. shores about fifteen years ago, people exercised in sweat suits and drab-colored leotards made of 100 percent nylon. This apparel did not move and stretch with the bodies that wore them. As the operator of several aerobics studios, Marx was well situated to see the need develop.
Description of S:	The wellness revolution is itself an entrepreneurial event: Women and men are taking control of their bodies, cutting the fat, spinning off bad eating habits, and exercising to create lean, mean, active machines.
Members of E:	Robert Marx, husband, an architectural designer who subsequently joined the company
Size of V:	The company, which is privately held, reported revenues in 1992 of approximately $50 million.
Social Utility:	Marx gives generously of her time and resources to help young women entrepreneurs. She is also a board member of the American Society of Fitness.
Principal Source of Venture Capital:	Cash flow from her aerobics studios

An estimated 25 percent of the 164 million adults in the United States consider themselves active fitness enthusiasts. Fitness has become part of their lives. Approximately 26 million participate in an aerobic activity. With the evolution of the fitness revolution, fitness bodywear has become a staple of the American wardrobe. It reached sales of $2 billion in 1992, and sporting goods stores as well as department stores have created women's bodywear departments. Videos and other information and exercise products are also carried in these new departments.

One of the leaders who caught the wave early and has since directed its course is GILDA MARX, who leapt into the fray in 1977 and has built the largest company in the industry. Tired of drab-colored leotards made of 100 percent nylon, Marx set out to create a new fabric that would stretch and flex when a woman did. What she came up with in 1977 was Flexatard, a shiny, colorful fabric that moved and stretched with a woman's body.

However, the leotards Marx fashioned out of the new material didn't impress retailers. "One retailer told me nobody would ever buy my leotards," Marx recalls. But customers proved the retailer wrong, and Marx's Flexatard has since boosted worldwide sales at Los Angeles-based Gilda Marx Industries, Inc., to more than $50 million. A visionary with an eye for innovation, Marx has expanded her business to include audiotapes, videotapes, children's exercise wear, and exercise bras, among other fitness-related products. And her merchandise is sold in more than 5,000 retail outlets as well as in her own Gilda Marx boutique in New York City.

Marx got into the fitness market through dance. "When I was in my early twenties," she explains, "I choreographed a show for a group of women doing a benefit in Los Angeles. The woman who asked me was a student of mine at the dance studio I taught in my teens. The women loved my training routine and asked me to begin teaching them, so I started teaching classes in my home."

She charged the women for the lessons, but she did not think of the dance training as a business. That came only after a woman asked her to open a dance studio with her. Somewhat shakily, Marx broke off on her own and opened Gilda Marx of Encino in 1977, her first studio. This put Marx on the windowsill of one of the biggest revolutions ever to hit our shores. And she caught the wave early.

Rebecca Matthias

Name of Company:	Mothers Work, Inc.
Location:	Philadelphia
Date Founded:	1982
Description of Business:	Designs, develops, and produces upscale maternity clothing, which it sells through sixty-five company-owned stores.
Description of *P*:	Pregnant working women need to find attractive, classic apparel to wear to their offices and work sites.
Description of *S*:	A chain of small, well-stocked maternity apparel stores in high-traffic metropolitan areas caters to this growing need.
Members of *E*:	Rebecca Matthias, founder
Size of V:	The company achieved an initial public offering for its common stock in May 1993 and in early 1994, its market value was $57 million.
Social Utility:	Board of the Philadelphia Chamber of Commerce; Young Presidents Organization
Principal Source of Venture Capital:	The founder's savings of $10,000

"Never give up. Never. Never. Never." Winston Churchill's famous exhortation to the British during World War II is appropriate in reflecting on REBECCA MATTHIAS's entrepreneurial journey. With a Master's degree in civil engineering from the Massachusetts Institute of Technology, Matthias started her career by going to work in her husband's computer software company, where she remained for two years learning the business.

After moving to Philadelphia, Matthias became pregnant. When she could not find suitable maternity apparel, Matthias thought she saw a business opportunity in the sale of maternity clothes by direct mail. With $10,000 in savings, she spent $3,600 to print 3,000 catalogs, $2,900 on advertising and office expenses, and $3,500 on inventory. Rather than rent mailing lists, Matthias ran print ads in *The Wall Street Journal* and *The New Yorker*. The business plan was a disaster. Matthias got lots of catalog requests, but no orders. The clothing in the catalog was a spring line, but in March, when she ran the ads, women were projecting their summer apparel needs, and the orders did not materialize.

Undaunted, Matthias telephoned some of the women who had ordered her catalogs and asked them what products they would like to see. They responded that her catalog should be in color, rather than black and white, and the selection should be broader.

Back to the drawing board went Matthias, but the new and improved catalog didn't earn back its costs, either.

Quit? No way. Matthias discovered that her business plan was wrong. The maternity market is a small niche of the women's apparel market. And the number of women who like to buy through the mail is an even smaller amount. Plus, finding a pregnant woman's name by renting mailing lists is not economic because she is no longer pregnant by the time you have developed a marketing piece and mailed it to her.

Many people would have withdrawn from this marketplace, but not Matthias. She figured that the best way to reach her customer base was through retail stores and that the most economic way to get into retailing was by franchising. Matthias sold her first franchise in 1984 and over the next year she sold ten more.

But the business model was still unprofitable. She was selling apparel to her franchisees at wholesale prices, while her original business plan had been structured to sell at retail. Mothers Work's cost structure was too high. The solution: Open company-owned stores and vertically integrate backwards into manufacturing.

Matthias began buying back franchises while locating cut-and-sew subcontractors, of which there are now twelve. All garments are designed and graded in-house on a computer-aided design system. This departure in her business plan required venture capital, for which the company went to private and state-owned funds (Pennsylvania is one of the few states that offer venture capital to its citizens). The financings carved a big chunk out of Matthias's ownership but enabled her to finance the business plan that was right for the market. For the fiscal year ending September 30, 1992, Mothers Work earned $501,000 on sales of $19.1 million; and profits were up by more than 100 percent midway through 1993.

Jessica McClintock

Name of Company:	Jessica McClintock Fashions, Inc.
Location:	San Francisco
Date Founded:	1969
Description of Business:	Sells women's and children's clothing, bridal gowns, and perfumes through fourteen company-owned stores and through retailers including J. C. Penney, Macy's, and Marshall Field's.
Description of *P*:	Young women in an increasingly unromantic age felt the need for romantic feminine apparel for proms, weddings, and special occasions.
Description of *S*:	Plugging into the nostalgia market, McClintock's clothing speaks of another time, another place—perhaps the 1890s—with inspiration from her New England grandmother, who taught McClintock sewing.
Members of *E*:	Ben Gollober, vice president
Size of V:	The company reports sales of more than $150 million per year.
Social Utility:	She donates her time and money to the United American Heart Association, the Human Campaign Fund, the YMCA, Chinatown Schools of the Sacred Heart, the San Francisco Bay Area AIDS Association, and a host of other local organizations and charities.
Principal Source of Venture Capital:	$5,000 in personal savings

"I've always looked at life from a romantic point of view," JESSICA MCCLINTOCK admits. "I love soft things. I surround myself with romantic music . . . classical, most of the time. My home is very romantic—eighteenth-century French furniture, antiques, curtains everywhere."

From that starry-eyed perspective, McClintock has built a $150 million-plus fashion empire. Her signature special-occasion dresses, rich with nostalgia and feminine detail, are many a career woman's cup of tea when romance is on her mind. She designs for proms, every party that ever existed, and weddings. "There's dressing little girls for their birthdays. I supply the marketplace in a very strong way for those lifestyles," she said.

McClintock's designs have long been best-sellers in U.S. and European department stores. Recently, she has expanded the company into the retail business, opening fourteen Jessica McClintock boutiques, including a new store in Horton Plaza in San Diego.

The watchwords guiding her design career are "focus, focus, focus," she said. "Don't keep running around; focus, only do it better. And for twenty-six years, that's how I have run a very successful business. My mind tells me there is always room to do a better beautiful dress. That's my challenge."

Born in Maine and raised by her mother and grandmother, an excellent seamstress, McClintock moved to California with her first husband. When he was killed in an accident, she and her son Scott returned to the East Coast. Three years later, after a "marriage to the wrong man," she went back to California.

She took a friend's advice and became a partner in a fledgling company called Gunne Sax. Within a few months, as McClintock's prairie dresses romanced flower children everywhere, she bought out her partner.

Gunne Sax is still McClintock's best-selling line. Her other divisions include Gunne Sax for Girls; Jessica McClintock Contemporary Apparel, Collections, and Bridal Wear; and Scott McClintock Dresses and Sportswear.

In the anti-ostentation 1990s, customers want value as well as good designs, McClintock believes. Her party dresses range from $100 to $250; bridal gowns are $250 to $500.

"When I got started, I did everything myself," she recalls. "I'd sell out one production and use the money to buy cloth for the next. I'd deliver cloth to seamstresses, then go home and design garments for them. Production runs of twenty garments became fifty garments, and in about three months I was designing three or four collections and taking them to Joseph Magnin in San Francisco. I did everything—wrote my invoices, packed the garments, and delivered them. I never took anything for granted, and still don't."

And today? "Now I have a dozen showrooms around the country, computers, an ad department, and 300 employees. I design about 4,000 new garments a year. We ship to 10,000 accounts, mostly in the United States. I have to plan two full seasons ahead, keep track of the seasons in progress, and analyze what worked or did not work in seasons past.

"I'm not a workaholic, but I put in similar hours. But fashion design is not work to me, it is my fun, my life. I'm up at six, at work by eight, break half an hour for lunch—usually at my desk to look at fashion magazines so I can keep my eye on what's happening—then spend the rest of the day in the workroom making sure my designs are going the way I want.

"I do fifteen to twenty designs a day, which my assistants immediately fabricate. Sometimes they're perfect the way they are, other times they need to be reworked; a skirt needs to be revised, or something else. I have three designers who help me as I revise, do swatches, make sure all the fabrics are ordered. When the fabrics come in, I check them personally. We go through an enormous variety of materials—linens, silk jacquards, charmeuses, knits, appliqués, watercolor crepes, velvets, buttons, and miles of lace."

Clearly this entrepreneur has reached the summit and could relax a bit. But McClintock personifies the axiom that for the successful entrepreneur the chase is the goal.

Joyce Meskis

Name of Company:	Tattered Cover Books, Inc.
Location:	Denver
Date Founded:	1974
Description of Business:	It is one of the largest bookstores in the country, boasting over 155,000 titles.
Description of *P*:	To any bibliophile or avid reader no amount of books can ever be enough. Most major bookstores carry an average of 20,000 titles and offer aisles of books, but no place to sit, relax, and browse.
Description of *S*:	Joyce Meskis has created a 40,000-square-foot book lover's paradise with comfortable couches and chairs, space to spread out and read, and various plants and ferns to give the store a comfortable, and cozy, down-home feeling.
Members of *E*:	Joyce Meskis, president
Size of *V*:	1992 sales are estimated at $7 million.
Social Utility:	Meskis set up the Rocky Mountain Book Fair; sponsors literary programs; encourages staff to read at the women and children's center; has story-telling open to the public; and devotes her time, energy, and funds to libraries.
Principal Source of Venture Capital:	Money borrowed from anyone who would lend it to her

As a child, JOYCE MESKIS wanted to be a college math professor when she grew up. As she put herself through Purdue University and then the

University of Denver, she found herself working in bookstores and libraries. While she was still intent on becoming a professor, she shifted her major from math to English. She loved to read and to be around books.

As she was working toward her Master's degree, she married a man with whom she had two children. She was still working for a library and a bookstore as she raised her two daughters. When her marriage didn't work out and she and her husband divorced, Meskis decided to drop out of school. She realized that she was already doing what she loved best and decided to get on with her life. With her half of the assets granted to her in the divorce, Meskis opened up a small, 1,000-square-foot bookstore in Parker, Colorado, a small suburb 20 miles south of Denver. When the expected growth of the community never materialized, Meskis realized that she had to get out of Parker and move closer to Denver. When she heard that the Tattered Cover Bookstore in the upscale Cherry Creek area of Denver was for sale, she combined her diminutive savings with money borrowed from virtually anyone who would lend it to her and bought the 950-square-foot bookstore in 1974. By 1986, Meskis had expanded seven times and changed locations twice, finally ending up at her current location across from the Cherry Creek Mall.

One must visit the Tattered Cover Bookstore to understand the grandiosity of Meskis's vision. Her profound love of books and her commitment to share this with the public has translated into a 40,000-square-foot shrine to more than 155,000 different books. With over 9,000 different publishers on file, customers can order virtually any book that cannot be found in the labyrinth of shelves at Tattered Cover.

The only thing that one might have a hard time finding at Tattered Cover is an empty easy chair or couch on a Sunday afternoon. Floor space becomes a valuable commodity on such days as customers lounge and sprawl around the vast space that Meskis has made available to them. With all of its cozy nooks and crannies, Tattered Cover has been designed to draw people into its down-home atmosphere. Under absolutely no pressure to buy, customers can comfortably browse for hours. Trust and support are what her knowledgeable staff of 320 successfully bring to customers. All personnel have been carefully selected and trained, and share Meskis's passion for books. In addition, Tattered Cover puts out a series of publications, ranging from new non-bestseller lists to new business publications designed to keep her customers informed of a few of the 50,000 new titles that will come out each year. Book signings, readings, and in-house programs on various topics and by various authors are all regular features at the Tattered Cover Bookstore.

Joyce Meskis reaches out to all readers with an open and gentle hand, offering something for everyone. Her philosophy is summed up in this statement: "As long as there's one more person out there who's interested in reading one more book and can get it with our help, we will be a part of their reading lives."[1]

1. Sharron Nelton, *Nation's Business*, March 1992, p. 39.

Hinda Miller
Lisa Lindahl

Name of Company:	Jogbra, Inc.
Location:	Williston, Vermont
Date Founded:	1977
Description of Business:	Manufactures women and men's sports support equipment.
Description of *P*:	As the running craze took off during the seventies, active women began looking for a more supportive bra.
Description of *S*:	Constructed the first sports bra for women, using high-performance fabric made of lycra and cotton to give women greater support and launched the first women's sports bra company.
Members of *E*:	Hinda Miller, president and co-founder Lisa Lindahl, co-founder, left company in 1992
Size of *V*:	Figures unavailable. Company reports growth of 30 percent annually since 1982, when total sales reached one million. Estimated total sales in 1992: 10 million.
Social Utility:	Jbi sponsors the Susan G. Komen Breast Cancer Foundation's "Race for the Cure" and supports the United States Volleyball Association and the U.S. Women's Volleyball Team.
Principal Source of Venture Capital:	SBA loan of $50,000; $30,000 from Hinda Miller's parents

As physical fitness and exercise began to grow in popularity in the United States in the late 1970s, more and more people began to hit the pavement and started jogging. The cardiovascular craze brought in a whole new line of sportswear, ranging from sneakers to sunglasses. One product that had been overlooked for years was an athletic support bra for women. While men had always had athletic supporters, there was nothing available on the market for active women.

When LISA LINDAHL, a secretary at the University of Vermont by day and a student of educational administration by night, complained to her sister about the problems that women joggers faced, her sister responded jokingly that there ought to be a "jockstrap for women." While they both burst out in laughter initially, this conversation would be responsible for sparking the development of an entire industry known today as women's sportswear. Women used to try anything from pulling their bras tighter, to wearing two bras, using a smaller size, or even wrapping themselves with an elastic bandage. It was clear that women needed a better solution.

A friend introduced Lisa Lindahl to HINDA MILLER, who was a runner and a costume designer for the local Shakespearean festival. When the two met, it was the beginning of a turbulent relationship that would nearly destroy them and their business a number of times. While they both needed each other, they had a difficult time working together. However, they were both mature enough to look beyond their differences and realize that they had a winning idea and could really help each other achieve their own goals.

Lindahl and Miller put their heads together and created a prototype sports bra by sewing together two jockstraps. When they went to a local bank to pitch their new product for a loan, after the male banker recovered from blushing, he suggested they try the Small Business Association. Lindahl and Miller received a $50,000 SBA loan and an additional $30,000 from Miller's parents, and in 1977, Jogbra, Inc., was formed.

The prototype went through five design changes until it was finally perfected. Starting with an order of forty dozen bras, Lindahl sold twenty dozen to specialty stores in Vermont, and Miller sold the other half to stores down south. They also ran an advertisement in *Running Times* magazine. To their surprise, the bras were an instant success and sold out immediately. In the first year, sales were $500,000, and by 1982, sales reached $1 million. From that point on, sales grew on the average of 30 percent annually.

Success did not come easily; both Miller and Lindahl worked around the clock. Lindahl headed up the sales, while Miller concentrated on production and design. They both would work on marketing and managerial responsibility. Miller's spontaneous drive and Lindahl's cautious and tenacious nature caused this dynamic duo to lock horns on virtually every decision they had to make. However, because of their commitment to their product and to each other's own growth, they were mature enough to keep their eyes on the big picture and worked things out. They even created an advisory board so that they could gain impartial advice on their business decisions. Day by day, they hammered out their differences, and the company continued to grow.

By 1990, they decided to sell and become a part of Playtex Apparel, Inc., which was eventually bought by the largest company with a woman's name: the Sara Lee Corporation. Their decision to sell was based on practicality. By 1990, it became increasingly difficult to sustain company growth due to better capitalized, larger competitors. They needed more capital to fund a more aggressive advertising campaign and start building their inventory. While it was painful to sell out, they both agreed that it was the right thing to do.

Over the years, they have been responsible for introducing the Jogbra Sports Bra and a variety of sports-specific bras made of high-performance material. In addition, they have used groundbreaking biomechanical breast motion research patented in the Motion Control Requirement system to help guide customers in choosing their bra based on activity and breast size. Jogbra, Inc., also manufactures a line of supportive men's underwear called M.A.X. The Miller-Lindahl team has developed markets around the globe, including Canada, Japan, Italy, Spain, England, Sweden, the Netherlands, and Australia, creating and revolutionizing an industry worldwide.

Judi Sheppard Missett

Name of Company:	Jazzercise, Inc.
Location:	Carlsbad, California
Date Founded:	1969
Description of Business:	International dance-exercise franchise company
Description of *P*:	As a dance instructor, Judi Sheppard Missett noticed that people were not staying in her classes. At that time, there were only dance classes and exercise classes. Her class was not serving the needs of young mothers and housewives.
Description of *S*:	Missett recognized that women really wanted to combine having fun with staying fit. They never took dance classes to become professional dancers. Missett pioneered the first casual dance class geared to fun and fitness, thus combining her love for dancing and her desire to stay in shape.
Members of *E*:	Judi Sheppard Missett, president and chief executive officer
Size of *V*:	A multimillion-dollar top-ten franchise company
Social Utility:	Judi Missett has taught and trained more than 5,000 instructors who now own and operate their own Jazzercize franchises.
Principal Source Venture Capital:	Personal savings and revenue from her dance classes

From the age of three, JUDI SHEPPARD MISSETT knew that she wanted to be a dancer. By the age of twelve she was performing regularly and teaching over 100 students in her home town of Red Oak, Iowa. Today Missett stands tall as the president and CEO of Jazzercise International, responsible for helping 400,000 students in more than 13,000 classes worldwide to keep in shape every week.

Missett earned her degree in theater and dance from Northwestern University in 1966. After graduation, she toured with the Chicago Dance Company and taught dance lessons back in Chicago. She began to notice that she was having a hard time keeping students in her class. There were always people signing up but there were even more people dropping out. Housewives and young mothers were rotating in and out of her studio. Her jazz dance classes were demanding and challenging, as were all dance classes at that time. The problem seemed to be that the women who took her classes were not interested in becoming professional dancers but wanted instead simply to learn some new steps and stay fit. Realizing this, Missett decided to offer a casual dance class for fitness and fun. Fifteen students showed up for the first class. They loved it so much that each brought a friend to the next class, and so on. It was an instant success. For the first time, Missett emphasized fun over form. She removed all the mirrors in the studio and encouraged her students to enjoy the movement and exercise by not being critical of their form. At that time, exercise classes and dance classes were quite separate. By combining dance music and exercises in a casual format she was able to give her students what they had always been looking for.

In 1972, Missett, her husband, and her daughter, Shanna, moved to southern California, where Missett began to promote and develop her new jazz exercise techniques. She was able to get the YMCA-YWCA and other recreational departments to list her class in scheduled events for a small percentage of her class fee. When she sent out a press release, "New Dance Class Developed in Chicago," the local papers gave her all the publicity she needed. On the first day of classes she was greeted by more than seventy students. For the next five years Missett filled every class.

She became so busy that she would sometimes teach twenty two-hour classes a week. It became evident that she would have to teach others to help her lead the classes. She offered her top ten students lessons on how to teach the new form and it worked. Each one of the women was able to run her own class under the Jazzercise name and continue training with Missett for a small start-up fee and 20 percent of her studio's revenues. The franchise system worked well. By 1983, Jazzercise was incorporated and had a formal franchising organization in place. The instructors felt that they were running their own businesses and were making three times as much money as they would have if they were instructors for any other exercise or dance classes. By aligning franchisees, she allowed Jazzercise to spread around the globe, for whenever an instructor moved she could take the Jazzercise name with her. It gave her instructors an excellent opportunity to run their own businesses. All they needed was a low-budget room to rent and they were in business. By offering a low start-up fee, Missett has made Jazzercise accessible to virtually any woman who wants to start her own career and has given an opportunity to thousands of women who could never have dreamed of opening their own business. Although the 20 percent royalties remain high, *Entrepreneur* magazine still marked it as one of the top five low-investment franchises in 1993.

The success of Jazzercise paralleled the fitness boom of the early eighties. In 1980, one year after Jazzercise was incorporated, the total gross receipts from franchises were nearly $2 million. By 1983 that same figure had soared to $40 million! However, during the mid-eighties Jazzercise started to lose its momentum as numerous competitors popped up. Refusing to stand by and watch her company slip away, Missett launched a strong promotional campaign. Doing everything from television shows to writing her own book, Missett determined to build up both her own and the Jazzercise name. By 1988 she was appearing at the Superbowl halftime show, Hands Across America, and at an Olympic Festival ceremony at Dodger Stadium. Missett even tried her hand at cross-promotions. Whether she was gracefully leaping in front of the McDonald's in Red Square, Moscow, or at the White House with Arnold Schwarzenegger, she attracted attention wherever she went. Missett's campaign was successful, and today Jazzercise continues to offer women the same opportunity for fitness and fun through a variety of different adaptations of the basic program. In addition to the classes, Missett offers a twelve-week diet program, a variety of videotapes, and a full line of fitness wear and accessories. Missett is fit, and her business is fitter.

June Morris

Name of Company:	Morris Airlines, Inc.
Location:	Salt Lake City, Utah
Date Founded:	1984
Description of Business:	Offers discount air fares to travelers flying in the Western states.
Description of *P*:	There are many people who choose to drive or take the train to their destinations simply because it is too expensive to fly.
Description of *S*:	By offering rock-bottom prices, Morris Air has been able to attract an entirely new clientele to the airports and has actually doubled boardings in most of the cities it serves.
Members of *E*:	June Morris, chief executive officer David Needleman, president
Size of V:	The company was acquired in late 1993 for 3.6 million shares of Southwest Airlines common stock. The approximate market value of the issued stock was $120 million.
Social Utility:	Morris Air has made air travel accessible to many who could not afford it before, bringing more families together across the Western states. In addition, Morris employs over 1,700 people, including part-time help in Salt Lake City.
Principal Source of Venture Capital:	Proceeds of sale of travel agency; supplier's patience and sweat equity

JUNE MORRIS has taken off with her very own airline company, Morris Air. At a time when airlines are suffering and shutting down. Some would say that Morris is crazy to launch her new airlines company, but on December 4, 1992, Morris Air flew its first planes. Today, with over twenty planes and an expected $200 million in sales for the year, Morris stands poised to become a major player in the airlines industry. But for this sixty-two-year-old travel industry veteran, success is nothing new.

Growing up in rural Utah, Morris herded sheep in her youth. After marrying at an early age and playing housewife for a while, she took a job marking maps for the American Automobile Association. When AAA decided to open up a travel agency in Utah, Morris decided that this was what she wanted to do and expressed interest to her boss. She got the job, heading the first AAA travel agency in Utah. Following AAA, she worked for American Express Travel Services. When she met her second husband, Mitchel Morris, she decided to quit and stay at home. This lasted only six months before she realized that she was much happier working. With the encouragement and support of her husband, she decided to open her own travel agency. When her husband first suggested it, Morris said "No way," but with a little help from him she was able to open a one-person, one-room office at his photofinishing business. Morris says that she has "always had a little bit of competitiveness" in her and within a couple of years Morris Travel became the largest travel agency in Utah and one of the largest in the country.

One day, when a corporate client asked if there was a way to break down the billing into individual accounts and departments, Morris told him she would work on it. She borrowed her husband's computer consultant and worked with him on a program that could handle corporate accounts. At that time, there was no agent who could provide such services. When Morris finalized the program, it enabled her to attract big companies and brought her more business. In addition, Morris's was the first travel agency in Utah to implement the computerized airline ticket system that is universally used today.

During the late 1970s when the airlines were deregulated, Morris was concerned that corporations would start to go directly to the airlines and bypass the travel agents altogether. Since 80 percent of her business at that time came from business clients, Morris decided to focus on leisure travel. She hired a man by the name of David Needleman in 1984, and he now serves as president of Morris Air. Her son, Richard Frendt, and Needleman worked together with her and developed leisure packages to Hawaii. Needleman came up with the idea to charter planes and to try to offer the lowest air fares they could in order to attract as many people as possible. "We started with 180 passengers once a week and now we are doing about 150,000 passengers in a week," says Morris. This was the beginning of Morris Air. The charter business began to take off and they sold the travel agency, which at that time was doing more than $100 million in sales a year. Through the years Morris Air chartered various airlines, expanding their leisure packages to Alaska, Florida, and Mexico. Before they knew it, they had become so large that they couldn't abide by the charter rules. This prompted Morris to apply for an airline certification. Morris says, "When the paper weighed as much as the airplane, then you could get the certificate." She hired a man who was formerly a member of the FAA to work on the paperwork necessary to receive certification. With the help of him and his crew, Morris says, "We were able to get our certification in record time."

Morris Air has been able to succeed in a time when most airlines are suffering as the result of a number of factors. Following the lead of Southwest Airlines, Morris uses only one kind of plane for its short hauls, the 737-300. This keeps the cost of spare parts and inventory much much lower than it would be for a larger airline, which may have multiple aircraft, each with its own particular parts. The average cost of an engine is $2–3 million. By serving only muffins instead of meals on board, Morris is able to offer passengers a much lower fare. Furthermore, Morris chooses not to use the automated airline ticket system, thereby saving itself about $3 a ticket. Very important to Morris Air's success is the fact that it has been expanding steadily over the years but has been conservative with its expansion. Having its own airline is nothing more than a natural progression in a long series of carefully thought-out business decisions. Morris started small and has steadily grown for the past twenty-three years. Having absolutely no debt, Morris Air has no extra baggage to worry about and is therefore flying high today.

To young entrepreneurs Morris says, "Don't be intimidated if you don't know accounting or anything like that. You don't really need to know all that stuff. Start small and learn as you go. Learn from your mistakes." Morris is the first to admit that she doesn't know it all: "I rely on hearing everyone else's ideas." She says that she surrounds herself with intelligent people in an environment that encourages them to think. "We have intrepreneurs working within the company, building new programs, and doing neat things. If you give them the latitude, and you don't try to have everybody fit into a certain slot, and you let them create their own thing, you get the creative juices flowing and you get help from everyone. I think that more people should let the people that they work with come forth with their ideas and value everything that their people are saying."

Kathlene Mullinix

Name of Company:	Synaptic Pharmaceuticals, Inc.
Location:	Paramus, New Jersey
Date Founded:	1987
Description of Business:	Engages in research involving a brain chemical called serotonin.
Description of P:	The problems of schizophrenia, anxiety, migraine headaches, nausea, depression, and addiction may be caused by imbalances of serotonin in the brain. Conventional psychiatric drugs often cause unpleasant side effects.
Description of S:	Mullinix and her co-workers are attempting to locate and identify the many receptors or proteins that act as docking sites in brain cells to determine which of them relate to which malady, and then clone them genetically in drug form.
Members of E:	Eric Kandell and Richard Axel, who helped conceive the initial objectives of Synaptic John White, patent counsel with Cooper & Dunham, a wise advisor to the company
Size of V:	Synaptic is privately held, but a $12 million strategic investment from Eli Lilly probably places an estimated value of the company at about $75 million.
Social Utility:	Mullinix provides seminars to high schoolers and is on the board of Respite Services, Inc., which helps handicapped children.
Principal Source of Venture Capital:	$5 million venture capital invested by Adler & Co. and Athena Venture Partners

KATHLENE MULLINIX is into designer genes. One of the very few women to have launched a biotechnology company, Mullinix admits that she had greater hurdles to overcome than would a man in a similar position. "The venture capitalists who put in the initial capital said, 'Kathy, you can't be president. We'll do a search for a president. But you can be senior vice president,' " she said.

She didn't wish to block the investment, so Mullinix agreed and ran the company while the investors looked for a president. A year passed and Mullinix asked the venture capitalists to name her president and CEO. They responded, "Well you can be president, but not CEO. We will search for a CEO." Another year went by and they made her chief executive officer.

"When I was a young girl, my father encouraged me to 'Be your own boss,' " Mullinix said. "Then, when I had my first job, as a department store clerk, my manager told me that I had to take my lunch at a certain time. That rubbed me the wrong way, and I understood what my father meant."

Mullinix earned a bachelor of arts degree in chemistry from Trinity College in Washington, D.C., in 1965, and a Ph.D. in chemical biology from Columbia University in 1969. Following her post doctorate studies, she joined the National Institutes of Health in 1972 as a research chemist and became an assistant director of intramural programs there in 1979. From 1981 to 1987, Mullinix was vice provost of Columbia University. It was while she was at Columbia University that a molecular biologist and a neurobiologist approached her with an idea for a new company that they wanted her to run. The problem they wanted to solve was that drugs used to modulate the nervous systems produced unpleasant and some-times dangerous side effects. These side effects included weight gain, sexual dysfunction, and impaired motor function. Mullinix and her team believed that they could clone the genes that act as neurotransmitter receptors through molecular biology. In that way, they would develop disease-specific drugs that work on the nervous system, have long-lasting effects, and produce no side effects. "We presented our story without a business plan to Adler & Co., and Athena Venture Partners, an Israeli fund, and they agreed that we may have something. They put in the first round and have been terrific supporters ever since," Mullinix said.

Synaptic recently raised $12 million from Eli Lilly and Co., part of which is a research and development strategic partnering agreement, and part is venture capital. "We intend to form several partnerships such as this one because the established drug companies have much to offer us with the manufacturing and marketing capabilities. The revenue stream from licensing royalties, we believe, will become a significant number," Mullinix says.

Mullinix speaks to high school students to encourage them to do something important with their lives. Her advice in a nutshell: "Take a lot more chances with your lives than you think you should. Don't expect rewards on day one. There will be many hurdles set in front of you, but with patience and careful risk-taking, you will get around them."

Therese E. Myers

Name of Company: Quarterdeck Office Systems, Inc.

Location: Santa Monica, California

Date Founded: 1982

Description of
Business: Designs, develops, produces, markets, and supports computer software known as "utility programs" that enhance the performance of DOS-based operating systems.

Description of *P*:   IBM tried and failed to bring utility software programs to its users, and into that void leapt Quarterdeck and its archrival Microsoft to enhance the productivity of IBM and IBM-compatible personal computers.

Description of *S*:   Computers are machines. Software makes them functional. Productivity-enhancing software, such as the company's DESQview packages, makes the least expensive personal computer operate as if it were a sophisticated workstation.

Members of *E*:   Gary W. Pope, software guru and executive vice president

Size of V: The company achieved an initial public offering of its common stock in 1991. Its market value in early 1994 was approximately $50 million.

Social Utility: Quarterdeck donates its products to the Santa Monica Junior League, has sponsored the Big Brothers' Golf Tournament, and donates its software to inmates in out-of-state penitentiaries.

Principal Source of
Venture Capital: An initial loan of $20,000 from her mother was
                     supplemented by $7 million of venture capital
                     from Peregrine Ventures, Sevin Rosen,
                     Sequoia, and other established funds.

THERESE MYERS manages one of the best teams of software writers in the world. She got her training in this arcane business at AXXA, the wholly owned software subsidiary of Citicorp. Among her 300-person team there are no pressed suits and no Mercedes in the parking lot; the used desks were bought at auctions; and Myers' dog Andy wanders through the company's rented offices on Main Street in Santa Monica.

Myers ascribes her success to being in the right place at the right time. The big break for Quarterdeck came in 1986 when one of the first IBM clone-makers, AIR, shipped its state-of-the-art, 386 microprocessor with Quarterdeck's DESQview software bundled in. That break led to sales of $2.3 million in 1987. They reached $55 million in 1992, with profits of $9 million. Fifteen percent of the company's sales come from abroad, and the international sector is growing.

While Myers was a graduate student at Carnegie Mellon University, John Reed hired her for a summer internship at Citibank. On her first day, Reed's boss was promoted to president and tapped Reed to be his chief of staff. Myers could not know then that Reed would remain fond of her, and rehire her later, as he climbed the company ladder to become chairman and CEO of Citicorp in 1984.

She returned to Carnegie Mellon to complete a Master's degree in industrial administration. Fortunately, Arthur Young in New York was hiring nonaccountants and she was selected with only twenty-nine other junior hires to get an all-expenses-paid accounting course at Northwestern.

The New York Times profiled the program and featured Myers and one other trainee. A copy of the article fortuitously came into Reed's hands. He hired her back and encouraged her for the next eleven years as she worked in various Citicorp subsidiaries that were pioneering office technology.

Myers told the Los Angeles *Business Journal,* [1] "We were allowed to do anything we wanted" at Citicorp's AXXA unit in Brentwood, Califor-

1. Todd White, *"Stacking Success at Quarterdeck,"* Los Angeles *Business Journal,* June 29, 1992, p. 17.

nia, led by the brilliant Jack Scantlin, pioneer of automated teller machines and, earlier, one of the first radio pagers and workstation developers.

When AXXA was wound down, Myers left. She founded her own firm with three other Citicorp talents, programmers Jill Eastman and Mike Kuppin, and Gary Pope. They rented a one-room studio behind a Santa Monica beach house and began working for eighteen months with no salary, trying to develop fast reflexes.

The team spent $14,000 for two Vector Graphics personal computers, which they dumped soon afterward when IBM debuted its PC, the Quarterdeck foursome correctly betting that it and its Microsoft-brand system software would eventually become industry standards. They tied their fortunes to Microsoft's MS-DOS (disk operating system) software, vowing to enhance it in myriad ways.

"Putting a layer on top of DOS turned out to be *the* strategic idea of the eighties for software," insists Myers.

Quarterdeck's flagship DESQview and QEMM software have been particularly sought after by "power users" and corporations, such as Boeing, Ford Aerospace, General Motors, Philip Morris, Texaco, and Upjohn, which try to wring the most out of their microprocessors and programs.

"It's amazing that we're still here," Myers says when reflecting on the cutthroat competition in the computer software industry.

Josie Cruz Natori

Name of Company:	The Natori Company
Location:	New York City
Date Founded:	1977
Description of Business:	The company has radically changed the lingerie industry by bringing fashion excitement to what had been a traditional market.
Description of *P*:	Raised in the Philippines (a matriarchal culture, where women are frequently business owners), Natori was from childhood geared to make an important commercial statement very much identified with herself.
Description of *S*:	A successful investment banker at Merrill Lynch, Natori touched the flint to the match on a trip to visit her family in the Philippines when she saw the fine embroidery work of her countrywomen and brought some pieces back with her to New York.
Members of *E*:	Ken Natori, husband and president, who joined the company in 1985
Size of V:	The company is privately held, but reports sales of approximately $40 million per year.
Social Utility:	Natori is very involved in her extended community. She is on the board of Junior Achievement, the Philippine-American Foundation, Dreyfus Fund, Manhattanville College, and the White House Commission on Small Business.
Principal Source of Venture Capital:	$150,000 in personal savings

For JOSIE CRUZ NATORI, the effervescent Philippine-born entrepreneur who walked away from a stellar career on Wall Street (she was vice president in investment banking at Merrill Lynch) to build a global fashion empire, rules are made to be broken. Natori is best known for revolutionizing the lingerie industry by bringing fashion excitement to what had been a traditional market. She designed bustiers, camisoles, and tunics to be worn from the bedroom to the board room, changing the modern woman's perception of lingerie.

Considered a prodigy at the age of nine, when she played her first piano solo with the Manila Philharmonic, Natori came to the United States in 1964 to study economics at Manhattanville College and to continue her musical studies. After graduation, she joined Bache Securities as a stockbroker, later moving to Merrill Lynch. In 1971, Josie Cruz met Kenneth Natori, an investment banker, on a blind date. They married a year and a half later.

Meanwhile, back on Wall Street, Natori began looking for other opportunities. She says, "I was bored on Wall Street, and I was looking for something that I could control." During a trip home, she visited a group of highly skilled embroiderers, whose work was largely overlooked by the Philippine apparel industry. Natori began importing finely embroidered and appliqued cotton shirts, and showing them to retailers in New York. A Bloomingdale's buyer suggested she design the blouses as nightshirts. They were an instant success, and the Natori fashion label was born.

The first few years of the Natori Company were lean, with Josie showing the collections to buyers in the couple's apartment with baby Kenneth, Jr., watching from his crib. And in 1985, Ken Natori left his position as managing director of Shearson Lehman Brothers to join the Natori Company as chairman. But Natori's keen sense for women's changing ideas about lingerie and sleepwear was perfectly timed. "Women were becoming more aware of their bodies," says Natori. "They were exercising and wanted to show off the results of their hard work. They also wanted to show their femininity at the office. My silky camisoles and embroidered bustiers were the antithesis of the 'dress for success' look, and women were ready for them."

Today, Josie and Ken work side-by-side in a grand office suite overseeing a staff of over one hundred employees. Their factory in the Philippines produces much of the company's products, with other design and production facilities in New York and a Natori boutique in Paris.

The world of Natori products continues to grow. In addition to Natori Foundations, the company has recently introduced Natori Jewelry and a Natori shoe collection. The Natoris continue to pioneer new ideas in business, fashion, and lifestyle. "I got my drive from my maternal grandmother and father, who had their own businesses," Natori says. However, she has gone further than they ever dreamed. Through August 1993, the Natoris sponsored "Infra-Apparel," an exhibition at the Metropolitan Museum of Art's Costume Institute in New York, which documented the influence of lingerie on ready-to-wear clothing since the 1800s.

Lane Nemeth

Name of Company:	Discovery Toys, Inc.
Location:	Pleasant Hill, California
Date Founded:	1978
Description of Business:	Sells a private-label line of educational toys, games, tapes, and books on a party-plan basis.
Description of P:	The paucity of educational toys that were available for infants and accessible to their parents and grandparents
Description of S:	Party-plan selling is a marketing channel directly into the home; the inventory is unique, not in stores, and has a high gross profit. It is financed by the customer, who places and pays for the order through a sales consultant, at which time the inventory item is put into production.
Members of E:	Jack Lauster, executive vice president Marianne Lundstrom, vice president, Finance
Size of V:	Although privately held and not required to publish financial information, it is estimated that Discovery Toys' valuation is about $100 million.
Social Utility:	The company has created 170 jobs at headquarters and 30,000 sales jobs across the United States. Nemeth is launching a nationwide public service campaign on the value of self-esteem in young children. She is also the founder of the Children's Advisory Council.
Principal Source of Venture Capital:	$25,000 borrowed from family members and friends

LANE NEMETH, now forty-five, worked for three years as the director of a state-funded day care center in Concord, California. When her husband's employer first moved them to Concord, Nemeth was basically a housewife who thought she might go to work. But she worked very hard and, she told *Esquire*, "I burned out on my work."[1]

One day in 1976, she went shopping for an educational toy for a friend's one-year-old son. She could not find one anywhere. So Nemeth went home, sat on the living room floor, and sketched out a business plan. The problem was the absence both of educational toys in the toy stores and of qualified sales personnel to describe the educational qualities of entertainment toys. Her solution: Select a line of educational toys and make the sales presentation in the home, explaining to the parent the skill that the toy is developing. "I grew up with this hugely idealistic view of the world," Nemeth says. "I really visualized our mission when my daughter was born. I didn't want her growing up in a world where kids could only communicate through anger and violence." Through Discovery Toys she hopes to help parents raise their children as peacemakers. "We choose and design toys that are nonviolent, and intentionally create cooperative game versions for most of our games that encourage children to work for a common goal." Operating out of her garage in the first year, Nemeth had sales of $280,000.

Along the way, there were some fits and starts, but the purpose of trouble is to instruct. In one instance, when Discovery Toys needed money very badly, it had to borrow at an interest rate of 27.5 percent per annum. At another time, the company underordered and was out of stock on thirty-five items. However, Nemeth stayed true to her mission and true to her staff. "The bottom line only matters if you do everything else right. Come at business with a high degree of ethics and quality and adhere to that, no matter what. You can win and the money will be there. Business is society. We touch an enormous number of people, and we have to touch everybody with care and concern, with gentleness and awareness."

The company has approximately 30,000 people (mostly women) in a multilevel sales force. The "educational consultant" who arranges the party receives a 26 percent commission on sales and a smaller cut on sales made by her recruits. Achieving sales goals is rewarded with cars, fur coats, vacations, and jewelry. The marketing format is not unique: Mary Kay Cosmetics, the Amway Corporation, Transart Industries, and others

---

1. *Esquire*, December 1984, p. 29.

have been doing it for years. What is unique is that here the product is educational—toys for the mind—and upscale. "We're not just selling product," Discovery Toys will tell you. "We're selling the healthy and happy development of children. That's the future. We're selling the future."

Today Nemeth is looking to spread her mission around the globe. Future markets include China, Latin America, the Pacific Rim, and Eastern Europe. Nemeth believes that her toys transcend all cultural boundaries. "I think parenting is our common bond. We all love our children; we all want them to be happy, successful, and self-fulfilled."

Jean O'Ffill

Name of Company:	Jet Tech, Inc.; Phoenix Metals, Inc.
Location:	Edwardsville, Kansas
Date Founded:	Jet Tech acquired 1981; Phoenix Metals acquired 1988.
Description of Business:	O'Ffill buys troubled, undervalued manufacturing companies, fixes them up, turns them around, and sells them—or keeps them.
Description of P:	Owners and managers of troubled businesses frequently have a poor understanding of the nature of the workout and turnaround process. They fear the worst. They are unable to make cuts. Buyers like O'Ffill who are fearless and sharp, come along, buy these cash-bleeders, and fix them.
Description of S:	Diagnose—sell assets—cut overhead—form a core group of tough, loyal managers—and develop a redirect-and-grow plan: These are the steps O'Ffill and other "grave dancers" take to restore companies to abundant health.
Members of E:	Ken Norcross, process scientist, senior vice president Denis Nelson, operations manager, executive vice president
Size of V:	Jet Tech's revenues are $12 million; Phoenix Metals' revenues are $3 million.
Social Utility:	O'Ffill establishes employee stock ownership programs that enable all employees to own stock in her companies after two years.

Principal Source of
Venture Capital: Supplier credit, bank loans, and customer
                              advances

When asked to give advice to young women entrepreneurs venturing forth for the first time, JEAN O'FFILL smiles and with a twinkle in her eye says, "When you are really, really devoted to business, forget about being married. It's just not fair to men."

The middle of three daughters, O'Ffill says, "I was the son of the family. The brother came along later, but until then, my father couldn't believe I was a girl. 'Good gosh! She's a girl!' was his attitude. So I got raised like a boy, and Dad instilled in me to learn math and learn to speak, because if you are going to make it in a man's world, those are the two skills you will need most.

"My father and I were very close. I revered him. But that didn't stop me from getting married at seventeen—for the first time—while I was in college. My second husband died. And the third one—don't even ask about him."

O'Ffill bought her first company, a textile machinery manufacturer, in 1984. It had sales of $14 million per year and was losing money. O'Ffill ran it for three years, then sold it in 1987 when sales were $22 million and profits reached $1.5 million.

"I'm a herder, I buy companies and make them well. I'm not a particularly good sustainer, I guess, because healthy, smooth-running companies start to bore me," O'Ffill explains.

In 1981 she bought Jet Tech, Inc., a manufacturer of waste-water treatment systems. It had sales of $3 million at the time and was losing more than $1 million a year. "The owners thought that nobody was dumb enough to buy it. But they hadn't met me yet. I bought it. It had a hundred-year-old name and some good products. Today it does $12 million a year on its way to $15 million and its earnings have grown from $160,000 in 1991 to $1.5 million in 1993. We have sixty-two employees," O'Ffill says.

Jet Tech's customers include most of industrial America that has environmental problems, such as food and beverage producers and film and semiconductor manufacturers. These include Borden, Jack Daniel's, Jim Beam, Kodak, and Ordia Foods, among others. "Municipalities used to pay to clean up the water, but they don't have any money, so the burden has been shifted to industry," she says. Jet Tech has expanded its sales abroad and has installed systems in Belgium and for three General Motors plants in Mexico. It is bidding on jobs in Israel.

O'Ffill bought Phoenix Metals, Inc., a metals fabricator, in May 1992. It had sales of $2 million and was losing money. "I'm running this sucker for now, and I'm going to turn it around and get back to Jet Tech. I've spotted a blower equipment company to buy for Jet Tech—it will add to our water purifying capability—and I'll be putting my energies into that this coming year. International companies are ten years behind the United States in waste-water treatment, and we're going to do some good business with them," she says.

O'Ffill shares her business philosophy: "I've got one mission in my life: to treat people properly and, at the same time, be able to make a profit. It's as simple as that!

"If I can point to one of my most successful management skills, it is that I share inside information with all my employees. They can see when we make money and when we lose money, how much I take home and where the cash is reinvested. They respect this sharing of information, and, because many of them are stockholders, I believe it has become the straw that stirs the drink in my companies."

Elisabeth Claiborne Ortenberg

Name of Company:	Liz Claiborne, Inc.
Date Founded:	1976
Location:	New York City
Description of Business:	This designer of women's clothing made by independent suppliers in the United States and the Far East sells its "better sportswear" merchandise through more than 3,000 specialty stores.
Description of *P*:	Working women want well-made, fashionable sportswear to wear to the office. They are busy, so they will shop mainly in the department stores. To be certain they are getting quality, women want a fashion image they can trust.
Description of *S*:	Ortenberg focused her line on the needs of business and professional women. To save costs, 65 percent of the manufacturing is done overseas. Distribution is direct to big department stores. And to maintain a fashionable high-quality image—and the prices of a "designer" label—Ortenberg has appeared frequently on the covers of magazines read by working women.
Members of *E*:	Arthur Ortenberg, Leonard Boxer, Jerome A. Chazen, co-founders
Size of V:	The approximately eighty-three million shares of common stock outstanding traded at an average of $23.50 in 1993 for an average market value of approximately $1.95 billion.

Social Utility: Fashion entrepreneurs are viewed, perhaps
                                   unfairly, as opportunistic. Ortenberg,
                                   however, has generated more than 2,500 jobs
                                   in the United States.

Principal Source of
Venture Capital: The four co-founders invested an aggregate of
                                   $250,000 to start the business.

ELISABETH CLAIBORNE ORTENBERG has distinguished herself as one of the best
entrepreneurs in America in an industry that has taken the toll of more
businesses and had more grown men crying in their pillows than any
other. In New York it's called the "rag business," and its function is to
design, produce, and deliver to merchants throughout the country the
clothing that we will select to wear.

Most apparel companies have been fly-by-night, here today, gone
tomorrow, primarily because they have addressed a trend or a look, and
not solved a problem. Liz Claiborne, Inc., is different. It solved a problem.
Simply stated, women in fast-paced industrial and financial companies
do not have time to shop for apparel and stay up-to-date with styles, yet
they cannot afford to look out of step at any time. The solution to this need
was a line of apparel between "classic" and "avant-garde" that was
designed for smart-looking, young women executives. But the line was
marketed like a service rather than a product. Instead of going to the
expense of opening and operating its own stores, where sales personnel
would be trained to service the customer, the company provided "Claiboards" to the retailers who stocked the line. As Irene Daria wrote in
Women's Wear Daily, "Claiboards [are] a trademarked concept using
sketches, photos, and printed explanations showing how merchandise
should be displayed in groups."[1] Claiboards explained to the salesperson
how to mix and match the apparel to maximize the appearance for the
customer. The sales and service tool said in effect, "Here's how to service
the customer so she'll keep coming back." Products in a competitive
marketplace keep selling and selling if the customer feels he or she is
receiving service, not because the product is unique, which with apparel
is not the case.

Jerome A. Chazen, one of the company's four founders, says, "We
sometimes fantasize about how wonderful it would be to have our own
stores. . . . Then the blouse that goes with group A [wouldn't] be on the

---

1. Irene Daria, "Claiborne Priority: Managing Its Growth," *Women's Wear Daily*,
June 26, 1984, p. 4.

other side of the floor." But this is unlikely to happen. Thus, the emphasis on sales training.

Liz Claiborne, Inc., may not have happened except for the fact that in February 1976 Jonathan Logan closed Youth Guild, a dress division in which Ortenberg had worked as a designer for sixteen years. Concomitantly, her husband, Arthur Ortenberg, phased out his consulting business, and they went into business together. They advertised for a production partner. This led to Leonard Boxer joining the fledgling firm. Jerry Chazen, Ortenberg's college roommate and a retailer, invested his share of the initial $250,000, but didn't join the company until it could afford him.

After eighteen months of operations, Liz Claiborne, Inc., was on its way to a $7 million year. The four partners felt they might be on to something big. They went on a three-day retreat to the Poconos to talk about "what success would mean, how it would change each of our lives, and whether we wanted those changes to happen," Chazen said. Two of the partners did not want rapid growth, but Ortenberg's argument was compelling, for Liz Claiborne, Inc., as well as for other rapidly emerging companies: "Once you shape a company to service the marketplace and your services are necessary, the company develops a compulsion of its own to grow." This statement says a great deal about entrepreneurial drive and motivation.

Dian G. Owen

Name of Company: Owen Healthcare Group, Inc.
Location: Houston
Date Founded: 1969
Description of
Business: Manages hospital pharmacies, owns and
                     operates retail pharmacies, manages hospital
                     materials, provides home infusion services,
                     and develops and markets computer software
                     for pharmacies.
Description of *P*:   Hospitals are not noted for their exceptional
                     management, and in the face of inexorably
                     rising health care costs, they need help in
                     running a tighter ship.
Description of *S*:   Owen Healthcare spotted the need of hospitals
                     to have some of their facilities, such as
                     hospital pharmacies, managed by outside
                     companies. Owen used the cash flow from
                     hospital pharmacy management to expand into
                     new businesses.
Members of *E*:   Jean Owen, co-founder and husband, who died
                     in a 1976 airplane crash
                     Carl Isgren, president
                     Harlan Stai, executive vice president
Size of V: The company is privately held, but with
                     revenues of $240 million in 1992 and the high
                     values the stock market puts on health care
                     service companies, the company could be
                     worth more than $150 million if it were public,
                     and still more than that in an acquisition.
Social Utility: Owen is an extremely active community service
                     volunteer. She is a board member of the West

Texas Rehabilitation Center, the Muscular
Dystrophy Association, and McMurray
College, and she is chairperson of the board of
St. John's Episcopal School in Abilene. Owen
Healthcare has adopted a nearby elementary
school.

Principal Source of
Venture Capital: A $25,000 loan from ex-in-laws

DIAN OWEN, chairman of the board, and her husband, Jean, founded Owen
Healthcare, Inc., as a hospital pharmacy management company in 1969.
When Jean Owen died in a 1976 airplane crash, Dian rejected buyout
offers and assumed control of the company, which at the time had sales of
$6.6 million. One of the potential buyers controlled sixteen of the
company's clients. When Owen rejected his offer, he pulled the clients
away to make the entrepreneur beg and forced him to be brought out.
Unfazed, Owen went out and signed up twenty-one new clients.

During Owen's tenure, gross revenues have grown more than 25
percent annually, from $6.6 million in 1976 to $240 million in 1992. The
company employs more than 2,000 people who serve more than 250
hospitals in forty states.

In 1982, the company hit the 100-client mark. Two years later, Owen
Healthcare surpassed its biggest competitor in size to become the premier
hospital pharmacy management firm in the country. The same year,
Owen Healthcare diversified into materials management and established
its Hospital Materials Services Division. In 1985, the company expanded
into the home infusion area and established Owen Home Infusion
Services.

Since 1985, the company has continued to develop new technology
designed to keep client costs down, for instance, Omega-R$_x$, a computerized pharmacy management system that implements and monitors
Owen's pharmacy programs, and HMS Supplyline, a proprietary data
base that assists hospital materials managers in making cost-effective
purchasing decisions.

Owen Healthcare's management team is employee-focused. Employees with children in day care centers are paid bonuses to cover the
costs of day care. Dian Owen formed an ESOP in 1985. Her goal is to have
the top management team 50 percent women. "My management style is
through an executive circle," she explains. "The top managers and I meet
in a circle and we process problems and solutions with one another until
we work things through. I set the goals. Management tells me how we're
going to reach them."

Linda Paresky

Name of Company:	Thomas Cook Travel 1989 Travel Education Centers 1975 Agenda, Inc. 1985
Location:	Cambridge, Massachusetts
Date Founded:	Crimson Travel 1965 (Merged with Thomas Cook) 1989
Description of Business:	Travel agency, training, and consulting companies
Description of P:	In 1965, 85 percent of the U.S. population had never been on an airplane.
Description of S:	Recognizing the enormous potential in the travel industry, Linda and her husband, David, co-founded Crimson Travel Services in 1965.
Members of E:	David Paresky, co-founder, Crimson Travel Christopher Hooson, co-founder, Agenda, Inc. David Paresky and Linda Paresky, co-owners, Thomas Cook Travel
Size of V:	Thomas Cook (1993) gross sales: nearly $2 billion. Travel Education Centers' billings: over $1 million
Social Utility	Trustee of Simmons College; board of directors, American Thyroid Foundation; board of advisors for the American Repertory Theater; Former appointee, Massachusetts Council for Arts and Humanities; president-elect, Massachusetts Women's Forum; member, International Women's Forum

Principal Source of
Venture Capital: Two desks and two phone lines paid for by the
                           couple

LINDA PARESKY, president of her senior class at Simmons College, was not quite sure what she wanted to do when she graduated in 1964. One of her English professors encouraged her to continue to study English and pursue her M.A.T. at Harvard University. Paresky says, "I grew up in an era where women didn't think broadly about career opportunities and were not always clear about what opportunities were available to them." While she was at Simmons College, she met her future husband, who was completing his law degree. He later went on to complete his MBA. The two established a travel company, organizing trips for college students. This would only be the beginning of a fruitful career in the travel business for Linda.

Paresky says that she was always a "starter of organizations." "I enjoy coming up with the idea that fits the need." She reflects to her college days, "When I was at Simmons, I founded the Roxburry Volunteer Tutorial Association, which was designed to organize college students to volunteer their time to tutor for inner city children." Her work with the community did not stop there. While she was in graduate school at Harvard University, she was asked to participate in a pilot program with the Boston public schools teaching high school English.

Although she says she really did not have one specific mentor, Paresky notes, "My parents encouraged me to trust my instincts and take risks." Her instincts guided her well when she decided to marry her husband, David Paresky. The couple has been happily married since 1963. Between his financial and legal background and her outstanding organizational and leadership skills, the two formed one of business's most formidable partnerships.

In 1965, with two desks and two telephones, they decided to open up their own travel agency in Harvard Square, Cambridge, and named it Crimson Travel. Initially, they focused on student and family travel packages and then moved toward corporate travel. Business grew rapidly and steadily. However, frustrated by the lack of qualified or trained personnel in the travel industry, Linda Paresky put her teaching and organizational skills to work, and in 1975, opened up the Travel Education Center, a school for individuals interested in working in the travel business. What could be better? If you can't find good staff, build a school and train them yourself! Even better: Charge them for it. The Travel Education Center provided Crimson Travel with a pool of well-trained travel professionals to choose from while offering an opportunity for hundreds of students to gain excellent training for a career in the travel business. Today, Travel Education Center operates in three states, is nationally accredited, and graduates over 600 future travel agents every year.

This was just the beginning. Her instincts would prove to be right once again. In 1976, she recruited Christopher Hooson, whom she thought was incredibly talented, to serve as the director of her new travel school. He eventually left to work for a different company. However, nine years later, he returned to Paresky with a new business idea. The two formed a partnership and opened Agenda, Inc., in 1985, which provides training design and consulting for tourist boards and other companies in the travel industry. With an employee training program that could not be beat, and a two-person management team that would impress any outside investment company, Crimson Travel was poised to make its mark on the travel industry. By 1988, Crimson Travel was the largest travel agency in New England. The Pareskys knew that they needed to expand nationally to better serve their corporate accounts, and decided to merge with Heritage Travel in 1988, making Crimson/Heritage the sixth largest travel agency in the United States. At that time, Thomas Cook Travel was ranked eighth and had the international and worldwide presence Crimson/Heritage was looking for. Consequently, the following year, the Pareskys took advantage of an opportunity to merge with Thomas Cook Travel, taking over full management of the nationwide company, and formed the third largest travel agency out of a total of 30,000 in the United States. Today, Thomas Cook Travel has over 300 offices, 3,500 employees, and gross sales of about $2 billion. Thomas Cook Travel is now owned 100 percent by the Pareskys after a recent buyout of the remaining interest in the company from the estate of Robert Maxwell.

Paresky has proven herself to be a remarkable entrepreneur and manager. By 1988, she had earned her Ph.D. in educational and developmental psychology with a minor in organizational development. Why did she pursue a Ph.D. after starting three companies? Paresky says, "I felt the need to grow myself. . . . It was for my own self-actualization." While she was working on her own personal growth, taking courses in the evening, she was acquiring the skills necessary for her travel agency to grow even further. Her understanding of people and organizational talent was essential in the merger of the three travel companies. She says that it was a merger of three different companies and that she worked to organize them into a "single corporate culture," focusing on quality and customer satisfaction. Furthermore, Paresky's studies and experience have helped ensure her staff maintains a level of competence and confidence in their work and that they feel comfortable in their ability to take advantage of opportunities and solve problems efficiently and effectively.

Paresky's advice to young entrepreneurs: (1) Choose a field you enjoy and people you enjoy working with, because you will spend a lot of time with them; (2) listen to your customers: A complaint is an opportunity for continuous improvement and organizational learning; an unmet need is an opportunity for a new product or service; (3) treat customers, vendors, and employees with honesty and integrity; (4) create an environment that empowers everyone in the organization to have a sense of ownership—for internal and external customer satisfaction—and unleash the creative potential of everyone in the company; (5) achieve a balance between work, love, and play; set personal and organizational goals; (6) be prepared to work long and hard; (7) give back to the community; (8) make a difference; (9) change the paradigm from command and control management to a supportive leader model; (10) model the values you espouse.

There are two kinds of people who need positive reinforcement: those who need it and those who don't! If there was ever a ten commandments of business management, it is the ten empirically proven commandments of Linda Paresky.

Rachel Perry

Name of Company:	Rachel Perry Cosmetics
Location:	Chatsworth, California
Date Founded:	1973
Description of Business:	Manufactures natural skin care products.
Description of P:	Natural skin care products were virtually nonexistent during the early 1970s. All skin care products used synthetic and chemical ingredients.
Description of S:	Rachel Perry developed skin care products that used only natural ingredients.
Members of E:	Rachel Perry, founder and president
Size of V:	$10 million
Social Utility:	Rachel Perry does not test on animals and uses sustainably harvested ingredients in order to preserve and protect the world's tropical rain forests. In addition, for every product that is sold, Rachel Perry donates 10 cents to an environmental organization.
Principal Source of Venture Capital:	$1,200 borrowed from a friend

While the cosmetics business has always interested RACHEL PERRY, her main ambition was to be a singer and songwriter. She started her career at age 15 working for Coty, where she learned about skin care and cosmetics and became one of Coty's youngest sales representatives. She continued to sell cosmetics in order to pursue a career as a singer and songwriter. After working for Coty, she worked in department stores demonstrating various cosmetic products and then gave facials at various Beverly Hills salons. Through her experiences in the cosmetics industry and as a student of biochemistry, endocrinology, and nutrition, Perry was able to develop a course on facials, facial massage, and skin care that she could teach from her home. Combining her knowlege of the skin with a bit of intuition, Perry developed a four-step technique for facials. The first step was epiderm abrasion, which required a facial scrub. At that time, Perry could find only synthetic facial scrubs and none of them were adequate to do the job she wanted to do. She decided to experiment in her home kitchen by combining various natural ingredients that she knew were good for the skin and tried to come up with a facial scrub of her own. She did, and with the combination of sea kelp, sea salt, honey, and almond meal, she created the industry's first natural facial scrub. This would eventually launch her into her very own cosmetics and skin care company, Rachel Perry Cosmetics.

Perry says of this scrub, "It was so pure you could have eaten it."[1] She put her mixture into little labeled jars and gave them to all the students in her class. They ate it up. One of her students realized that it helped control her acne and convinced her husband, who owned a health food store, to carry the product. Within a short period, the product sold out. Encouraged by the public's response, Perry borrowed $1,200 from a friend and began making more facial scrub in her kitchen sink and selling it to other health food stores. When she decided to do a check on her product in the stores, she noticed that her scrub had started to "beard up." Because the scrub was made up of entirely natural ingredients, its shelf life was relatively short. With very little money, Perry hired a chemist to come up with a way of prolonging the life of her natural facial scrub and continued making the product. She did all of the selling, packaging, labeling, and shipping out of her home. Business was slow for the first four years, and it remained a sideline to her song writing. But the business started to grow in spite of itself. She had three products, the Sea Kelp-Herbal Facial Scrub, Violet-Rose Skin Toner, and Lemon Mint Astringent, and they all started to sell in volume. From her kitchen she moved into her garage and from there into four more garages.

She met a piano player named John Meyer, who became her husband and vice president of Rachel Perry cosmetics. Meyer helped focus the company and became actively involved in marketing. Meyer pushed Perry into trade shows and into hiring distributors to make Rachel Perry

---

1. Gayle Sato, *Enterprising Women*, March/April 1990, p. 86.

nationally known and eventually a major player in the natural skin care products industry.

But things were not that easy. Within a few years she divorced John Meyer and promoted a woman who had worked her way up in the company to vice president. Not really knowledgeable about marketing, she hired an outside marketing agency whose brokers were paid by the number of stores in which they were able to get the product placed. Perry was very unsure about this move, but she unwisely agreed. What resulted was chaos. Virtually overnight, her product was in 9,000 stores, with only twenty-one sales reps to support them. She was producing more product than she could sell and was supporting her sales reps with their expense accounts. There was really no management in the company. "It took me a long time to believe that I am the president of this company and that I do have the last word," she says. "In the end, I'm going to do what I want for my products and what I think is best." By 1983, Rachel Perry Cosmetics was heading for disaster and consequently Perry reorganized the company. To do that she had a lot to learn. She was an artist and did not know anything about running a company. But in reality she knew enough. "I've learned that you have to rely on your own intuition, which is half judgment, half experience. If you have a strong gut feeling about something, it usually turns out. If I allow myself to be talked into something, 90 percent of the time it's wrong." "Trust your instincts," she says. "Don't allow anyone to intimidate you, and don't feel that executives know more than you do just because you don't have much business experience. Even if you aren't an accountant, you probably know more about what's good for your company than anyone else. That's not to say I never make mistakes, but at least they're my mistakes."[2]

2. Ibid., p. 89.

Robin Piccone

Name of Company:	Piccone Apparel
Location:	Los Angeles
Date Founded:	1986
Description of Business:	Swimwear and sportswear designer known for its dramatic, body-conscious silhouettes and seductive style.
Description of *P*:	Neoprene, commonly used to make surfers' wet suits, caught Robin Piccone's attention. The body-conscious and "athletically seductive" quality of this synthetic rubberized material, combined with the surfer craze, inspired her to create an entire swimwear line from this product.
Description of *S*:	Robin Piccone brought her designs to Body Glove, a forty-year-old Hermosa Beach wet-suit company, and became the first designer to have a licensing agreement with the company. She revolutionized the swimwear industry with her use of neoprene.
Members of *E*:	Robin cites her husband, Richard Battaglia, and her mother, Rita, as people who have been instrumental in the business since its inception in 1986.
Size of V:	Privately held. The total revenues for 1993 are estimated at $10 million.
Social Utility:	Local school decorating committee, City Hope, Woman of the Year, $100,000 to Pediatric AIDS, supports AIDS project of Los Angeles.

Principal Source of	
Venture Capital:	$300,000 of personal savings and her mother's retirement money

ROBIN PICCONE has appropriately been dubbed the "queen of neoprene." In 1986, she sent shock waves through the swimwear industry when her athletic and sexy swimwear hit the beaches of California. Heads turned as women who wore her newly constructed swimwear paraded down the beaches. Within one year she had sold over $1 million in swimwear and distinguished herself as a top-notch designer on the cutting edge of the swimwear fashion industry.

This was not the first time Piccone had made a statement in the swimwear industry, however. After she graduated from the Los Angeles Trade Technical College in 1979 she landed a job working as a cutter at Cole of California, a major swimwear design and manufacturing company. Piccone had originally wanted to get into the fashion industry but settled for the job at Cole. She worked her way up to the position of assistant designer and was responsible for creating two of their most successful suits. After a couple of years with Cole, she was recruited by Bobby Brooks swimwear division in New York, where she spent five years as head designer in charge of developing the division's line from start to finish. Before setting out on her own, she worked as the head designer for Daffy, for which she created the popular "Mickey Mouse" bathing suit.

In 1986 she decided it was time to start her own company. She had been experimenting with neoprene and was impressed with the way it hugged the body. After drawing up the designs for a line of swimwear made of neoprene, she approached the president of Body Glove, Robbie Meinstrell, and signed the first licensing agreement with the forty-year-old Hermosa Beach company for a swimwear line.

Out of her Venice Beach apartment she opened her Body Glove Swimwear store. The whole thing was a family affair. Her mother helped with the initial investment and worked as the bookkeeper. Her husband, Richard Battaglia, former actor, with no prior retail experience, headed up the sales effort. All three of them, with the help of an aunt, did everything from making the patterns, cutting the fabric, and sewing the samples, to answering the phones, packing and shipping the goods, picking up pins, and sweeping the floors. They worked very hard. It is said that even when their garage flooded, they would be standing on boxes, diligently working to get the orders made up and shipped out.

Robin Piccone Swimwear evolved from ideas generated while she was working for Body Glove. The Piccone Swimwear line uses colors and styles that were not suitable for the Body Glove image. Body Glove was athletic and sexy. Robin Piccone's own line is both more serious and glamorous with a retro-modern look to it.

Piccone's love for the fashion industry has also led her to start her own sportswear line, and this has sent more shock waves through the pages of fashion magazines. Her combination of comfort and elegance has captured the hearts of fashion editors and the orders have been rolling in. She has shifted to lycra and more modern fabrics and has created a line of clothing to fit her own active lifestyle.

Piccone says that she is influenced by "everything around me: colored marking pens, old movies, and, especially in fabric selection, functional objects for other industries—like a rubber donut that I found on the floor of an auto repair garage."

Sheri Poe

Name of Company:	RYKÄ, Inc.
Location:	Norwood, Massachusetts
Date Founded:	1987
Description of Business:	Designs, develops, produces, and markets athletic shoes exclusively for the women's market.
Description of *P*:	Poe's fight is against violence toward women, and the arena that she selected is athletic shoes. Her premise is that exercise and running bolster the wearer's immune system and keeps her healthy; the warrior spirit is awakened in her.
Description of *S*:	RYKÄ, Inc., is poised to become one of the most unique consumer products companies in the world because it has adopted a cause—ending violence against women—and because the benefits of its success will accrue to women who have been violated and to people offended by this violence.
Members of *E*:	Poe's grandmother
Size of V:	The company is publicly held with $12 million in sales in 1992 and a projected $18 million in 1993. Its market capitalization in early 1994 was $14 million.
Social Utility:	Seven percent of the company's profits are pledged to the RYKÄ ROSE ("Regaining One's Self-Esteem") Foundation, which channels money to groups helping women who have been victims of violent crime.

Principal Source of
Venture Capital: $4 million raised via an initial public offering

SHERI POE is one of the nation's most progressive entrepreneurial women. In 1987, at the age of thirty-four, Sheri founded the women's athletic footwear company, RYKÄ, Inc. Despite warnings from friends who cautioned her not to try to compete with the footwear giants in this male-dominated industry, she started RYKÄ from the kitchen of her house and grew it into a publicly held, multi-million dollar corporation and a model of corporate citizenship. RYKÄ has become a leader in the women's athletic footwear industry.

Poe identified the market niche for women's athletic shoes and pioneered an exclusively women's footwear company. She had aspired to have her own business and discovered a need in the women's market-place—a result of her not being able to find an athletic shoe that fit her properly. At that time, women's athletic shoes were only scaled-down versions of men's shoes, lacking the high arch and narrow heal that is characteristic of a woman's foot. She persevered for over a year to find start-up funds and finally met an investment banker, who was also having a problem with the fit of her workout shoes. This woman helped Poe take RYKÄ public, raising $4 million in one week.

Having started her company in the midst of the October 1987 stock market crash, Poe managed to keep RYKÄ afloat despite very difficult economic times, quality control problems with initial shipments of shoes, and financial challenges. In a few short years, RYKÄ has grown from a small start-up to a core brand in the sporting goods industry with distributors in more than fifteen countries, and remains true to its mission of developing shoes exclusively for women.

As president and CEO of RYKÄ, Poe decided she needed to do more than make great shoes *For Women, By Women*™. She wanted to give her company a "soul" and a conscience that reflected her concerns. Poe wanted to help other women avoid the pain that she had experienced, as a rape survivor of over two decades. Her vision led her to create the RYKÄ ROSE™ Foundation (Regaining One's Self-Esteem™), a charitable non-profit organization committed to ending violence against women, through its funding of education/awareness, prevention, and treatment programs. Additionally, ROSE serves to empower women who are survivors of violent crimes to regain their self-esteem and to rebuild their lives.

Poe hopes that by sharing her personal story, other women will be encouraged to seek help. She broke her long-held silence after reading that Oprah Winfrey had testified before Congress on her experiences as a childhood survivor of sexual asault. For Poe, nearly twenty years had passed, but she took a courageous and healing step toward her recovery by finally disclosing the rape to others, including her parents and her children.

As a silent victim, Poe had battled bulimia for ten years. The results were chronic hepatitis, liver damage, and a forecast from her doctors that she would not live to the age of thirty, never have children, and never hold a normal job. The shocking news propelled Poe into action—with an incredible drive to live. She had survived the attack and she was not going to let it kill her. Poe turned to exercise, which became her personal salvation. It changed her life and, years later, gave her the idea of starting RYKÄ, when her athletic shoes were causing her physical pain. She has further defied doctors' predictions by giving birth to, and raising a family of, four children.

With the success of RYKÄ and the growth of the ROSE Foundation, Poe now helps other survivors take control of their lives and achieve a sound body, mind, and spirit. In keeping with its commitment to women, RYKÄ has pledged to partially underwrite the activities of the ROSE Foundation. RYKÄ's advertising campaign has integrated the message of the RYKÄ ROSE Foundation with the RYKÄ brand. The ads conclude:

> In exercise, it's often said, "No pain, no gain."
> In this case, the gains will also come
> when there is no pain.

Barbara Gardner Proctor

Name of Company: Proctor & Gardner Advertising, Inc.

Location: Chicago

Date Founded: 1970

Description of
Business: The company, specializing in urban and diversity marketing, is one of the most respected marketing agencies in the country.

Description of P: Proctor realized that large advertisers wished to appeal directly to the black consumer but needed guidance to do so. She also wanted to protect the black community from ethically dubious advertising pitches.

Description of S: The company designs, develops, and implements advertising campaigns for large consumer products companies to reach the black community. Billings exceed $25 million annually.

Members of E: Melody Bather-Gardner, vice president
Gordon Lendner, creative art director

Size of V: The company is privately held, but its dominant position in its niche would fetch a higher-than-expected valuation, perhaps greater than the size of its billings.

Social Utility: Proctor is a beacon for women entrepreneurs to follow the world over.

Principal Source of
Venture Capital: An $80,000 SBA loan. She told the bank officer to call various advertising agencies and ask what they would have to pay someone with her credentials. That's how he arrived at $80,000.

BARBARA GARDNER PROCTOR has achieved financial and professional success without sacrificing her ethical standards. "In the public-trust category," she told *The Wall Street Journal*, "the advertising business is in a dead heat with the used car salesman. And justifiably so. Advertising's only goal seems to be to move goods and services at a profit."[1]

She decries the effect of advertising on women, claiming that they have fallen prey to dubious pitches for psychoactive drugs and sleep inducers that have very little medicinal value. Women smokers, she says, are targeted and encouraged by advertisers as well. Sounds like a soap-box orator or some flake who calls up radio talk shows?

Not at all. Proctor is the owner of one of the fastest-growing advertising agencies in the country, Proctor & Gardner Advertising, Inc. It reaches the black community for Kraft, Inc., Jewel Food Stores, and American Family Insurance. One of Proctor's most memorable and personally satisfying campaigns was the assistance it provided Jewel Food Stores in the early 1970s. "Jewel had a lot of stores in the black community during a time of unrest. I got the Jewel account in December 1970, and the campaign we did for them was 'We know about pride.' " The campaign formed a bridge between Jewel and the black community.

Proctor has served as director of Ameritech; a director of Bingham Companies, Mid-City National Bank of Chicago, the Better Business Bureau, and The Executives' Club of Chicago; a trustee of Mundelein College, Northwestern Memorial Hospital, and Talladega College; and a committee member of sixteen different charitable and cultural organizations.

After a short career with Vee-Jay Records from 1961 to 1964 and a divorce, Proctor worked for three Chicago advertising agencies in the 1960s, rising to the level of copy supervisor by 1970. Then she was fired. She says that the agency wanted her to write an aerosol hair-color TV commercial that parodied the civil rights sit-ins of the time by calling it a "foam-in." She refused because it demeaned the civil rights advocates.

But why didn't Proctor just take a job at an another ad agency? She said, "I realized that I was going to keep getting fired if I lived up to my own principles; therefore, the only way not to get fired again was to start my own company."

1. Earl C. Gottschalk, Jr., "More Women Start Up Their Own Businesses, With Major Successes," *The Wall Street Journal*, May 17, 1983, p. 1.

With no alternative but to put her own ideas to work, Proctor formed her own advertising agency. The proof of the pudding for this single parent, who was put out on the street in 1970 for standing up for her beliefs, is a successful enterprise. President Ronald Reagan cited Barbara Proctor in his 1984 State of the Union address as an example of one of "the heroes of the eighties."

Clara Taylor Reed

Name of Company:	Mid-Delta Home Health, Inc.
Location:	Belzoni, Mississippi
Date Founded:	1978
Description of Business:	Provides home health care services to the elderly and ill.
Description of *P*:	Nursing homes can be sad and lonely places in which to spend the twilight years of one's life. The vast majority of the elderly and the infirm say they would prefer to remain at home. But with no one to care for them, this option is frequently removed.
Description of *S*:	Home health care services allow patients to preserve their dignity along with answering their health care needs. Mid-Delta has a paralegal on staff to provide legal services as well.
Members of *E*:	Maxine Netz, nurse, supervisor, troubleshooter
Size of *V*:	The company is privately held and not required to publish its financial statements. Sales are in excess of $14 million.
Social Utility:	In addition to having founded a needed and socially useful business, Reed is chairperson of the board of trustees of her church, Evans Chapel United, and choir soloist; president of the Parents, Teachers, Students Association PTSA, and a board member of the Mississippi Valley State College Foundation.
Principal Source of Venture Capital:	$1,000 in personal savings

When in 1978 CLARA REED opened the doors of her home health agency in the small town of Belzoni, Mississippi, she had no idea how instrumental she would become in meeting the health needs of the Mississippi Delta. Concerned about the health problems and needs of the community, Reed organized Mid-Delta Home Health, Inc., which provides health services to patients who are essentially home-bound, under the care of a certified physician. Reed says, "Home health care can be an alternative to a nursing home. After patients are referred to our agency, we teach them how to care and deal with their illness. This enables patients to stay at home, where they will probably live longer and be happier."

Reed began her nursing career after graduating in 1963 from Mississippi Valley State College's Licensed Practical Nurses Program. She later entered the college's Registered Nurses Program and graduated in 1970 with an associate degree in nursing. She received a B.A. degree in gerontology in 1990.

Mid-Delta has become not only one of the greatest resources for providing complete health care needs in Mississippi, but a source of employment as well. With well over 370 employees in twelve offices in a six-county area, Reed finds the reality of being a black female entrepreneur a rewarding experience.

"I have always worked hard," Reed says. "That's nothing new to me. Starting my own business was an idea that came to me when I was a nurse at the local hospital. We were understaffed and I had to work seven days a week. I just felt I needed to control my own destiny. So, that's what I did."

Reed was raised by a single mother, Ethel Lidell Taylor, who taught school. "During cotton harvest season, school would let out at twelve and Mom and all the children would go to the fields and pick cotton. I helped Mom since I was four years old because I was the oldest of three children. I helped to cook and take care of the kids. I milked five cows a day and walked five miles to school. . . . Mom died when I was seventeen. She is my inspiration for everything I do. Had she had the opportunities she gave me, she could have gone very far with her life. I'm very proud of her. She's like the wind at my back pushing me on." Reed's daughter is now interning at Mid-Delta, and her husband joined as director of physical facilities several years ago.

To gain a marketing edge over potential competitors, Reed recently put the company through a strenuous accreditation and overall evaluation procedure with CHAPS. The company had to meet 600 very tough standards, and it did. No other home health care company in Mississippi has a CHAPS accreditation.

"Under health reform we will do all right," says Reed. "Hospitals are discharging patients sooner, and that trend will continue. They're discharging maternity patients with C-sections after one day, so we're fixing to introduce a new maternity service. I believe we're well positioned for the future."

Judith Resnick

Name of Company:	Dabney/Resnick, Inc.
Location:	Los Angeles
Date Founded:	1989
Description of Business:	The company is an investment banking, brokerage, and money management firm.
Description of *P*:	Bankrupt and troubled companies are not always dead and buried, although most investors run from them as if they carried the plague. In many instances, a crisis-ridden company represents an opportunity for a keen-eyed manager to turn it around and realize values. Judith Resnick spots the fallen angels from among the dying frogs and invests in them with her firm's and her clients' capital.
Description of *S*:	Collect an experienced team of research professionals that has the skill to locate and evaluate undervalued securities and then market that skill to investors.
Members of *E*:	Neil Dabney, partner David Millison, director of research
Size of V:	Dabney/Resnick, Inc., is a closely held investment banking firm that is not required to publish its financial statements. If its valuation is worth one-tenth of its favorable press, you can be sure that the company is very valuable.
Social Utility:	Board of Directors, City of Hope; La Mission West Childrens Foundation; LA Women's Foundation
Principal Source of Venture Capital:	Self-funded corporation

JUDITH RESNICK was raised in an affluent Los Angeles family. She married and divorced young, raised two teenage daughters, and never worked a day in her life until she was forty-one. Her father died suddenly in 1977, and her sister and mother were killed in a plane crash shortly thereafter. Her father's former partners stopped paying her royalty income from a bowling alley her father had bequeathed to her. Suddenly Resnick was destitute.

She sold her house and lived off the proceeds for a while. Then she looked for work. The problem was she had no work experience; in fact, the only form of work she knew was investing her royalty income. Resnick observed how her broker had continually lost money for her while earning commissions for himself. She knew she could do better than that.

After being turned down by several well-known brokerage houses, a manager at Drexel Burnham Lambert took a chance on her, and Resnick ran with the opportunity.

"I made a list of everyone I knew on the earth and called them,"[1] Resnick said. Then she called people she didn't know. Selling mostly Treasury bonds and municipal bonds, Resnick earned $106,000 in her rookie year. By her third year, she had earned $750,000. "I just didn't have time to make excuses for myself," she says. "I guess I didn't know I was oppressed."

Drexel's sky-rocketing success in the mid-1980s created Resnick's next opportunity. The firm's institutional high-yield desk was doing so much business that small brokerage firms couldn't even get through to place orders. One of those clients was a regional Florida brokerage firm trying to buy 150 bonds in the fall of 1987. The call was passed to the retail side, and Resnick did the trade. "That was when I realized I could put together a dealer desk and give small brokerage firms and investors Drexel's ideas in junk bonds."[2]

Resnick called Drexel's legendary deal-maker, Michael Milken. She told him she could handle small clients like the Florida brokerage and keep them from going to other firms for junk bonds. Two weeks later, Milken hired her. That was early in 1988; in her first year on the job, she sold $200 million in bonds to small institutional clients. She was joined by two high-yield trainees and former institutional salesman Neil Dabney.

Then disaster struck. The Securities & Exchange Commission

---

1. "I Didn't Know I Was Oppressed," *Forbes*, Gretchen Morgenson, March 15, 1993, pp. 140–141.
2. Ibid.

brought the roof down on Drexel. Eight months prior to the SEC investigation, Dabney and Resnick did not like what they saw and decided to open their own firm. A local bank was willing to gamble on them, and several hundred of Resnick's and Dabney's clients were set to move their accounts. Dabney/Resnick was approved by the NASD and opened for business in Beverly Hills in July 1989. The firm consisted of six employees.

Spooked by terrible publicity in the media, the junk-bond market collapsed just after they set up shop. This turned out to be an opportunity in disguise. Most junk bonds had become bargains. While most brokers and most of the business media were telling people to get out of junk bonds, Resnick and Dabney urged their clients to buy. The market rebounded and their clients' returns were phenomenal.

Always conservative, Dabney/Resnick paid off its bank debt after just four months in business. Now, with a couple of years of handsome returns on its high-yield portfolios—up 36 percent in 1991 and 39 percent in 1992—Dabney/Resnick has expanded its money management for high net-worth individuals and corporate finance. Last year, the eighty-person firm traded approximately $2.5 billion in bonds and also advised on about $1 billion in leveraged buyouts, restructurings, and financings.

Neil Dabney attributes his partner's success to this, "Fear of failure or rejections will not enter her mind," he says. "She believes in herself and those around her; that we will succeed even if it looks overwhelming on the surface."[3] Resnick says that raising children alone taught her all that she needed to know about business.

The highly regarded Nelson's "Top 20" Money Managers lists Dabney/Resnick as the second-best performer for the three-year period 1991–1993 with a phenomenal average annual return for their clients of 21.7 percent per annum. The high yield, more than 700 percent better than typical savings accounts' yield over the same period, is attributable to Resnick's faith in her ability, and that of her teammates, to find, analyze, and invest in companies that others give up on.

3. Ibid., p. 141.

Anita Roddick

Name of Company:	The Body Shop, Ltd.
Location:	London
Date Founded:	1976
Description of Business:	Operates a chain of more than 1,000 natural cosmetics retail stores throughout the world.
Description of *P*:	Roddick identified a major paradigm shift among young women consumers who, she believed, sought to make a social awareness statement with their cosmetics purchases. The Body Shop permits its customers to give something back to the planet by buying and using products whose raw materials are farmed and harvested by tribes of poor hunter-gatherers in the underdeveloped regions of the world.
Description of *S*:	The Body Shop promotes human rights, environmental concerns, indigenous rights, and investment in the poorer regions of the world with every sale of its bubble bath and jojoba shampoo.
Members of *E*:	Gordon Roddick, chairman of the board
Size of *V*:	The company achieved a public market for its stock in 1983, and its capitalization in early 1994 was $624 million.
Social Utility:	The list of The Body Shop's socially useful achievements exceeds that of any fifty industrial corporations combined. Here is a sampling:

   * Employees are paid a half-day a month for
     community volunteer time.

                 * The company dispatches employees to
                    rebuild Romanian orphanages.
                 * Body Shop employees replant the cactus
                    that its Mexican Nanhus grow to make
                    sisal sponges.
                 * Customers are encouraged to fill out
                    antitorture and other petitions while
                    shopping.

Principal Source of
Venture Capital: A £4,000 bank loan

ANITA RODDICK is recreating the language of responsible business. The Body Shop's basic business is cosmetics, which solve problems relating to beauty and health. Roddick repackaged them for the soul.

Much of The Body Shop's approach seems aimed at making customers feel good rather than look good. Its packaging shuns elaborate cardboard boxes in favor of simple plastic bottles with plain labels. Customers are encouraged to recycle these bottles by bringing them back for refilling. To further set itself apart, the company sells its products in individual Body Shop stores rather than in department stores or pharmacies. The company has achieved a significant moral victory over its competitors, who have only recently begun to heed the wake-up call in this $20 billion market.

"The Body Shop did sound a wake-up call," says William P. Lauder, general manager of Origins.[1] Lauder, the thirty-one year-old grandson of the company's founder, Estee Lauder, freely acknowledges that some aspects of Origins' business plan, such as donating a portion of its sales to charity, were inspired by The Body Shop. Meanwhile, Estee Lauder is rapidly expanding the number of outlets dedicated to selling Origins. The products went on sale in August 1990, and there are now 100 Origins stores. Estee Lauder has plans for 500 by 1995.

The Body Shop, which opened its first store in the United States in 1988, has also started an ambitious expansion program that calls for 500 stores in three years.

While cosmetics with natural ingredients have long been available from small Mom and Pop stores, Roddick has taken the fad sector mainstream with a duplicable marketing plan.

Roddick is creating an entire generation of consumers who will not

1. Trish Hall, "Striving to be Cosmetically Correct," *The New York Times*, May 27, 1993, p. B-1.

buy a product unless the jar is returnable for refills and the ingredients have botanical names. Animals may not be used to test The Body Shop's products. Employees will not offer customers shopping bags; Body Shop customers know enough to bring their own.

The Body Shop was conceived as a means to make a living. Roddick and her husband, Gordon, presented a business plan to their banker and he loaned them £4,000. They spent six months looking for a small store in Brighton and even longer to locate product.

"This was the hardest thing in the world because I went about it all the wrong way," recalls Roddick.[2] First she tried the big-contract manufacturers. She wrote to them, rang them, and visited them with the raw materials she wanted in the products. But they were interested only in large quantities and she had a total of about £700 to invest. She was forced to consult the Yellow Pages for smaller companies. Here she found a local laboratory that liked the concept and had a very good herbalist who preferred natural ingredients.

Everything was done on a shoestring with no concession to aesthetics. Roddick chose plastic "hospital" bottles because they were so cheap. They painted the shop in green paint because it covered everything, even damp spots.

The Roddicks filled the shop with a small range of preparations, all carefully labeled by hand, and put up a large handwritten notice saying "OPEN."

The first day, they took in £100, more than enough to cover the projections. Feeling confident that his wife could make a go of the store, Gordon left for an eighteen-month horseback ride from Buenos Aires to New York. When he returned to England, a chain was emerging. The image was firmly in place, and Roddick has never diluted it. Her business style is inimitable and her energy is indefatigable.

2. Nicky Smith, "Italian Brio + British Phlegm = The Body Shop," *Working Woman*, November 1984, p. 39.

Barbara Nyden Rodstein

Name of Company:	Hardin Industries, Inc.
Location:	Los Angeles
Date Founded:	1982
Description of Business:	Designs, develops, and manufactures high-quality, solid brass decorative bath fixtures and accessories, which it sells through multiple marketing channels in forty-six countries throughout the world.
Description of *P*:	Economic necessity was the mother of Hardin Industries. Nyden Rodstein's husband's business failed when the bank demanded full repayment of its loan on a Friday in February 1982. "By Monday, we took what little I had in personal savings and started Hardin Industries. It was that or starve," Nyden Rodstein explains.
Description of *S*:	"As an eleven-year-old in Chicago, I collected junk and sold it. I knew that brass only cost a few cents per pound. So, one day, when I priced bathroom fixtures and saw that the brass ones were selling for $350, I told my late husband, 'There's a lot of fluff in this business.' That's how we selected the brass fixture business."
Members of *E*:	Barry Saven, executive vice president Phyllis Schwartz, vice president, Marketing Robert Lutz, vice president, Operations
Size of *V*:	The company is privately held, with sales of $25 million.

Social Utility: Nyden Rodstein is a human buzz saw of
                            community activities, including the American
                            Women's Economic Development Corporation,
                            for which she raises and contributes money to
                            assist young women in completing college and
                            starting businesses. "Our average investment
                            per woman is $140 and their average annual
                            income in their first year of work is $14,000.
                            Now *that's* a rate of return for you," Nyden
                            Rodstein says. She is also a director of the
                            Joffrey Ballet, and her honors have included
                            The Leukemia Society's Woman of the Year
                            and Century City Chamber of Commerce
                            Woman of Achievement awards, among many
                            others.

Principal Source of
Venture Capital: $5,000 in personal savings

My motto is "Just do it," says BARBARA NYDEN RODSTEIN, who launched what
has become the largest manufacturer of decorative brass fixtures in the
world a mere eleven years ago. She had no choice but to just do it because
her late husband's tool manufacturing business had just been shuttered
by its bank.

"But we live in a country where nobody has to stay down. If they
don't want to," Nyden Rodstein contends. "That's what I tell the young
women in the NABW program. Finish school. Get a job. Then pick the
business you would like to go into."

In Nyden Rodstein's case, she picked a very old and established
industry, bathroom faucets and fixtures. Many of her competitors started
more than 100 years ago. "If I operated my business the way they do
theirs, it would take me 100 years to get to where they are. And I don't
have 100 years," she says.

Hardin Industries sells through independent sales reps to more than
2,200 plumbing fixture dealers in the United States, and in the forty-six
countries where the company sells its products, it goes through dealers,
wholesalers, reps, and joint-venture partners depending on the country.
Hardin has five product lines, two of which, Metropolis and Top Brass,
are at the very high end in terms of price points. The Metropolis line is like
artwork; it features an art deco-inspired frosted glass faucet. The other
lines include simple brass faucets, porcelain colonials, and swan-neck
spouts complete with wings.

"Eighty percent of our end users are women," she explains, "and we
know that they like to redecorate every five years. Our marketing pitch is

'Why knock out a wall when you can change faucets and fixtures for less money and still achieve your new look?'

"If we sold to men, we'd be a pretty sorry company. Men walk around in the same suit and tie for years, unless their wives or girlfriends change their outfits. Since many of our competitors are male, they don't understand what we're doing. This has left a very wide niche for us."

Born into a poor but hardworking Chicago family (her father was a truck driver), Nyden Rodstein began working at age 7 delivering newspapers. She soon added watching children to her résumé, then collecting junk and selling it. "When I was fourteen, I lied about my age and got a job in a factory. That's why I've always liked factories."

Two people stand out in her memory as pushing her to do something important with her life. Ms. Cal Markou, her seventh grade teacher, was Nyden Rodstein's most important mentor. "Somebody I really wanted to achieve for," she says. "And my mother was my other great mentor. She encouraged me to read. At one point in my teenage years, I was reading five books a week."

Nyden Rodstein's mother, a waitress, was really quite unusual. "My mother told my siblings and me to pick any religion we wanted. We didn't have to have hers or our father's. But no matter which one we picked, we had to learn it and we had to defend it. She had selected the Baha'i religion; in fact, she was one of the founders of the Chicago chapter." Because she learned it and defended it, Nyden Rodstein, who selected Judaism, is currently taking Hebrew classes with the goal of becoming a Bat Mitzvah.

Nyden Rodstein has been blessed with strong mentors, a working partnership with her husband, and the insight to see a niche in the market of her choice. But she wouldn't have gotten as far as she has, which is literally to the top of the heap and still going, if she hadn't been willing to "just do it."

Fran Sussner Rogers

Name of Company: Work/Family Directions
Location: Boston, Massachusetts
Date Founded: 1983
Description of
Business: This consulting firm helps companies to put together work-family programs.
Description of *P*: Recent statistics indicate that women are better educated than men; more women than men graduate from college and women make better grades than men. But women have fewer employment opportunities because corporate America, which is heavily male-dominated in the power positions, assigns the role of family care to women. These corporate norms, which deny and frustrate the talents and contributions of women in the workplace, represent a serious productivity drain for America.
Description of *S*: There is a great opportunity for the country to increase worker productivity by removing the barriers to contributions by women and parents. Rogers' company trains corporations to adapt to worker needs by introducing dependent-care programs and less-than-full-time hours for women (and men) with parenting responsibilities. It works to remove the cultural barrier that assumes that women with family responsibilities cannot succeed.
Members of *E*:   Charles Rogers, husband and president of the consulting division
                     Phyllis Swersky, president
                     Rebecca Haig, senior vice president

Size of V:	The company is privately held, but its gross income is estimated to be $40 million.
Social Utility:	Rogers gives time and resources to the Children's Defense Fund, the Urban League, civil rights organizations, and the homeless, among other causes.
Principal Source of Venture Capital:	Personal savings

When FRAN SUSSNER ROGERS' first child developed asthma, she had to begin doing part of her work for an educational consulting firm at home. As a result, she was pressured and then written off by the company's executives.

"I knew I could be a good mother and get my work done, but the company didn't," she says. So she began a consulting business of her own from her home. She counseled individuals and companies on resolving conflicts between work and family. The business allowed her more flexibility and control over her life than she had had before and the opportunity to work on issues she cared about deeply.

"We've always said we started out as a mission that became a business. Now we're a business with a mission," she says. When Rogers' children were ages 5 and 2, she moved the business out of her house and into an office building. Today, she and her staff work with more than ninety companies a year. "The desire to get rich or produce a big, successful company was not the goal. It's just a wonderful by-product of doing wonderful work," she says.

Work/Family Directions creates and manages dependent-care programs for more than 100 companies, including IBM, AT&T, and American Express. Services range from advice on where to find appropriate day care and elder care to a counselor-staffed telephone consulting service that helps parents motivate their children, solve learning problems, and select schools. Work/Family also trains managers to be sensitive to family issues and conducts research on the changing demographics of the labor force.

Rogers captured her first big client in 1983 when IBM asked her to develop a nationwide day care referral service for its employees. With start-up funds from IBM, Rogers set up a team and a data base. Soon, other *Fortune* 500 companies knocked on her door. The business, which has offices in San Francisco and Chicago, has grown from eight employees and $2 million in revenues in 1985 to 240 employees and nearly $40 million in revenues in 1993.

"The market for helping employees deal with family issues is pretty big, and it's untapped," Rogers says.

Indeed, only about 7,000 of the 78,000 U.S. companies with more than 100 workers offer employees some form of child care support such as referral services for day care, on-site day care, or after-school programs, according to the Families and Work Institute, a New York research and consulting firm.

Yet child care is a pressing need for many employees. In a 1991–1992 study of ten companies conducted by the Families and Work Institute, 33 percent of employees reported difficulty locating child care.

Child care is just one segment of the market, however. Experts in work and family issues say that the need for elder care will explode in the next decade. About 10 percent of employees today are responsible for an aging relative, says Dana Friedman, co-president of the Families and Work Institute. Based on employee expectations in companies she's surveyed, that figure will jump to 40 percent by 1997. "It is going to be huge," Friedman says. "And we find that there's a more significant work impact from elder care than child care because it's not just [finding] a place to put your elderly relative. It's medical, and legal, and health, and in-home [services], and transportation."[1]

Rogers developed the confidence that it takes to start a business from her mother, who shared responsibilities with her father in a small upholstery business that the couple ran. "They would process the day's requests at dinner and the emphasis was always on customer service," Rogers says. "The other great influence in my life was Eleanor Roosevelt. My family revered her as someone who could make a difference. She visited my home town when I was six years old and she left an indelible impression on me."

1. Elizabeth Levitan Spaid, "Companies Learn to Help Employees With Families," *The Christian Science Monitor*, July 22, 1993, p. 12.

Pleasant T. Rowland

Name of Company:	Pleasant Company
Location:	Middleton, Wisconsin
Date Founded:	1986
Description of Business:	Produces books that serve as the basis for the company's product line of dolls and other accessories that educate young girls about growing up in America in different periods of American history.
Description of *P*:	Toys that are educational and represent positive values are virtually nonexistent.
Description of *S*:	Pleasant Company brings to life the pages of American history through the use of its books and doll collections. Young girls can act out fictional stories with the dolls, clothing, and other accessories that are available through the company.
Members of *E*:	Pleasant Rowland, founder and president
Size of V:	$74 million in sales in 1992
Social Utility:	Pleasant Company incorporates community service as a part of its corporate mission, donating merchandise to various child-related charities in addition to providing young girls with an educational line of toys and books.
Principal Source of Venture Capital:	$1 million in personal savings

From the beginning, PLEASANT ROWLAND was always concerned with children's education. After graduating from Wells College in New York in 1962, Rowland spent six years in the classroom teaching elementary

264

school. She was discouraged by the lack of creativity and simplicity in children's educational textbooks and consequently developed some of her own material combining reading with other language arts.

Following her career as a teacher, Rowland became a television news reporter for KGO-TV in San Francisco. While working on a story about a new bilingual education program, Rowland met a publisher who became interested in the work she had done as a teacher and asked her to develop reading textbooks for his company. From 1971 to 1978, Rowland served as vice president of the Boston Educational Research Company, where she was responsible for creating such best-selling reading programs as *Beginning to Read* and *Write and Listen* (for Macmillan) and *The Addison-Wesley Reading Program* (for Addison-Wesley). Then in 1981 she became the publisher of *Children's Magazine Guide*, which was an index of magazines available for elementary school children. After eight years she decided to sell the magazine to R. R. Bowker because the doll company she had started in 1986 had grown larger than anyone could have ever imagined.

Today Pleasant Company grosses more than $74 million and reaches 19 million homes through catalog circulation. Rowland was inspired to create the American Girl's Collection after taking a trip to Colonial Williamsburg, Virginia. Combining her love for history and a strong belief in the educational value of toys, she invested $1 million of her personal savings to develop an entire package of reading books, dolls, and other accessories for girls from ages 7 through 12 who enjoyed both reading and playing with dolls. For the books she wrote, she initially created three heroines, each of whom lived in a different period of American history. In 1991, she added a fourth. For each one of these heroines, Rowland developed a doll and six different stories about them that focus on family, school, Christmas, birthdays, and summer and winter adventures. In addition, Rowland has created a clothing line for the dolls and matching clothes for the girls who play with them as well.

Although the Barbie doll was invented by a woman, it was acquired by Mattel, which is male-dominated at the top. In fact, the entire doll and toy industry is run by men. When they create a doll for little girls, it is, like Barbie, a highly sexual creation that encourages the little girls who adore it to think of their sexuality long before they reach puberty. "This takes away an important part of their childhood," Rowland says. Her dolls go directly against this trend. They are not sexual objects, but rather instruments of learning and adventure as well as playthings.

On reflection, it is easy to see how the male-run doll and toy companies overlooked this niche. Now they have to play catch-up, a brand-new game for them.

Sue Scott

Name of Company:	Primal Lights
Location:	Emeryville, California
Date Founded:	1986
Description of Business:	Designs, develops, and manufactures novelty, gift, and celebratory lighting that it sells through catalogs and sales representatives.
Description of *P*:	Tired of the same old holiday lights? Sue Scott thought we might be. She has just the cure for unimaginative decorative lighting.
Description of *S*:	Scott blends art, humor, and enterprise in her unusual celebratory and novelty lights by lighting up dinosaurs, lizards, trout, fried eggs, and other items.
Members of *E*:	Lucy Scott, mother, and Cynthia Scott, sister, both of whom have Ph.D.s in psychology.
Size of V:	The company is privately held, with sales approaching $10 million.
Social Utility:	Hardly a day goes by that Scott doesn't bend down to lift up a young woman who wants to do something with her life. She is a mentor in W.I.S.E. (Women's Initiative for Self-Employment), for which she has adopted a woman business owner for a year; she speaks for the San Francisco Renaissance Entrepreneurship Center; has sponsored a Russian businesswoman through the Center for U.S.-U.S.S.R. Initiatives; and has presented a talk in Hungary for the National Women's Economic Alliance Foundation.

Principal Source of
Venture Capital: $25,000 raised on her credit cards

It is intellectually challenging to compare fine artists and entrepreneurs. Both are highly complex and idiosyncratic personality types—very open to experience, highly observant, and prone to seeing things in unusual ways, extremely curious, accepting of unconventional thoughts, appreciative of complexity, highly independent in judgment, thought, and action, self-reliant, and not responsive to group standards and controls. In fact, tell an artist or an entrepreneur that she can't do something and you have touched a nerve that triggers a reflexive, "Heck if I can't. I'll show you!"

But the artist tries to change the world alone, while the entrepreneur brings forth her solutions by working with others. "As an artist," says Sue Scott, "it took me months to complete one of my sculptures. As a businesswoman, I can make things happen in minutes with one phone call. I like the action."

Scott came to entrepreneurship at age 32, following years of sculpting large steel pieces and putting food on the table by working in galleries. "I was making $10 an hour working in a Santa Fe gallery and sculpting at night. The work became a drudge and it began to show in my sculptures. They were dark and heavy. I felt dark.

"I don't know why," she recalls, "but I put a light in my last piece, and that lit a spark somewhere deep inside me. I packed up my kids, dogs, and cats and lit out for San Francisco. In four days I was in business designing lights. The drive to do it was so sudden I named my company after the emotion—primal."

There were voices in Scott's childhood that said, "You can do it, Sue. You don't need a safety net." Her paternal grandmother was "probably one of the first feminists," Scott says. "She worked—bought and sold property." Raised in Appalachia, dirt-poor, she ran away with a traveling salesman, and, six husbands later, settled in Phoenix. Scott was raised in Phoenix under the watchful eye of her grandmother, who explained leverage to the young artist ("who would ever think I would use the word?") and told her to work smart and "don't get suckered."

After designing and producing her first novelty lights in 1986, Scott went to trade shows to display her wares. She signed ninety-five sales representatives across the country to carry her line. Today her largest marketing channel is catalogs, through which she sells everything from Camperland for RV owners, who enjoy lighting up their campsites, to Christmas tree lights for Neiman Marcus. "Entrepreneurship?" muses Scott, "It's like art. Both groups translate chaos into beautiful solutions."

Cheryl Shuman

Name of Company:	Starry Eyes Optical Services, Inc.
Location:	Sherman Oaks, California
Date Founded:	1984
Description of Business:	Designs, develops, and produces eyeglasses and sunglasses for movie stars and movie producers, which it sells to them in their homes and on location. It also sells glasses to the public via infomercials and through the QVC Network, a home shopping cable TV channel.
Description of *P*:	Shuman discovered that celebrities require specialized, personalized, and customized services in purchasing their sunglasses.
Description of *S*:	The public wants to wear the glasses that it sees the stars wear. In a 1992 test run on QVC Network, for instance, in 2½ minutes Shuman sold 5,000 frames of the kind Nick Nolte wore in *Cape Fear*. Shuman has created a market where none existed before.
Members of *E*:	Christine Brown, executive assistant
Size of V:	The company is privately held, with sales of more than $20 million per year.
Social Utility:	Shuman actively supports the Make a Wish Foundation, frequently taking the children to movie sets. She recently donated one dollar of every frame sold on QVC to Midwest Flood Relief.
Principal Source of Venture Capital:	$14,000 borrowed on her credit cards

CHERYL SHUMAN says she is a "terrible businessperson," but in fact her knack for locating niche markets exceeds that of any Armani-clad, kilty-loafered MBA marketing consultant on either coast. "I'm never satisfied with normal. And if you tell me I can't do a certain thing, I'll go out and prove you wrong. I guess that's why I'm a good ferret," says Shuman.

Shuman grew up dirt-poor in London, Ohio. She didn't know she was pretty until she entered a beauty contest in a borrowed dress when she was fourteen and won the $50 first prize. But before that, when she was less than ten, Shuman collected puppies by reading *Pennysaver* ads and sold them to Dr.'s Pet Center, a pet-store chain. Along with crocheting sweaters at night for sale at flea markets and collecting field mice for sale to research labs, Shuman made $12,000 a year. As a young teen, Shuman provided shopping services for her neighborhood by collecting stocks of coupons and buying thousands of dollars of supermarket products at steep discounts. By age 15, she had received national recognition as the "Coupon Queen."

Just as her modeling career was about to hit high gear in 1983 with an invitation to fly to Italy and work for Laura Biagotti, Shuman's car skidded and hit another head-on on her way to the airport. Shuman shattered her face and fractured her leg. She would no longer model.

"I used this near-death experience to think about doing things I should have done sooner. One of these things was to find and meet my natural father," Shuman said. "I found him in Los Angeles. So I packed up my little girl, and off we went. Before I left home at fourteen, my mother had told me to learn a trade. Fortunately, I had an optician's license, which enabled me to get a job fairly quickly in an upscale retail optical store in Los Angeles.

"One day a shabbily dressed black gentleman walked into the store and the other girls wouldn't wait on him. But I did, and he turned out to be Michael Jackson. I could tell he was uncomfortable, so I said, 'Wouldn't you like me to take several dozen pair of sunglasses out to your house so you could make a selection in private?' He said yes. We talked for four hours and I told him my life story. He made some phone calls. And one day a prop manager came into the store and said he was working on a Shirley MacLaine TV miniseries."

That gave Shuman an idea. She said she would come to the set with lots of samples and take orders. He agreed. Shuman quit her job and by taking $14,000 in cash advances on her credit cards and convincing suppliers to give her ninety-day terms, Shuman was in business. She lobbied studios for work, grossing $3,000 in her first month, $14,000 in her second. When she makes a house call or studio call, Shuman charges

$300 per hour and sells an average of six pairs of sunglasses to each customer at around $300 each. Clients have included Denzel Washington, for the glasses he wore in *Malcolm X*, and Arnold Schwarzenegger, who needed twenty pairs of sunglasses for $4,000 plus $2,000 for a day on the set of *Terminator II*.

QVC Network heard about Shuman and signed her to a seven-year contract to be Starry Eyes' exclusive retail outlet. She now sells more eyeglasses and sunglasses in one hour on QVC than the typical optical store sells in a year.

The journey to the top of the fashion eyewear market is only beginning for Cheryl Shuman, but the trek from her dirt-poor home in rural Ohio with the outhouse 100 yards away at this point seems like many lifetimes ago.

Muriel Siebert

Name of Company:	Muriel Siebert & Co.
Location:	New York City
Date Founded:	1967
Description of Business:	The company is a discount stock brokerage firm.
Description of *P*:	Someone once defined a pioneer as a person lying face down in the sand with arrows in her back. Well, Muriel "Mickey" Siebert has many "firsts," but no arrows in her back, though she's heard a few whiz by her ears. Siebert was the first woman partner of a brokerage firm, the first woman to own a stock brokerage firm, the first woman superintendent of New York State's Banking Department (not one single bank failed on her watch), and the first woman to take over a municipal credit union and effect a turnaround.
Description of *S*:	Siebert got the call to service New York State a mere two years into the start-up of her discount brokerage firm. When she returned to her firm five years later, it was in shambles. Three of her employees had walked out with tapes of her customer lists, and she had to rebuild the entire company in every department. Why did she bother to do it a second time? "As the only woman owner of a Stock Exchange firm, I felt an obligation to finish the job I started," Siebert explains.
Members of *E*:	Her team of loyal, experienced employees
Size of V:	The company is privately held and does not publish its financial statements.

Social Utility: In 1990, Siebert established the innovative
                                        Siebert Entrepreneurial Philanthropic Plan
                                        (SEPP) to share with charities half her firm's
                                        net profits from new securities underwritings.
                                        The SEPP plan offers issuers of securities, or
                                        institutional buyers of new issues, the
                                        opportunity to help charities in their
                                        communities by designating the recipient of
                                        the SEPP donation. In 1991, Sepp's first year,
                                        donations totaled $310,000. As of the the
                                        second quarter of 1993, total SEPP donations
                                        approximating $2 million had gone to charities
                                        across the nation. "Society's needs in the
                                        1990s seem overwhelming," Muriel Siebert
                                        says. "However, with a great deal of hard
                                        work and a little luck, I feel that my SEPP
                                        program can make a difference. It is our way
                                        of giving back and helping to make the 1990s
                                        the Decade of Decency."

Principal Source of
Venture Capital: Personal savings

With $500 to her name and no college degree, MURIEL SIEBERT went to Wall
Street in 1954 to become a world-class financier. Merrill Lynch turned her
down. Bache & Co. hired her as a research analyst at $65 per week. Six
years later, she made partner at Stearns & Co.

In 1967, she opened Muriel Siebert & Co., the first woman-owned
brokerage firm. Now, though comfortably situated as chairman and
president of Muriel Siebert & Co., a discount brokerage firm, Siebert
continues to make a point of breaking the rules on Wall Street. There are
no don't-rock-the-boat navy blue business suits for her. She wears
colorful clothes in bold prints, and she has a good reason. "It's an
important part of my business," she says. "I play up to my image. I like
bright clothes and purple dresses and suede pantsuits. I like them and the
press loves it. And it's me anyway."

Her image includes that of outspoken trailblazer. During a recent
financial writers' conference, Siebert recalls, two young women approached
her and said, "It is so nice to have you speak for us." Though they are
infinitely better prepared than she was in 1954, the young women trying to
break into Wall Street have her strong sympathy. "It is very discouraging to
come out of a place like Harvard and not go anywhere," she says.

Having gone "somewhere," Siebert is deeply satisfied with her
accomplishments in the finance industry. "I own myself; nobody else
does," she notes. "That's a pretty good spot to be in."

A favorite word of Mickey Siebert's is "risk." She has advised: "The men at the top of industry and government should be more willing to risk sharing leadership with women and minority members who are not merely clones of their white male buddies. In these fast-changing times we need the different viewpoints and experiences, we need the enlarged talent bank. The real risk lies in continuing to do things the way they've always been done."

Mickey Siebert not only proves what she preaches, but she *practices* it too. "Risk" could be her middle name. Her best-known gamble made historic waves in 1967 when she applied to become the first woman member of the New York Stock Exchange. Although she had risen to a partnership in a leading Wall Street brokerage firm, and had made big money for colleagues, her effort was patronized, ridiculed, or openly opposed by many men on Wall Street. She was turned down by nine of the first ten men she asked to sponsor her application.

Before considering her for membership, the Stock Exchange imposed a new condition: She needed a letter from a bank saying that it would lend her $300,000 of the near-record $445,000 seat price. But banks would not commit themselves to lending her the money until the Stock Exchange first agreed to admit her! It took many months to overcome this double bind and find the needed bank loan and sponsors. Siebert was finally elected to membership on December 28, 1967. On December 28, 1992, she celebrated her twenty-fifth anniversary.

Siebert is a founding member of The Women's Forum, an organization of 250 preeminent women in the New York area that has expanded into an international leadership network. Among the honors she has gained, Siebert has received the Financial Women's Association's Community Service Award for her SEPP program; New York City's Lifetime Achievement Award; the Benjamin Botwinick Prize in Business Ethics awarded by Columbia Business School in recognition of her SEPP program, and to honor an individual in business who exemplifies the highest standards of professional and ethical conduct; the White House Conference on Small Business Award for Entrepreneurial Excellence; the first national Emily Warren Roebling Award from the National Woman's Hall of Fame; the Equal Opportunity Award of the NOW Legal Defense and Education Fund; the Spirit of Achievement Award of Albert Einstein College of Medicine; the Outstanding Contributions to Equal Opportunity for Women Award of the Business Council for the United Nations Decade for Women; the Women's Equity Action League Achievement Award; and the YWCA Elizabeth Cutler Morrow Award. And in 1992, she became the first woman fellow at NYU's Stern School of Business.

Although she never graduated from college, Siebert has been awarded eight honorary doctorates.

Judy Sims

Name of Company:	Software Spectrum Corp.
Location:	Garland, Texas
Date Founded:	1983
Description of Business:	The company is a leading national reseller of microcomputer business software and a provider of related technical services. The company's customers are primarily large corporations with a significant number of microcomputers.
Description of *P*:	Information-based products—those that require technical services and training—are the razors and blades of today's marketplace. Sims recognized this need as the microcomputer marketplace was developing.
Description of *S*:	Software Spectrum provides product sales and technical support through a superbly trained field sales force located in twenty-nine cities near the company's 5,100 corporate clients.
Members of *E*:	Richard G. Sims, president Roger J. King, vice president, Sales
Size of V:	The company's 4,144,959 shares traded over the counter in early 1994 at a market value of $67.3 million.
Social Utility:	Member of the International Woman's Forum and the Young Presidents Organization. On the advisory board for the Center for Nonprofit Management. On the board of directors for Girls Incorporated of Metropolitan Dallas.

Principal Source of
Venture Capital: The company raised approximately $2.5 million
                                    in venture capital from Summit Ventures,
                                    Geocapital, and other funds after an initial
                                    $40,000 investment.

JUDY SIMS, a certified public accountant by training, rose through the ranks
from 1977 to 1985 to become the first woman audit partner with the firm of
Grant Thornton. Her husband, Richard, also a CPA, left his position as
controller of International Power Machines in 1983 to launch the company. Judy also participated in the start-up on weekends, holidays,
vacations, and in the evenings. She followed her $40,000 investment and
joined up full-time in 1985.

On an economic battlefield strewn with the wreckage of numerous
computer software distributors, the Simses discovered the solutions
required by their clients and responded to them by fielding a well-trained
sales and technical support team. Today, with sales exceeding $219
million, the company has more than 400 employees, of whom 200 are
administrative, service, and support personnel, 70 are in telemarketing
and customer service, 60 are integrated service personnel, 40 are account
executives, and 30 are marketing and sales administration personnel.
Name another company in which more than 90 percent of the personnel
are in sales and service!

The company works on very narrow profit margins: 13.4 percent in
1992, up from 12.9 percent in 1991 and 12.4 percent in 1990. These narrow
margins do not permit much room for error. Competitors with retail
selling space to pay for cannot meet Software Spectrum's prices.

But selling microcomputer software is not like selling TV sets or
electronic appliances. Computers can be made obsolete by their manufacturers on a few months' notice. Software Spectrum maintains very low
inventory levels, having only twenty-two days of inventory on hand in
1992.

Where did Sims develop such a sharp pencil and so acute a knowledge of marketing computer software? While attending Texas Tech
University, Sims worked one summer in a tiny Fort Worth tuxedo rental
shop. Rather than wait for customers to come into the shop, Sims studied
the society pages, noting which couples announced their engagements,
then calling on them to pitch rental formal wear from her shop. The tactic
worked well, and Sims pulled it out of her memory bank when she
adopted the idea of selling software door to door to large corporations.
She started cold-calling on local businesses and landed Dallas-based

Electronic Data Systems early on. GTE, Mobil Oil, and others followed suit.

By streamlining the entire software procurement process and offering competitive pricing coupled with a high level of services, Software Spectrum saves its customers time and money and eliminates many of the problems commonly encountered in the microcomputer software environment. Software Spectrum adapts its procurement services to the specific purchase procedures requested by its customers and provides accurate and timely delivery of products. Software Spectrum is the leader in providing corporations with a comprehensive plan to achieve customers' software management goals. Software Spectrum created ASSURANCE, a PC software management process and the corresponding implementation services to help customers optimize the advantages of the right-to-copy license agreements that are available from many software publishers. Among its other services, the company offers its customers software selection assistance, technical support, publications containing timely product and software industry information, product research, upgrade assistance, and an extensive series of seminars, networking, and application development.

"You've got to stay focused on your mission to make it in this market," says Sims. And door-to-door selling is her mission.

Patricia Pompili Sklar

Name of Company:	Landmark General Corporation
Location:	Novato, California
Date Founded:	1979
Description of Business:	The company sells calendars.
Description of *P*:	Calendars used to be given away by businesses for promotional purposes.
Description of *S*:	When Patricia Sklar and Spencer Sokale got together to look at some pictures that Sokale owned of the building of the Golden Gate Bridge, the beauty of the pictures inspired them to turn them into a calendar and start their retail calendar company.
Members of *E*:	Spencer Sokale, co-founder John Draper, chief executive officer
Size of *V*:	1992 gross revenues were estimated at $20 million.
Social Utility:	Many of the Landmark calendars are devoted to health issues, wildlife issues, and the environment. Proceeds from the various calendars are donated to appropriate charitable causes.
Principal Source of Venture Capital:	$10,000 borrowed from private sources and paid back in one year

PATRICIA SKLAR was born and raised in San Francisco. After attending the San Francisco College for Women, where she earned her degree in elementary education, she found a job teaching grade school. During her years as a teacher she met her husband and ended up putting him through school and helping him to start a business. Nine years later, she divorced him. By this time, she realized, her husband controlled everything—all the money and all the decisions. She had given all the financial responsibility to him. She had always wanted to get into business because she saw it as the only means of making more money. After the divorce, this seemed the only alternative.

Sklar says that her mother was a role model for her. "We never really had money when I was growing up. My mother always worked. She had to. She was a waitress, banker, bookkeeper, and even worked in collections. She really held the family together. My father worked nights as a bartender." Sklar embraced her mother's tenacious work ethic and, with her partner, Spencer Sokale, incorporated Landmark General in 1979.

An entrepreneur at heart, Sokale had been trying to sell Golden Gate Bridge memorabilia, namely pieces of the cable wire used to support the massive structure mounted on wood. While she was a teacher, Sklar had her own little venture going. She was trying to produce her very own roller disco review show. However, she encountered unforeseen costs and decided to get out of it while she could. This made Sklar cautious in the calendar venture. Sklar and Sokale did not spend a single penny until they had received at least 17,000 orders from local San Francisco shops. "I knocked on every door until I got the orders I wanted," she says. They did, and within a short time Sokale's beautiful pictures of the construction of the Golden Gate Bridge had become a huge calendar success. With a lot of work, Landmark Calendars was on its way.

"It was not easy," says Sklar. "We had a hard time getting a handle on operations. There were all kinds of challenges. We had computer transition problems. Financing problems." However, Sklar says, "Business is problem solving." If business is problem solving, Sklar has shown herself to be a solution producer. Today she says that she has a "well-run" operation. She has learned to be an effective and efficient manager. "We take care of business. We are also cautious and pay close attention to the economy. . . . You just have to do what it takes and be creative."

With a line of more than 350 calendars today, Landmark has proved its creativity and ability to stay on top of current trends. She and Sokale have also shown their concern for the greater community by donating a portion of the proceeds from sales of calendars devoted to health issues, the environment, and wildlife preservation to various funds and awareness-raising organizations. Sklar, who grew up in San Francisco, cradle of the 1960s, says: "For the last few years, the crises we've seen in this country seem to be bringing out the best in people. They're volunteering and getting involved more than has been seen in a long time. We feel that by donating proceeds to worthy causes, we're doing our part as business executives and concerned individuals."

Betty Smulian

Name of Company:	Trimble House Corp.
Location:	Atlanta
Date Founded:	1962
Description of Business:	Designs, develops, and manufactures quality outdoor commercial lighting as well as gaslights for the traditional market.
Description of *P*:	Betty Smulian was looking for a certain chandelier for her home in 1962 but couldn't find it.
Description of *S:*	An industrial designer by training, she bought the necessary raw materials and bent, hammered, sawed, and soldered her own chandelier.
Members of *E:*	Jim Smulian, president, who came into the business after it was taking off
Size of V:	The company is privately held, with sales in excess of $10 million.
Social Utility:	Smulian has numerous community service interests, including a board membership on the Georgia Chamber of Commerce, the International Business Fellows, the First Union Bank-Atlanta, and the American Jewish Committee.
Principal Source of Venture Capital:	Personal savings of $5,000

BETTY SMULIAN is the firstborn child of two firstborn parents and today her firstborn son is actively involved in Trimble House. "I believe more is expected of firstborn children. They are prepared for greater responsibility, and they shoulder it."

Nepotism is supported and endorsed in women-owned businesses. "Sons and fathers sometimes don't get along well in business, but sons and mothers are a great team. We believe in nepotism," says Smulian, echoing the philosophy of literally dozens of women entrepreneurs with adult children.

Smulian was one of the first women to earn a bachelor of science degree in industrial design, which she earned in her hometown of Philadelphia at the University of Pennsylvania. She married Jim Smulian after graduating and, she explains, "We moved to Atlanta because it looked like a good place to start a family."

Smulian's father was treasurer of Pep Boys and, according to Smulian, "My mother tackled every community service in town—the Temple, PTA, Hadassah—she was constantly in motion. I was very close with my aunts and uncles as well, and they worked too. Everyone I knew was busy." And Smulian is a busy businesswoman today, in her thirty-first year captaining her own ship. Trimble House branched away from the residential lighting market in the 1960s to move exclusively into commercial outdoor lighting. It now has thousands of accounts throughout the country, served by the company's sixty employees. It recently launched a line of traditional gaslit lanterns, which it sells through public utilities.

Linda D. Sonntag

Name of Company:	SyStemix, Inc.
Location:	Palo Alto, California
Date Founded:	1988
Description of Business:	Pioneering new therapies that harness the body's hematopoietic (blood-forming) cells to treat disease. SyStemix is developing proprietary cellular processes and products that capitalize on the ability of purified populations of hematopoietic cells to restore an array of disease-free, vital cells to patients whose blood and immune cells are diseased, damaged, or destroyed.
Description of P:	The problems for which SyStemix is seeking solutions include bone-marrow, breast, ovarian, and other forms of cancer; blood-borne genetic disorders; AIDS; and other autoimmune disorders.
Description of S:	The company was granted a fundamental patent for the separation of stem cells from bone marrow and for the cells' composition. These cells are believed to be the "parent" cells of all blood cells, including immune system cells, red blood cells, and platelets.
Members of E:	Linda M. Burch, vice president, Business Development John Schwartz, senior vice president and general counsel Ron Hoffman, M.D., vice president—Research John Gardner, Ph.D., vice president—Development

	Hugh Lewis, vice president—Operations Didier Lanson, Ph.D., vice president—European Operations
Size of V:	The company's revenues are around $7 million per year, derived primarily from lab tests. Its market value was $179 million in late 1993.
Social Utility:	Board member, San Francisco Film Society; trustee, University of California Art Museum. Sonntag supports a variety of social causes near and dear to her.
Principal Source of Venture Capital:	Capital gains from her previous venture and personal savings

Sometimes entrepreneurial companies' darkest nights end with their brightest days. Operating with just $181,000 in cash in March 1991, SyStemix raised $38 million in an initial public offering six months later. One month later, the U.S. Patent Office granted the company a patent on *the* hematopoietic stem cell. Then, two months later, in December 1991, Sandoz, the Swiss pharmaceutical giant, bought 60 percent of SyStemix for $392 million. To find the source of this incredible run of good fortune, look no further than the company's chief executive officer, LINDA D. SONNTAG. "My father escaped Nazi Germany in 1936 and emigrated to South Africa, where I was born and raised," Sonntag said. "He saw oppression and other images and events in South Africa that must have reminded my father of Germany, because he continually told his children to prepare ourselves with the skills to be able to leave some day. Our passport was education."

A native of South Africa, Sonntag earned a Ph.D. from the University of Witwatersrand and studied at the Weizmann Institute in Israel. At the age of twenty-five, Sonntag was a professor of genetics. She did further post doctoral work at the University of California, San Francisco with Dr. Herbert Boyer, the co-founder of Genentech, Inc. Sonntag was given business responsibilities along with scientific duties at Agrigenetics Research Corp. "She learned fast," said David J. Padwa, Sonntag's boss at Agrigenetics. "Coming out of an R&D environment, Linda was negotiating contracts, talking to financial guys, and dealing with business issues better than most nonscientific people ever dreamed they could do. We knew she would run her own company some day. It was just a matter of time."

"David Podwa trusted me with responsibilities beyond my skills at the time," Sonntag said. "He was a terrific mentor to me. He put opportunities in front of me."

The success of SyStemix bodes well for the eventual victory of scientists armed with genetic engineering skills in combat with autoimmune disorders and various cancers. The company's fundamental work is in using the body's own cells to fight disease. The immediate goal is to isolate a patient's stem cells and then grow them outside the body, where they can be coaxed into differentiating and/or being genetically modified with inserted genes. This technology ultimately aims to develop universal donor cells, enabling a cell-farming industry that will cryogenically bank cells for emergency needs. Presently, the company has a mouse model that is proving effective in investigating the pathogenesis of HIV infection. The company's mouse is the only animal model now available to study HIV infection in the setting of human organs.

Deborah Szekely

Name of Company:	Rancho la Puerta, Tecate, Baja California, Mexico, 1940 Golden Door, Escondido, California, 1958 The Eureka Foundation, Washington, D.C., 1990
Location:	See above.
Date Founded:	See above.
Description of *P*:	"It used to be that people needed to learn about fitness and living healthful lives. Today, it's all about survival," says Deborah Szekely.
Description of *S*:	With the help of her husband, Ms. Szekely founded a summer camp in Tecate, Mexico, dedicated to the study of exercise, nutrition, and serene living—a philosophy inspired by a sect of Dead Sea Essenes. Originally called the Essene School of Life, the camp became known as Rancho la Puerta. Eighteen years later, the Szekelys opened Golden Door, guided by the same principles. From helping individuals sustain their own lives, Deborah Szekely founded the nonprofit Eureka Foundation, dedicated to sustaining the community at large by supporting disadvantaged children and families in inner cities.
Members of *E*:	Deborah Szekely, founder and president, the Eureka Foundation Edmond Szekely, co-founder of Rancho la Puerta and Golden Door Alex Szekely, president, Rancho la Puerta and Golden Door Livia Szekely, landscape and architecture consultant

Size of V:	The two spas are privately held. The company does not disclose any financial information. The Eureka Foundation's CEOs cumulatively manage budgets in excess of $101 million.
Social Utility:	Whether building profitable companies or nonprofit organizations, Ms. Szekely works in human services. When the Inter-American Foundation needed a new chief, she sought and won the job over many other experienced executives. As IAF boss, she searched Latin America and the Caribbean for the best self-help groups that work to aid the poor on survival strategies, family life, and overall community reinforcement. She is a principle delegate (representing the United States) to the Inter-American Commission on Women. Among the many leading nonprofit boards on which Ms. Szekely serves are: the Center for Science in the Public Interest, the National Council of La Raza, Partners for Livable Communities, Youth Service America, and the Women's Economic Alliance. She is an honorary board member of the San Diego Center for Children and a national sponsor of the Save the Children Federation.
Principle Source of Venture Capital:	The Rancho la Puerta spa was funded by the couple's personal holdings and investments.

"The first third of life is devoted to being a child, growing and learning in school and at home. The next is spent working hard as you can and being rewarded for it. The final third is perhaps the most important: taking a role in making the world better for the next generation. It's something that has always been the work of the elders in any society," says DEBORAH SZEKELY, founder of the world-renowned Rancho la Puerta and Golden Door spas and now of the Eureka Foundation.

Szekely has overachieved on each of life's three stages because she plunged into each stage with her unique and explosive mix of energy, innovation, and insight. Growing up in Tahiti, she learned as a child the mature "pleasure of being helpful." With her mother, a registered nurse, she constantly went deep into the back country to help native people live more wholesome and spiritual lives, and eat natural, healthy, growing things. "I grew up a fruiterian," she says. Schooled early in the mysterious interaction of mind and body, she cultivated a kind of second sight that later inspired novelist/scientist Aldous Huxley to use Deborah and her brother as the models for the athletic young psychics in *The Island*, the novel that became a founding document in the human potentials movement. She learned early to combine scientific medicine with healthy lifestyling and inner healing.

Her work and her rare vitality came to the attention of Hungarian philosopher Edmond Szekely, who studied natural living experiments all over the world, and found nature's best in Tahiti. At thirty-five, he fell in love with Deborah, who was seventeen. In 1940, newly wed, Deborah found herself in California headed south to the border in her vintage (1928) Cadillac, loaded down and on the way to meet her husband in Tecate, Baja California. She drove up to her new home, a one-room hut, ten feet by thirty, hunkered down in the middle of a vineyard called Rancho la Puerta. The hut had holes for windows, one door, and a dirt floor. Rent was $10 a month. When cows hungrily rubbed up against the walls at night, the Szekelys discovered their hut had once been used to store hay. Now it served as the management base for The Essene School of Life, a pioneer American spa of Spartan simplicity: "$17.50 per week; bring your own tent; no running water; no electricity; neither gym nor swimming pool, but a great mountain for climbing plus a river for swimming; goats (no lactose) for milk and cheese; an exciting organic vegetable garden—the West Coast's first, yielding a generous harvest." Spreading the word of their experiment in harmonious living with nature—everything from herb tea/fruit juice drinks to biofeedback eventually got pre-tested there—the Szekelys poured out ideas in a monthly newsletter for $6 a year. By the end of World War II, over 100 members had signed up in half a dozen countries and came in each summer for the six-week program. Most of the nutritional, meditative, and lifestyle habits later adopted by several hundred growth centers and now by hundreds of U.S. spas started there or got some of their earliest tests there.

In 1958, the Szekelys opened a posh new spa, Golden Door, an hour or two north up in Escondido, California, now just west of I-15. Since Rancho la Puerta had been upgraded by years of improvements, guests at both spas now paid $250 a week. U.S. leaders and their wives, film stars, government officials, Fortune 500 company executives, and the press often got to know one another by spending a week together at the Door. With their privacy always protected, never leaked to gossip media, an international network of Deborah's friends began to form a kind of innovative underground. People who had shared the tortures of sore muscles and 1200-calorie days developed lasting friendships.

Then, in 1969, the California Commissioner of Highways came with a big check and an invitation to retire early. Under eminent domain, Ms. Szekely was informed, her Golden Door would be shut down. Against the advice of her bankers, accountants, friends, and family, she made a startling decision. As she recalls it, "Newly divorced, soon to be fifty, sole support of two children, and in my hand a tempting pot of gold from the State of California—I chose to risk all. I put everything I had on the line, and then borrowed $2 million more [a considerable sum in those days] to create the foremost Japanese inn and garden outside of Japan, again against counsel, for this was a time when Japan was not viewed with respect." Like other entrepreneurs studied by researchers, Ms. Szekely is not a risk-seeker but a visionary driven by an idea that needs to come into being. Entrepreneurs hate risks but beat the odds by extra effort and genius.

Golden Door, on 177 acres of awesome beauty, grows its own organic fruit and vegetables and glorious flowers. For thirty-five years, its inner circle of steady friends around the world have even shared its line of non-allergenic, totally fresh cosmetics, actually cosmeceuticals. If you don't use up a $45 vial of skin cream in a year, they refill for free. These spa-healthy skin-builders are dated like milk and contain not only the traditional biologicals like aloe vera, but the most advanced, new scientific discoveries like AHA, the Alpha Hydroxy Acids. In survey after survey, the Door wins out as the world's premier fitness spa. Other entrepreneurs who found spas tend, in prudence, to hire away a Door-trained manager or chef, rather like a vineyard manager taking his cuttings from a famous variety of grape. In her book *Secrets of the Golden Door*, Ms. Szekely reveals the spa foods that she and her innovative chefs have developed to keep healthy eating from being a pain or a bore.

When she turned sixty, Ms. Szekely turned the spas over to her children. She had a new vision of her mission, in the volunteer sector. Like many businesspeople, she'd already done years of community leadership work, and like many other entrepreneurs, she is more a builder of organizations, an innovator, than a money zealot. She heard about—and captured—a tough job as boss of the Inter-American Foundation. The IAF, then little known, was set up by Congress to encourage the self-help movements so desperately needed by poor people in the Caribbean and Latin America. Ms. Szekely is an expert in nonprofit strategy, with a rare gift for spotting ways to help people help themselves, fulfilling their own potential by working with others. When she resigned as CEO of IAF in 1990, she shocked friends with her firm resolve to apply the lessons she'd learned south of the border to the inner cities right here in the United States. "My time in Washington proved as energizing and joyous as my early years at Rancho la Peurta because—to my delight—my contribution to this Inter-American funding/learning laboratory was every bit as needed as rewarding," she says, just stating the facts. "It was my own learning lab for my next endeavor."

Next was the Eureka Foundation, based on a fresh strategy. With her practiced eye, she tracked the best models of inner-city human service organizations, everything from homes for the homeless groups to child care. In a parallel but similar search, she set up ways to identify the strongest natural leaders, often people struggling without adequate organization, know-how, or confidence. Then she brought the two together so that the best executives could go train themselves in the best organizations, wherever they were. Each city's crop of Eureka-picked managers or leaders—called Fellows—go to the best of the organizations as tuition-paying learners who then keep in touch with their teachers when they go back to their own cities. With fifty-four of her Eureka Fellows now graduated and going full blast in Los Angeles, Detroit, and San Diego, Ms. Szekely's Washington-based Eureka headquarters now works with more than eighty model agencies in twenty-five states, plus Washington D.C., Puerto Rico, and Vancouver. Beaming with her seventy-two years of vibrant living, Deborah Szekely lays it on the line: "I am reenergized as I watch Eureka building neighborhoods one leader at a time. Solutions to the problems that plague the inner cities are within reach and, where once I was committed to spreading the doctrine of fitness, today I work with equal dedication for this nonprofit 501C3. It is the simplest, most effective, and least expensive solution that I know of to the loss of the extended family. We're nourishing the root system: our young."

Heida Thurlow

Name of Company:	Chantal Cookware Corp.
Location:	Houston
Date Founded:	1971
Description of Business:	Manufactures high-quality enamel-on-steel cookware, sold at fine department specialty stores throughout the world.
Description of P:	From her own experience in the kitchen, Thurlow was frustrated with the quality of cookware available in the United States. She didn't want to choose between beauty and function; she wanted both.
Description of S:	After sampling the various models of German enamel-on-steel cookware in her own kitchen, Thurlow was able to design her ideal set of cookware, one that combined elegance and utility with the highest quality enamel-on-steel.
Members of E:	Heida Thurlow, president
Size of V:	1992 sales were over $10 million. Consumer products companies whose products catch on in the market are frequently valued at prices in excess of their revenues by the public or by strategic acquirers.
Social Utility:	Chantal has discontinued its red enamel cookware because of the effects the production of this color has on the environment. They only use recycled paper. Chantal also offers a no-smoking clinic to employees and offers employment to visually impaired and sheltered women trying to get back on their feet. The company has an extensive in-house recycling program.

Principal Source of
Venture Capital: Start-up capital provided when Heida sold her company back to the family for $25,000, plus a $50,000 bank loan secured through a woman loan officer.

Leaving West Germany to be with her husband, HEIDA THURLOW moved to Houston in 1971. Before coming to the United States, Thurlow had completed a degree in mechanical engineering and economics and worked in her parents' company, which made refractory materials that lined furnaces used to melt steel. From the earliest age, Thurlow had watched and learned from her mother's unyielding drive and energy. Thurlow characterizes her mother as a "fighter." "She would always say 'Where there is a will, there is a way.' I'm the same way." And a fighter she is. Always dreaming of starting and running her own company, Thurlow tried her hand at importing hand-painted dinnerware from Argentina and selling it to stores such as Pier 1 Imports. Within a short time, because of economic problems in Argentina, Thurlow was forced to move on. Now a single parent with two kids, Thurlow had to find a job that was going to help pay the bills. When she tried to apply for a job as a mechanical engineer, she was rejected by her male American contemporaries and could not find a job in her field of study. That did not stop Thurlow. She quickly went back to importing. This time she tried clay baking dishes from Germany, but this enterprise also failed, as her main supplier went out of business.

A fighter and an entrepreneur at heart, Thurlow forged ahead and sought out new ideas for a business. Frequenting cookware stores and department stores, she noticed that there was only one U.S. manufacturer of the enamel-on-steel cookware that was so popular in Germany. Instead of importing the pots from Germany to be sold, Thurlow ordered samples from every manufacturer of enamel-on-steel cookware in Germany and tested each one herself. She found that the most useful and durable of the pots were ugly and that the most beautiful pots weren't practical. Combining the best features of the pots she had tested and developing some new feature improvements herself, Heida Thurlow created her ideal set of cookware, which combined "elegance with function" in the highest-quality enamel-on-steel.

But this did not happen quickly or easily. "They laughed at me," says Thurlow, who went from bank to bank trying to secure a loan. "It did not stop me. I just kept on looking until I finally found a woman loan officer who believed that a woman could start her own business, and I got a $50,000 loan." Thurlow adds an interesting aside: "Out of all the banks that I had gone to, the only one that is still in business today is the bank that had made me my initial loan." Thurlow used the money to develop a roaster and steamer, and when she brought the prototype to the best enamel-on-steel producer in Germany, they too laughed at her and told her that her design of stainless steel handles could not be realized. She found out later that they simply did not want to change their ways. When she finally had her first finished product in hand, its lid was from Japan, its handles were from Scandinavia, and the pot itself was made in Germany. All three parts were assembled in Houston. Now that she had a product the problem was how to market it. Thurlow describes the market as "very difficult." She had a very hard time getting anyone to buy her new roaster and steamer and had to rent a stand at a local flea market to sell the leftover inventory from her import business in order to stay afloat.

But Thurlow believed in herself and her product and did not give up. She says, "It's so easy to quit; success often takes longer than you had ever expected. But the longer you stay with it, the more you learn about the different angles of it. If things do not seem to work one way, you begin to ask yourself, 'How about this way?' and before you know it you know more about the business than your competitors do." This fierce determination brought her to Chicago in 1979 and got her noticed at her first trade show. Thurlow remembers: "The first day I got there I had a small booth, and not a single person stopped by to look at my roasters." She knew that she did not have the name or the size to get noticed so she tried a different approach. "That night I went to Michigan Avenue and bought the most outrageous outfit that I could find. The next day I wore it, and everyone stopped by my booth to comment on it, and I would say 'Well, how about looking at my roasters too?' " Her strategy worked and got the attention of Chuck Williams, head of the Williams-Sonoma gourmet cookware chain. Williams placed an order for several hundred pieces, giving Heida Thurlow the break that she was waiting for. A few years later, the full line of Chantal Cookware was introduced. Today there are over 300 pieces in the Chantal line in six enamel colors plus stainless steel. It is the leading enamel-on-steel cookware in the United States and is popular in Europe and Japan as well.

As the first woman CEO of a cookware company, Thurlow has this advice for young women entrepreneurs: "Stop waiting for someone else to do it for you. Take a calculated risk, do a little research. Develop a good rapport with a bank that you know has a history of lending money to small businesses. You may not need it at first, but you may need it later. Believe in yourself and your idea and 'Just do it!' " If there was ever an example of how persistence pays, it is the story of Heida Thurlow.

Susie Tompkins

Name of Company:	Esprit de Corps
Location:	San Francisco
Date Founded:	1968
Description of Business:	Designs, develops, and produces classic apparel for teenagers, women's and children's shoes, and, most recently, a line of women's apparel that it sells through thirty-one company-owned as well as franchised stores and in more than one hundred Esprit boutiques within upscale department stores.
Description of P:	The company was the first apparel firm to capture the spunky, youthful, carefree look of California kids. It was the first environmentally conscious firm using naturally colored cotton, low-impact dyes, chemical-free finishes, and economically disadvantaged artisans.
Description of S:	It reinvented fashion advertising by using youthful employees rather than models in its ads. Sales grew to nearly $1 billion.
Members of E:	Corrado Federico, president
Size of V:	The company is privately held and not required to publish financial information.
Social Utility:	Through direct employee involvement and with its profits, the company promotes environmental auditing, meals for hundreds of AIDS victims, the suicide crisis line, tutoring refugees, and counseling homeless youth.
Principal Source of Venture Capital:	Personal savings initially; twenty years later, she dug into her savings once again to fund a buyout.

SUSIE TOMPKINS started Esprit de Corps in 1968 delivering products out of her station wagon. A year later, her husband, Doug, joined the firm. Susie gave the company its designs and her remarkable sense of color and style and, most important, its mission. Although socially responsible marketing statements are in vogue in the 1990s, they were way out ahead of the times back in 1968. Doug gave the company its business leadership. The two were generally considered the most successful business couple in the country as sales broke through the $800 million mark by the early 1980s.

The company slumped in 1987 when manufacturing costs got out of hand and consumers did not respond to concomitant higher prices. Esprit was unprepared for the slide because it had sunk its capital into opening more than thirty expensive, new, free-standing stores.

Doug and Susie began arguing openly over the direction, management, and objectives of the company. Susie argued that the Esprit customer was now an adult and that the company should follow her apparel needs. Doug held onto the goal of serving a continuous supply of youthful customers. The dispute carried over into their marriage, which fizzled. In March 1988, *The Wall Street Journal* gave a blistering report of Doug's notorious office affairs. The board asked both of them to step down and moved Corrado Federico up to CEO. Susie took a two-year vacation from Esprit. Each continued to own half interest in the company.

In 1989, Susie agreed to give Doug a four-month option to raise the necessary financing to buy her out. She contested the appraised value, and the board gave them an ultimatum: One 50 percent owner had to buy out the other or they would put the company on the auction block.

Major international apparel companies circled Esprit like piranha moving in on a dying cow. In the eleventh hour, Susie raised the necessary financing and took control, becoming the major shareholder in the process.

Can entrepreneurs do it the second time around? There have been a few, but you can count them on the fingers of one hand. Susie took over in the middle of an economic crisis that was followed by the recession of 1991. She swiftly closed stores and refocused the company according to her vision. The employees, who yearned for her return, fastened onto that vision. She is clearly the glue that makes Esprit work. Happily, the company rebounded and is reporting upticks in sales and cash flow to the enthusiastic applause of her employees, customers, and investors.

Maria Elena Torano

Name of Company: Maria Elena Torano and Associates

Location: Miami

Date Founded: 1980

Description of
Business: Provides management consulting and environmental cleanup services to corporations and government agencies.

Description of *P*:   The essence of the economic justification for the management consultant is that bureaucratic underlings are afraid to tell their bosses that they are out of step with reality for fear of losing their jobs or, at a minimum, their vertical mobility. An outside consultant can bring a fresh, truthful report to the organization, thus circumventing the barriers that prevent change and innovation from occurring. The greater the complexity of a situation, the greater the need for a consultant and the higher its fees. Torano takes on the toughest problems in the nation and succeeds at solving them.

Description of *S*:   Torano brings solutions to the problem of unwinding the savings and loan mess and to the environmental cleanup problem.

Members of *E*:   Ed Romero, mentor and owner of one of the largest Hispanic-owned companies in the country

Size of *V*:   1992 revenues are believed to be $15.4 million.

Social Utility: Torano is dedicated to helping Hispanic women. She is the founding chair of the National

Hispana Leadership Institute, director of the
U.S. Hispanic Chamber of Commerce,
founding member and officer of Hispanic
PAC, director of the Latin American
Management Association, an appointed
member of the U.S. Commission on Minority
Business Development, and a member of the
Smithsonian Institution Task Force on Latino
Issues.

Principal Source of
Venture Capital: A $20,000 SBA mini-loan

MARIA ELENA TORANO says it's all about *coraza*, which, translated into English,
means "armor." To understand what Torano means, one must examine
the life she has led. Born in Havana, Cuba, Torano says she learned to be
a strong woman from her mother. In 1959, when Fidel Castro took over
Cuba, she was living with her husband at her family's home in Boca
Ciega, some 30 miles from Havana. Their Cuban-style home had recently
been expanded to accommodate the two families. However, on Mother's
Day that year, Castro's soldiers raided her family's home, taking away all
their possessions. Her father, a government official, had no recourse
because the revolutionaries were now in charge.

As life in Cuba became more and more intolerable, Torano and her
husband, Arturo, moved to Florida. Recruited by the CIA, Torano's
husband and brother joined forces with other anti-Castro nationalists to
form an army of exiles called La Brigada 2506. They were sent to
Guatemala to be trained for an air and sea attack on Cuba that was
intended to oust Fidel Castro. On April 17, 1961, five ships set sail
from Nicaragua and arrived at Bahia de Cochinos, better known as the
Bay of Pigs. Unfortunately, the American air support never came and
most of La Brigada 2506, including Torano's husband and brother,
were captured and imprisoned in Havana. Back in Florida, Maria Elena
Torano was pregnant with their second child. Her second son nearly
died of a blood clot and was thought to be retarded. She was all alone
with two children to care for, and suffered from emotional and physical
stress. When her husband was finally released a year later, he came home
to find his wife hospitalized, suffering from internal bleeding. She had
been doing anything she could to keep the family afloat, including
bagging clothes for a dry cleaner, selling baked goods, and selling
pantyhose.

When her husband returned, he resumed his job as a tobacco broker
for the General Cigar Company. The family moved first to Connecticut

and then to Puerto Rico. In Connecticut, Torano passed a merit-system exam that enabled her to be a child welfare worker, and after moving to Puerto Rico she worked for Eastern Airlines as a reservationist. When she returned to Miami, she took a job with Jackson Memorial Hospital and in her free time volunteered in the development of Calle Ocho and in the building of Domino Park. Her husband continued to travel for his business, and this put a strain on the couple's relations. In 1977 she was recommended for a job in Washington as the associate director of the U.S. Community Services Administration. When her sons refused to move north and because her husband was always traveling, she left her sons to grow up with her parents, returning each week to visit them. Three years later, after her service was completed in Washington, she decided to open up her own PR firm and named it META for Maria Elena Torano and Associates. *Meta* also means "goal" in Spanish. By this time she had divorced her husband and remarried. Her second husband would die in 1989, and in 1992 she would marry for the third time.

In 1986, while on an assignment to help the Small Business Administration organize an educational program, she stumbled upon an item that described the advantages offered to minorities in bidding for government contracts. Torano won her first Small Business Administration 8(a) contract—as a management consultant—the same year. That assignment was to provide computer software to the Defense Contract Audit Agency, and Torano subcontracted it to a software developer. META had found its destiny. META went on to find success on two parallel tracks: management consulting services as an 8(a) contractor, and in environmental cleanup.

The company employs 260 people in ten offices in the United States and is responsible for ongoing projects in Malaysia, Indonesia, Guatemala, and Honduras. Recently, most of META's management work has been for the Resolution Trust Corp., the agency responsible for dealing with the multibillion-dollar mess that the savings and loan industry left behind. As 100 percent owner of META and 51 percent owner of its subsidiary METEC Asset Management, Inc., Torano is managing and liquidating more than $373 million in RTC assets.

"Maria Elena has done a very good job for us," says Lamar Kelly, RTC's senior vice president for asset management and sales. "In short, she is a charming and astute businesswoman who will tell you exactly what's on her mind."

But what about the environmental services part of her company? The RTC will be wrapped up within a couple of years, and META's 8(a) certification is set to expire in 1995, Torano points out. So she has been building up the environmental business to survive the transition. "For the next twenty to thirty years, environmental cleanup is where the opportunities will be," she says. "That's our long-term strategy."[1]

Her mentor in both sides of the business has been Ed Romero, president of the nuclear waste management company Advanced Sciences, Inc., in Albuquerque, New Mexico. When Torano received her first 8(a) contract, she subleased Washington office space from Romero's operation there. "I anticipated that she would be successful," he comments, "because she's hard-driven."

Right now, Torano is driving for expansion to $25 million by 1995. "That's my comfort level," she says, "and it would be manageable."

---

1. Rich Mendosa, "Maria Elena Torane and Associates," *Hispanic Business* 134, June 1993, p. 126.

Kay Unger

Name of Company:	Gillian Group
Location:	New York City
Date Founded:	1972
Description of Business:	Designs, develops, and manufactures moderately priced women's apparel that is sold through department store boutiques and specialty retailers.
Description of *P*:	Working women require innovative wardrobes that make a serious yet fashionable statement about the wearer. Unger's customer is thirty-five to fifty years old and generally commands an important position in her corporation and community. Her clothing has to make a classic statement to amplify and underscore her role.
Description of *S*:	Gillian Group has become one of the most successful manufacturers and marketers of women's dresses in the country largely because of Unger's attention to detail and keen observation of her customer.
Members of *E*:	Jon Levy, partner
Size of *V*:	The company is privately held and not required to publish financial statements. With sales of more than $150 million, the company would probably be worth about two-thirds that amount if acquired or one-half taken public.
Social Utility:	Unger is a member of the board of trustees of the Boys and Girls Club of America and is a director of the Epstein Fine Arts Fund, founded by her father in 1954 to assist deserving students in the arts.

299

Principal Source of
Venture Capital: $30,000 in inheritance money

Following her graduation from Washington University and the Parsons
School of Design in 1967, KAY UNGER went to work for the fashion designer
Jo Copeland. From there she moved on to Geoffrey Beane and finally Teal
Traina. It was while designing fashions at Traina that Unger realized she
had a fashion statement of her own to make. She began designing at night
and selling her clothing on lunch breaks, and in 1972, as she tells it, "I bit
the bullet and quit my daytime job, found a loft, and hired an assistant—
someone to cut and drape the clothing—and a sales rep." She found it
impossible to do everything, and Jon Levy and another friend (who later
left the partnership) joined her. Levy handled finance, administration,
and retail facilities issues.

Unger traveled extensively in the early years, always meeting with
potential customers and listening to their needs. How they saw themselves was important to Unger, and the self-image differs from region to
region. "What a woman wears to the supermarket in Dallas she would
wear to a wedding in Chicago," says Unger.

The Gillian customer works, has a family, travels, and has dinner
out. "My biggest challenge," says Unger, "is making sure my designs
keep up with her busy lifestyle." Unger has a lot in common with her
customers. She works a twelve-hour day, is married, raises two sons,
travels to the Orient on business, and vacations in Europe.

A Gillian customer picks up a card at the time of purchase with a
photograph of her dress or suit on it. The card also includes suggestions
for shoes and accessories to wear with the dress. Using information to
expand her customer base, Unger is designing a direct mail catalog tied
into different department stores where there is a Gillian boutique.

The Gillian line is known for its bold color combinations, quality
fabrics, and striking prints. The Gillian trademark reflects Unger's original childhood goal: to become an artist.

Patti Upton

Name of Company:	Aromatique, Inc.
Location:	Heber Springs, Arkansas
Date Founded:	1982
Description of Business:	Designs, develops, produces, and markets decorative fragrances, bath products, containers, candles, and accessories, which it sells to department and specialty stores.
Description of *P*:	Air freshness is an oversimplification of the problem for which packaged fragrances are a solution. People have childhood memories of certain fragrances—the smell of Christmas, of apple pies baking in the oven, of trees budding in the spring—that they seek to replicate in their homes.
Description of *S*:	With a keen sense of smell and an awareness of consumer needs, Upton packages and sells memories.
Members of *E*:	Richard H. Upton, husband and business mentor
Size of V:	The company is privately held and is not required to publish financial statements. With 1992 sales of $62 million, the company is arguably worth a medium-level eight figures.
Social Utility:	Patti Upton and Aromatique have generously contributed to the National Multiple Sclerosis Foundation, the Vincent Lombardi Cancer Research Fund, the March of Dimes, and the Nature Conservancy.
Principal Source of Venture Capital:	$10,000 of her inheritance

PATTI UPTON, a University of Arkansas beauty, may not have gotten a classic college education—she told her parents back then, "If you'll just let me stay one more year, I'll buy books"—but she is a crackerjack entrepreneur. She has built Aromatique into the largest producer of potpourri in the country, with a 100-product line featured in 5,000 stores in twenty-seven countries. The company occupies 350,000 square feet in fourteen buildings in Heber Springs, Arkansas, where it employs nearly 500 people.

Although experienced executives from Estee Lauder and Max Factor have joined the company, several of the key management positions were filled by friends and relatives who Upton persuaded to join Aromatique when it was a mere start-up.For instance, her father, Dr. J. A. Pulliam, is in charge of production. Chad Evans, who now oversees purchasing, began at the company gathering wood shavings part-time with the Uptons' children. Buddy Proctor, a family friend, developed the company's process for freeze-drying roses.

Then there is Ronnie Fair, son of friends of the Uptons; Patti approached him upon his earning a degree in accounting. She said to him, "I started a little business and I want you to do my accounting work. There's only one catch to it—you can't charge me anything because I don't have any money. But if I ever make any money, I'll take care of you then." Shortly thereafter, Fair joined the company as its controller, and he was later followed by his wife Sharon, Aromatique's publicity director.

Many fragrance companies could have gathered wood shavings, pine cones, bay leaves, and berries, spritzed them with one of their aromas, and asked Bloomingdale's for two feet of shelf space. But they didn't. It was too simplistic. Corporate executives *never* implement simplistic business plans until they have to simply because an entrepreneur has taken too much market share from them. The decorative fragrance business is about $250 million a year at wholesale, and wood shavings and dried berries are not precious commodities; so one can only imagine how fragrant Aromatique's gross profit margin is.

Upton began the business somewhat on a whim, although the characteristics for personal achievement were like a flint in search of a match all along. A friend with a gift shop asked her to design a fragrance basket that captured the smell of Christmas. Upton delivered the order, and before she had gotten in her car to drive home, her friend called out to her for a reorder.

Upton keeps stretching the company's capabilities and testing new fragrances and packaging while limiting the number of retail locations the company sells to. She sees the retailer as the selling force. "Good clients build repeat customers," she says.

Gae Veit

Name of Company:	Shingobee Construction, Inc.
Location:	Loretto, Minnesota
Date Founded:	1980
Description of Business:	The company is a general-purpose construction company specializing in the construction of commercial buildings.
Description of P:	Construction companies are fairly common, but Shingobee Builders is most certainly not. It was launched by a member of the Crow Creek Sioux tribe, by a woman, and in an environment where women are not supposed to achieve commercial success. Three obstacles were overcome by this unique company—minority status, gender status, and the unlit path of entrepreneurship.
Description of S:	Veit has built one of the most consistently praised construction companies in the Northwest.
Members of E:	Thomas Godlewski, executive president Keith MacDonald, president of Operations Loren Kjersten, vice president
Size of V:	The company's sales were $11.4 million in 1992. It is privately held and does not publish detailed financial information.
Social Utility:	Veit was named Female Entrepreneur of the Year in 1992. She is giving assistance to other minority and Native American entrepreneurs.
Principal Source of Venture Capital:	$1,000 in personal savings and a $5,000 loan

GAE VEIT is no one to be taken lightly. "I was playing racquetball with a guy once," she recalls, "and I put him in the hospital when I accidentally hit him in the face and split his lip."

For twenty years she worked as an office manager for an excavation company run by her former father-in-law before launching out on her own with $1,000 in personal savings and a $5,000 bank loan.

Veit credits personal contacts and networking as the keys to her success. "The client wants to see who they are dealing with. And in a male-dominated business, I certainly stand out."

Shingobee is an Indian word that means "beautiful evergreen tree." Like the tree that is her company's logo, Veit never stops growing. She hires primarily minority workers, and their earnings spread throughout their Native American communities. She provides a role model for the next generation. This is essential because the average annual gross receipts of Native American-owned companies are only about one-third the combined average of all other American companies.

Shingobee's capabilities speak for themselves. US West has given the company twenty contracts. Shingobee built a 22,000-square-foot dining hall, kitchen, and medical training facility for the Minnesota Air National Guard, an Olympic-size ice skating rink in Eden Prairie, Minnesota, and two city parks for the town of Plymouth, Minnesota.

Veit says the hardest part of being a minority woman in the construction business was gaining "credibility." She says when she first got started she would send men out to do her bidding and marketing. However, Veit says, times have changed and she now "feels more comfortable" in the old-boy network. "Government-forced goals have helped considerably," she claims. "Affirmative action programs have opened the doors to minorities and women." While Veit says that these programs have helped her get contracts, it has been her commitment to quality and her friendly service that have kept them coming back. Veit believes that "women are natural managers. They are not dictatorial. We're good team builders and work cooperatively." She says that today people are seeking her out not because she is a woman but because they enjoy working with her and her associates.

Gae Veit characterizes her industry as highly stressful. Deadlines have to be met on time and, as she says, "Things can get a little hectic around here." As a result, she has hired a corporate chaplain for her co-workers and their families to help them though the trying times.

In Native American communities, women are not pushed to succeed in business. In the male-dominated construction industry, especially, women-owned companies are rare. Gae Veit did not let these drawbacks or any others, for that matter, stand in her way. As she quotes from Philippians 4:13: "I can do all things through Christ which strengtheneth me."

Lillian Vernon

Name of Company:	Lillian Vernon Corp.
Location:	New Rochelle, New York
Date Founded:	1951
Description of Business:	Sells housewares and novelty items via mail order. In 1992, it expanded into outlet stores.
Description of *P*:	Lillian Vernon is a pioneer among women entrepreneurs. Needing income and determined to run her own business, she launched a housewares marketing business on customer financing—mail order—forty-three years ago. Running fast to stay one step ahead of the competition, Lillian Vernon now has sales within an eyelash of $200 million per year.
Description of *S*:	Lillian Vernon offers the customer the opportunity to buy utilitarian products from the comfort of their homes. Catalogs provide information on price, size, and colors. Today's retail salesperson frequently cannot do that and must call the manager for assistance.
Members of *E*:	Fred P. Hochberg, president and chief operating officer
Size of V:	The company's market value in early 1994 was $167.2 million.
Social Utility:	The company donates funds and merchandise to more than 500 charities, including a 40-foot container of linens to Florida hurricane victims, blankets for New York's homeless, and 7,000 teddy bears for hospitalized children.

Principal Source of
Venture Capital: $2,000 of her wedding gift money

Perhaps the Lillian Vernon Corp. rather than giant corporations should be the subject of case studies in business schools. After all, it cuts to the very heart of what the successful entrepreneurial company is all about—launched with a mere $2,000, started by someone without business experience, selling nonproprietary products, and using a "trust-based" marketing channel—in other words, mail-order marketing.

As a pregnant housewife, LILLIAN VERNON, a refugee from the Nazis, launched Lillian Vernon Corp. by placing a $495 ad in *Seventeen* magazine for purses and belts that she had purchased. Women entrepreneurs in 1951 were a rare commodity (and continued to be so for almost thirty years), and they did not believe that they could raise venture capital, which was true if statistics mean anything. Most of them started businesses based on trust; that is, send me your money and I will send you in return a product, a franchised territory, a dealership, a training program, or a cosmetics line for you to sell to your friends and neighbors. The economic name for this is the law of reciprocity, which is the essence of all commerce: I will cooperate with you as long as you cooperate with me; but if you defect, I will defect until you begin cooperating with me again. As long as there is clarity up front, as long as both sides understand what they are selling or paying for, the shipment terms, and the guarantees, if any, then the law of reciprocity governs every single commercial act in which either payment is made in advance or goods or services are provided in advance.

How then does a company like Lillian Vernon Corp. succeed when other retailers of gifts, housewares, decorative items, and children's products fail?

In the first place, direct mail marketing is an information-based form of selling. Information is conveyed to the customer about the products in the catalog to a degree that arguably exceeds the amount of information the typical retail store clerk can communicate to her customer. Second, information is collected about the customers, including demographic data and data on purchasing habits, and this information (in the computer age) can be used to target market products back to them. Consumer advertising does not collect customer information.

In addition, a large and responsive mailing list can be rented to other companies that want to reach the same market.

But that doesn't explain Vernon's genius. She was the first entrepreneur to personalize products, knowing that vanity is a powerful magnet and that most people will not return gifts with their names on them. She implemented brilliant product line and channel extensions, producing private label products for Max Factor, Elizabeth Arden, Avon, and Revlon (1956), launching spin-off catalogs—Garden Products and Lilly's Kids (1980)—and opening factory outlet stores (1989).

In the meantime, Vernon has maintained tight cost controls by opening a highly automated warehouse and demanding low product costs. The company's gross profit margin actually improved by one-half of one percent over the last three years, one of the most widely used measures of product freshness and operating efficiency.

If you are searching for excellence in business, look no further than Lillian Vernon. In other words, put Vernon and the CEOs of the five largest gift companies together at the starting gate. Give the five men $5 million; give Vernon $50,000. Vernon will beat the socks off them.

Adrienne Vittadini

Name of Company:	Adrienne Vittadini, Inc.
Location:	New York City
Date Founded:	1979
Description of Business:	Designs, develops, and produces a line of popular-priced women's sportswear, which it markets through multiple marketing channels.
Description of P:	Vittadini looks at the vast number of potential customers for her sportswear and the large number of women's apparel manufacturers trying to reach them and she comments, "The one who taps the customer on the shoulder and says 'Look at us' will get the business."
Description of S:	Vittadini says "Look at us" through multiple marketing channels so that her company touches the customer on the shoulder with many fingers.
Members of E:	Gianluigi "Gigi" Vittadini, who left the stewardship of his family's pharmaceutical business in Milan when his wife's business reached $10 million in sales in its third year.
Size of V:	The company is privately held but reports sales of approximately $200 million per year.
Social Utility:	Adrienne Vittadini contributes her time and resources to the Sloan Kettering Foundation, AMFAR, the New York City Ballet, City Meals on Wheels, the CFDA, the New York City Opera, and Pediatric AIDS.
Principal Source of Venture Capital:	A small personal investment

Perhaps the world's most famous—not to mention successful—knitter, ADRIENNE VITTADINI, started out on her own in 1979 because her husband Gigi was "traveling a lot, spending one week in New York, the next in Milan. We had to make a decision," she says. "Either I had to give up my work and travel with him, or he would have to become more involved in my business." She won the tug-of-war, and Gigi, by making the right move.

Vittadini's knit sweaters took the world by storm, and the company grew by 50 percent a year during the 1980s. The elegant, "European" look that the company developed, with evening wear priced in the $125 to $500 range, touched a nerve, and American women snapped it off the racks all over the country.

In the European tradition, which Vittadini transported to New York, the company operates as a family, but with nonfamily members playing key management roles and treated as part of the Vittadini family.

Revenue growth with concomitant profitability is attributable to the company's brilliant moves into cross-merchandising, licensing, and developing multiple marketing channels. Its foundation was built on selling to U.S. department stores. From there it took its line to Canada, Europe, and the Far East. After that it opened twenty-seven Adrienne Vittadini stores and factory outlets. To drive customers into its retail outlets, the company launched a direct mail catalog with an 800 number to give the customers the option of shopping at home. That's six channels.

Then the management team tackled cross-licensing and struck deals with Revlon for perfume. Other licensing agreements will firmly establish the company as a lifestyle marketer rather than just a knitwear producer. Licensed categories include swimwear, scarves, handbags, cosmetic bags, sleepwear, lingerie, socks, belts, girls' wear, sheets, towels, a shoe line, and the newest one—wallpaper.

Willingness to partner rather than to plunge ahead de novo, a spirit of cooperation, and a faith in the law of reciprocity that governs many women-owned businesses have all been articles of faith at Adrienne Vittadini, where many fingers of many licensees touch the customer on the shoulder to say, "Look at us."

Terrie M. Williams

Name of Company:	The Terrie Williams Agency
Location:	New York City
Date Founded:	1988
Description of Business:	Provides publicity, public relations, and events planning for entertainment, sports, and corporate clients.
Description of *P*:	Celebrities, sports and entertainment personalities, and consumer products companies need to protect their reputations and require that their reputations be projected in the media in a positive manner that correctly interprets their mission to the public.
Description of *S*:	Williams is a nonstop, high-energy networker with an exceptional imagination and the ability and the trained staff to implement her ideas for her clients.
Members of *E*:	Rupert C. Ifil, vice president and general manager Joe Cooney, vice president and director of editorial services
Size of *V*:	The company is privately held and is not required to publish its financial statements.
Social Utility:	Williams is devoted to a handful of community services.
Principal Source of Venture Capital:	Private sources

TERRIE WILLIAMS graduated cum laude from Brandeis University and then earned a Master's degree in social work from Columbia University. For the next three years she worked at New York Hospital as a social worker. A stint as a volunteer at a radio station led her into the communications business. Ed Lewis, the publisher of *Essence* magazine, spotted her and brought Williams into his company, where in 1986 she became vice president and director of corporate communications.

After six years at *Essence*, Williams, then thirty-four, left to form her own firm. Not known for her timidity, Williams captured comedic actor Eddie Murphy as her first client. How did she do it? She asked for his business, sent him a proposal, called him, got the assignment.

She added Miles Davis and Anita Baker to her roster, and word spread of Williams's immense talent, huge Rolodex, and ability to get things done. Doubtless there was a void that Williams filled—black entertainers who wanted a black public relations agent, and consumer products companies that wanted to project a certain image in the black community.

Williams's clients read like a Who's Who of Important People and Companies. In sports, her company represents Jackie Joyner-Kersee, Willie Stargell, and Dave Winfield; in music, Anita Baker, Kathleen Battle, Richie Havens, Janet Jackson, and more; in film, *House Party*, *Glory*, *Sarafina*, *New York City*, Eddie Murphy, Wesley Snipes, Robert Townsend, and others; in events, Nelson Mandela's New York Welcoming Committee, The NBA "Stay in School Program," and others; and among corporations, Coca Cola Bottling of New York, Consolidated Edison, Essence Communications, Inc., Time Warner, and more.

Williams might never have flowered as a public relations entrepreneurs had she not accidentally seen an announcement for a course in public relations being offered at the YMCA. "It's not just about publicity," she says. "Public relations is the business of image building. It's my job to make certain that my clients are presented to the media in a manner they believe is balanced." Because there are a lot of media and because celebrities and consumer products companies are very busy, Williams is in constant motion servicing the needs of her demanding clients.

It's definitely not a business for those deficient in self-esteem and moxie, but Williams has what it takes. She has come into the public relations industry like a rocket and stood it on its head.

Lynn Wilson

Name of Company:	Lynn Wilson and Associates
Location:	Coral Gables, Florida
Date Founded:	1967
Description of Business:	An interior architectural design company
Description of *P*:	The need for people to express their personalities and commercial statements in attractive, efficient environments
Description of *S*:	Wilson developed a team that is responsive to the design requirements of corporate and individual clients.
Members of *E*:	Lynn Wilson, president
Size of V:	Annual gross sales are estimated at $250 million.
Social Utility:	Lynn Wilson is a strong supporter of the arts and sits on the Board of the Florida Ballet, the Metropolitan Museum of Art, and the World Symphony.
Principal Source of Venture Capital:	$200 and home office

LYNN WILSON grew up quickly when, at age 12, her father became very ill and then, four years later, passed away and her mother had to go back to work. Lynn found herself taking on the role of mother and father to her younger sister and learned to support and take care of herself. "I learned to discipline myself and fill my life with productive activity. . . . I have worked hard all my life." With two parents who had been in show business, Wilson initially pursued careers as a dancer, singer, model, actor, and artist. "I never planned on being an interior architectural designer. I was just as confused as the next kid when it came to knowing what I wanted to be when I grew up."

In the early 1960s she entered the University of Miami on a full academic scholarship. She kept herself busy maintaining her grades while at the same time working her way through school. In fact, *LIFE* magazine did an article on her life as a full-time student by day and a show girl by night. She did eight shows a week and was completing twenty-five to twenty-eight credits a semester, whereas the average student was taking only fifteen to eighteen credits a semester. She convinced the School of Architecture to let her skip the first two years of classes and be placed in junior- and senior-level architectural design classes by showing them her portfolio of the artwork she had been doing on the side. Thus in four years Wilson managed to complete both a degree in arts and sciences and a degree in architecture while supporting herself. She says that she learned to work on little to no sleep. "I would get back from my shows at three-thirty in the morning and would have to be in class by eight o'clock." To this day she still does not sleep more than four hours a night. In addition to her undergraduate degrees she completed her Master's in art history.

As soon as Wilson finished school she managed to land her first job as a draftsman at a large architectural design firm in New York. As at college, she found herself surrounded exclusively by men. "I had no mentor or role model to follow. I learned to rely on my own intelligence and hard work." She moved on to become the key designer for a firm that specialized in designing banks and hospitals and then became head designer for a more all-encompassing firm. Within these five years, Wilson also married, gave birth to three children, and assumed a leadership role in the two out of the last three jobs she had held. If that was not enough, at age 27 she decided to go into business for herself. And in 1967, Lynn Wilson and Associates was formed.

The company started in her home and Wilson did all her own drafting, typing, bookkeeping, and writing of contracts. Within a year, she moved into an office and slowly began building a talented staff that today numbers over 250. She borrowed nothing and characterizes herself as old-fashioned when it comes to her tactics and philosophy in business. "I believe in value, hard work, perseverence, patience. . . in being honest and honorable. . . . I don't believe in borrowing money and spending what you don't have." She feels that today we have taken the focus off value and placed too much emphasis on the "hype and presentation. The finished product is what has to be focused on," she asserts. In fact, Lynn

Wilson and Associates has never had a sales or marketing person. It has gotten work solely on referrals. Her marketing philosophy is simple: Offer a better product at a better price and business will come. "If you do what you do well and can offer the right price, they will hear about you real fast!"

By no means has her success come easily or quickly. As a mother of three, she found herself doing it all, running from softball games to soccer practice to ballet lessons to the office and back to parents' night at school. "I was supermom," she says. Lynn Wilson has worked long and hard and characterizes herself as "very detail-oriented and meticulous. It has been slow but steady," she says. In the long run this has paid off. Wilson loves what she does and continues to forge ahead today with the same vigor of her college days. She says, "Life is what you make of it, and, for me, living my life means exploring the edges of my talents and pushing the limits of my abilities. Not in a fanatical way," she adds, "but in a way to experience what I can do just as an athlete may try different sports. I chose the creative aspect of architectural design to challenge myself." She believes that everyone has something to give this world that will help enrich people and sees her buildings and designs as a means of touching people with beauty.

Trisha Wilson

Name of Company:	Wilson & Associates
Date Founded:	1975
Location:	Dallas
Description of Business:	Interior, architectural design company that handles commercial projects such as hotels, restaurants, clubs, office buildings, and executive offices
Description of *P*:	One of the requirements of America's building boom of the last two decades has been interior design consultants capable of transferring their clients' broad vision of the image they sought to convey into beautiful, yet utilitarian work space.
Description of *S*:	Wilson & Associates moved quickly to fill the need of its market for interior and architectural design.
Members of *E*:	Cheryl Neumann, chief operations officer Jim Rimelspach, design director Diane Montgomery, project manager
Size of V:	This privately held company chooses not to disclose its financial statements.
Social Utility:	Trisha Wilson is a firm believer in giving back to the community. Wilson & Associates has adopted a local high school that serves under-privileged kids. All employees are required to take part in the high school. Wilson's staff is involved in everything from mentoring students to planning high school dances.
Principal Source of Venture Capital:	$300 in personal savings and a home office

TRISHA WILSON graduated with a degree in interior design from the University of Austin, where, she says, she "just wanted to have fun. I had no intention of being a career person. I just wanted to make some money and work with my girlfriends." She began her career creating window displays and selling furniture at a local furniture store. For two years she worked on commission and learned the art of selling. But furniture was not the only thing she learned to sell. Knowing that she wanted to be more than just a "glorified salesperson," Wilson kept her eyes out for something new. As Wilson puts it, "I learned to take advantage of opportunities." And that is exactly what she did.

One day a customer came in looking for furniture for his home. After some conversation, she found out that he was opening a new restaurant in Dallas. By the time he had left, not only did he have new furniture for his home but also a new interior designer for his restaurant who had no prior experience at all. When asked what she knew about restaurants, Wilson remarked, "I know I can do it!" And she did it. The project was a big success and Wilson sought out other restaurants to design interiors for, setting up shop in her small private office, where she worked by herself for a couple years.

When Wilson heard that the real estate mogul Trammel Crow was going to build a very large new hotel in Dallas, she immediately wrote him a letter saying that she had some great ideas for the restaurants that would be built in the hotel. When he called back to ask her about her ideas, Wilson says, "I had no idea what to say. I just kept it together, made up a couple of concepts and told him about them." When he asked her how many employees she had, she said six, even though it was just herself at home at that time. As Wilson explains, "I knew I could do anything if I had the chance. I told him I had six employees because I did not want to give him the impression that I would not be able to handle it." As soon as she got the job she hired six new people and began preparations for the hotel job, her first big assignment. Five of the original six people are still with Wilson today.

Almost twenty years later, Wilson attributes her success to just keeping things simple and "not getting bogged down in details." She says, "I just put one foot in front of the other . . . and take things one step at a time." As a mentor to some MBA students at SMU, she laughs when she thinks about some of the questions she has been asked. One day one of her students asked her what kind of market studies and demographic data she used to decide to expand and move into new areas. She answered, "I have no plans. . . if it feels right, I go for it!"

While in London on a business trip, "feeling the energy of the city," she decided to call the manager of the hotel she was staying in, and told him that she was opening an office in London and would like to redo the rooms of his hotel. She had absolutely no plans for opening an office in London, but she knew that if she could get his business she would probably have to. When he gave her the OK, she proceeded to call the rest of the hotels in London whose names she found in the phone book of her room. Within three months Wilson's British clientele was so large that she did indeed open offices in London.

When asked about the future of Wilson & Associates, she remarks, "I'm not too sure. . . . I can't be limited by my imagination today. New opportunities and new ideas seem always to present themselves to me that are beyond my wildest imagination." As Wilson puts it, "I like to keep things open." In addition, she also attributes her success to keeping a positive attitude and not being afraid to ask dumb questions or try something new. "Just do it!" she remarks, "If something does not turn out, something better will." It is this attitude that has led Wilson to open up offices in Singapore, Johannesburg, Los Angeles, and New York. It is what has made Wilson & Associates one of the top five interior architectural design firms in the world. As Wilson puts it, "If you love what you are doing and believe in yourself," [the plaque on her desk reads in big bold letters] "IT CAN BE DONE!"